Bass Guitar

FOR

DUMMIES®

Bass Guitar For Dummies®

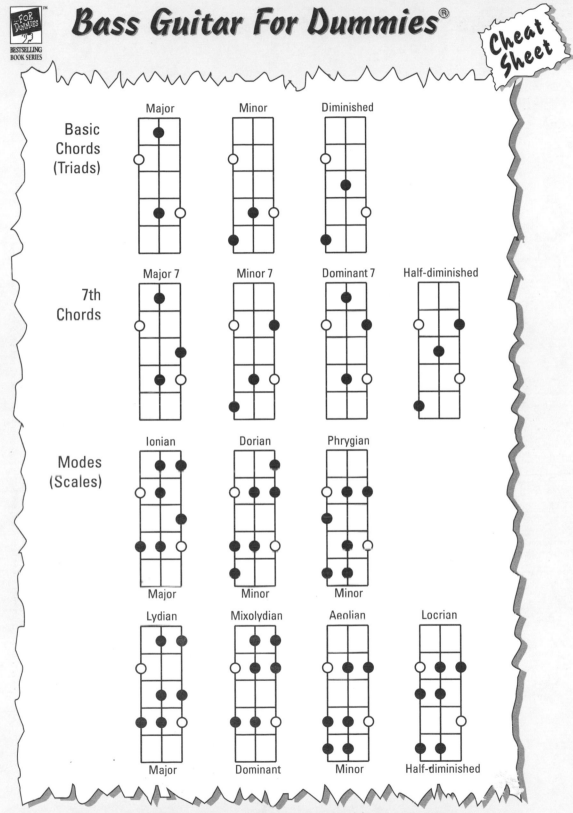

Bass Guitar For Dummies®

Cheat Sheet

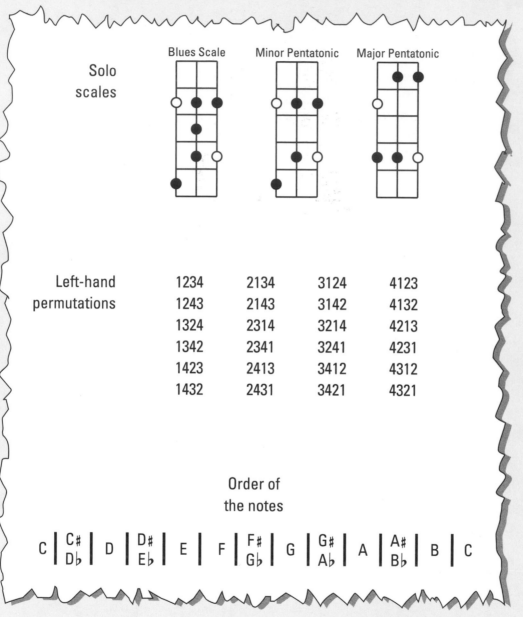

Solo scales

Blues Scale | **Minor Pentatonic** | **Major Pentatonic**

Left-hand permutations

1234	2134	3124	4123
1243	2143	3142	4132
1324	2314	3214	4213
1342	2341	3241	4231
1423	2413	3412	4312
1432	2431	3421	4321

Order of the notes

C | C# / Db | D | D# / Eb | E | F | F# / Gb | G | G# / Ab | A | A# / Bb | B | C

Copyright © 2003 Wiley Publishing, Inc.
All rights reserved.

Item 2487-9.

For more information about Wiley Publishing,
call 1-800-762-2974.

For Dummies: Bestselling Book Series for Beginners

by Patrick Pfeiffer

Foreword by Will Lee
Bassist, *Late Show with David Letterman*

Wiley Publishing, Inc.

Bass Guitar For Dummies®

Published by
Wiley Publishing, Inc.
111 River St.
Hoboken, NJ 07030
www.wiley.com

Copyright © 2003 by Wiley Publishing, Inc., Indianapolis, Indiana

Published simultaneously in Canada

For general information on our other products and services or to obtain technical support, please contact our Customer Care Department within the U.S. at 800-762-2974, outside the U.S. at 317-572-3993, or fax 317-572-4002.

Wiley also publishes its books in a variety of electronic formats. Some content that appears in print may not be available in electronic books.

Library of Congress Cataloging-in-Publication Data:

Library of Congress Control Number: 2003101911

ISBN: 0-7645-2487-9

Manufactured in the United States of America

10 9 8 7 6

1B/ST/RQ/QT/IN

About the Author

Patrick Pfeiffer is a professional bassist, composer, and bass teacher in New York City. He earned his bachelor's degree in music from Arizona State University, and his master's degree in jazz studies from the New England Conservatory of Music, where he studied with famed bassist Miroslav Vitous. Pfeiffer's solo CD, *Fruits and Nuts* (recorded with his group Phoenix), earned stellar reviews and a recommendation from *Bass Player Magazine*.

Besides performing and recording, Pfeiffer teaches bass guitar at the renowned *Katie Agresta Studio* in New York City and gives clinics on rhythm section playing for bassists and drummers. His former students include Adam Clayton of U2, and Alec Such of Bon Jovi. Pfeiffer has played and/or recorded with Phoebe Snow, Slam Steward, Paul Griffin, Babatunde Olantunji, Sheila Jordan, George Russell, Margaret Whiting, Joe LoVano, Hernan Romero, the Marvelettes, and the Gary Corwin All Stars, to name a few.

He also wrote "In Search of the Groove," a groove manual for bassists.

Dedication

This book is dedicated to my soul mate and wife, Lisa Ann Herth Pfeiffer.

This book is also dedicated to the memory of an extraordinary man: Paul Griffin . . . musician, mentor, and friend.

Author's Acknowledgments

I am eternally grateful to Lisa Pfeiffer for her never-ending love, support, and wisdom during the writing of this book (and always). I'm honored and privileged to have worked with three outstanding bass players on this book, without whom I would not have been able to accomplish this feat. A thousand thanks to Crissy Walford, who tirelessly worked to make sure that my points came across clearly, and to Nicolas diPierro, who created all the technical figures, sometimes under nearly impossible deadline pressure. Also thanks to Chris Jisi, my technical editor, whose expertise, enthusiasm, and thorough knowledge of all things bass kept me out of trouble.

Special thanks to Pam Sourelis (not a bass player yet, but probably soon) who put my writing into proper style, and also to Tere Drenth. I am very grateful to the folks at Wiley Publishing, Inc., who put in long hours on this project: my acquisitions editor Tracy Boggier, my project editor Allyson Grove, copy editor Greg Pearson, and art director Shelley Lea. I also wish to thank Matt Wagner, my agent, without whom this book would not have happened, and Marla Marquit Steuer (yet another wonderful bass player) for pointing the right folks into the right (my) direction.

I'm honored and grateful to have an incredible studio team: David B. Meade on drums, Lou DiNatale on keyboard, and MP Kuo, the sound engineer at Uptime Studios in New York City. Many, many thanks to Steven Schlesinger (for the great photos), Katie Ulanov (for the use of the Green Bass), Katie Agresta (for always being there), Ursula Pfeiffer and Wilhelm Pfeiffer (for believing in me and helping me pursue what I really love), Andreas and Mark Pfeiffer (for their encouragement), Michael Tobias (for the wonderful MTD basses), Michael Carolan (yet another wonderful bassist), Reiner Hoffmann (for my first bass), Marjorie Herth, Robert Miller, Will Lee (for always finding the time to give me encouraging advice), Adam Clayton (for putting his trust in me), Lawrence, Loys, and Sanford Green (my other family), Ronnie Carritue, Hilmar Stanger (my first bass teacher), Dennis Sexton (another great bass teacher), and David Sokol (of Euphoria Studios). And a very special thanks to LuLu for being a constant source of unconditional love.

A special thanks also goes to Gurumayi Chidvilasananda and the Sidha Yoga Foundation, and to Daisaku Ikeda and the SGI family.

Publisher's Acknowledgments

We're proud of this book; please send us your comments through our Dummies online registration form located at www.dummies.com/register/.

Some of the people who helped bring this book to market include the following:

Acquisitions, Editorial, and Media Development

Project Editor: Allyson Grove

Acquisitions Editor: Tracy Boggier

Copy Editor: Greg Pearson

Acquisitions Coordinator: Holly G. Grimes

Technical Editor: Chris Jisi

Media Development Specialist: Kit Malone

Editorial Manager: Michelle Hacker

Editorial Assistant: Elizabeth Rea

Cover Photos: © DiMaggio/Kalish/CORBIS

Cartoons: Rich Tennant, www.the5thwave.com

Production

Project Coordinator: Erin Smith

Layout and Graphics: Seth Conley, Joyce Haughey, LeAndra Hosier, Stephanie D. Jumper, Tiffany Muth, Mary Gillot Virgin

Proofreaders: Andy Hollandbeck, Carl W. Pierce, Robert Springer, Brian H. Walls, TECHBOOKS Production Services,

Indexer: TECHBOOKS Production Services

Special Help: Mary Yeary

Publishing and Editorial for Consumer Dummies

Diane Graves Steele, Vice President and Publisher, Consumer Dummies

Joyce Pepple, Acquisitions Director, Consumer Dummies

Kristin A. Cocks, Product Development Director, Consumer Dummies

Michael Spring, Vice President and Publisher, Travel

Brice Gosnell, Associate Publisher, Travel

Suzanne Jannetta, Editorial Director, Travel

Publishing for Technology Dummies

Andy Cummings, Vice President and Publisher, Dummies Technology/General User

Composition Services

Gerry Fahey, Vice President of Production Services

Debbie Stailey, Director of Composition Services

Contents at a Glance

Table of Contents

Foreword

For bassists or bass wannabes, *Bass Guitar For Dummies* takes you on a tour of the instrument and explores all avenues of bassdom. Of the myriad tools available for bassists, *Bass Guitar For Dummies* is at the pinnacle of them all. Never before has such a complete anthology been assembled. It's like having an unlimited ticket for all the rides at BassLand!

Patrick Pfeiffer, great communicator of bass guitar has laid it all out for you to enjoy. *Bass Guitar For Dummies* can be read laterally, literally, or "loiterily." In other words, cover to cover, in order, or at your leisure; when you have a couple of minutes, just read a page, or a chapter. It's not too deep, not too heavy, but it's all good information and a lot of fun. So dig in, and enjoy *Bass Guitar For Dummies!*

All the Bass,

Will Lee, bassist, *Late Show with David Letterman*

Introduction

· ·

Shake the earth with deep, sonorous vibrations. Be the force that relent-lessly drives the music. Rumble like the ominous thunder of an approaching storm. For you, it's not enough just to be heard; you need to be *felt*, too. You need to play bass.

Imagine your favorite music without bass. It doesn't work, does it? The bass is the heartbeat of the music, the foundation for the groove, and the glue holding together all the different instruments. You can hear the music sing as it's carried along by the bass groove. You can hear the music come to life. You can feel the vibrations of the low notes — sometimes subtle and caress-ing, sometimes literally earthshaking — as they propel the song. The bass is the heart.

Leave center stage to the other musicians — you have more important work to do. The limelight may be cool, but bassists *rule!*

About This Book

You can find everything you need to dominate the bass in *Bass Guitar For Dummies* — from the correct way to strike a note, to a funk groove in the style of Jaco Pastorius. It's all here.

Each chapter is independent of the others. You can skip the stuff you already know and go straight to the parts that interest you, without feeling lost. To find the subject you're looking for, just check out the table of contents. You can also look up specific topics in the index at the back of the book. Or you can read this book from front to back and build up your bass-playing skills step by step. Either way, just remember to enjoy the journey.

I structure *Bass Guitar For Dummies* so that you can decide for yourself how far you want to take your skills on the instrument. I checked out the entrance requirements for music schools and conservatories, and included informa-tion that will fulfill those requirements (without getting too theoretical — after all, you don't want to spend all your time theorizing . . . you want to *play*). However, this book goes well beyond the minimum requirements and shows you how to actually *apply* all this information to real-life bass playing. I show you how to play in different styles and how to create your own grooves and solos so that you don't have to copy someone else's bass line note for note.

No bass guitar? No problem. *Bass Guitar For Dummies* doesn't assume that you have your own bass. If you don't, just head over to Part VI to find out how to choose the right bass and accessories to get started. If you have a bass already, you can start with the maintenance section in Chapter 15 and find out how to set up your instrument so that it's easier to play.

You don't need to read music to figure out how to play the bass guitar. (You can unknit your eyebrows now . . . it's true.) So how can you get the information you need from this book?

- ✓ **Look at the grids:** The grids are pictures of the notes you use on the fingerboard of the bass guitar. The grids show you where the notes are in relation to each other and which fingers you use to play them. The grids also provide you with an additional advantage: If you use the grid to finger a certain pattern of notes, you can then transfer the same pattern (fingering and all) onto any other section of the fingerboard to play the note pattern in a different key. That's why reading music isn't necessary. The notes on a page of regular music notation look completely different for each new key, but if you use the grid, you'll find that, as far as note patterns go, one size fits all.

- ✓ **Read the tablature:** *Tablature* is a shorthand notational technique that shows you which string to strike and where to hold the string down to sound a note. The short name for tablature is *tab* (just in case anyone asks).

- ✓ **Listen to the CD:** You can hear all the exercises and grooves that are shown in the figures. You can listen to the sound of a groove, and then take a look at the grid and the tab, put your hand in the right position on the fingerboard, and reproduce the sound.

  After you master a groove, you can pan your stereo to one side to get rid of the sound of the bass, and then play the groove in the example with just the drums (real drums, not a machine). Or you can create your own groove in the feel and style of the example.

- ✓ **As you improve, try reading the music notation:** As you get better, you can look at the notation and begin to learn to read music. After you figure out how to play a few phrases, you quickly discover that reading musical notation is not so difficult after all, and that it even makes your musical life easier.

Conventions Used in This Book

I use a few conventions in *Bass Guitar For Dummies* to help keep the text consistent and make it easy to follow. Here's a list of those conventions:

- ✔ **Right hand and left hand:** Instead of saying *striking hand* and *fretting hand,* I say *right hand* for the hand that strikes the string, and *left hand* for the hand that frets the note. My apologies to left-handed players. If you're left-handed, please read *right hand* to mean *left hand,* and vice versa.

- ✔ **Up and down, higher and lower:** Moving your left hand up the neck of the bass means moving it up in *pitch* (moving your hand toward the body of the bass). Moving your left hand down the neck means moving it down in *pitch* (moving your hand away from the body). I use the same principle for the right hand. Going to the next *higher* string means playing the string that has a higher sound (the string closer to the floor). The next *lower* string is the string that has a lower sound (the string closer to the ceiling). Just think of whether the sound is higher or lower and you'll be fine.

- ✔ **Triple music notation:** In the figures, the music for the grooves and the exercises is printed with the standard music notation on top, the tablature below, and the grid next to them. You don't have to read all of them at the same time (good heavens, that would be worse than reading piano music). Simply pick the one you feel most comfortable with, and then use the others to double-check that you're playing the groove or exercise correctly. Of course, you can also listen to the CD to hear what the music is supposed to sound like.

- ✔ **The numbers:** In the text, the numbers between 1 and 8 (1, 2, 3, 4, 5, 6, 7, and 8) represent notes in a chord or scale. The designation *7th,* on the other hand, refers to a particular chord, such as a major 7th chord. Finally, the distance between two notes (the interval) is called a 2nd (second), 3rd (third), 4th (fourth), and so on.

Not-So-Foolish Assumptions

I assume that you want to play the bass guitar, but I don't assume anything else. No matter what style you're interested in, this book covers them all. It doesn't even matter whether you want to play a four-, five-, or six-string bass. The grids featured in this book can be used for any bass guitar, and the shapes of the patterns never change. All you have to do is read this book with an open mind, and I assure you, you'll be playing bass . . . and quickly. Of course, you can learn even more quickly if you use this book in conjunction with private lessons from a bass guitar teacher. And any experience you've had playing another instrument won't go to waste, either.

How This Book Is Organized

This book is organized so that you can get the information you need easily and quickly. For efficiency, I group the chapters into eight parts.

Part I: The World According to Bass

If you're just beginning to play music, you'll want to start right here. Part I contains three chapters on the basics you need to know before starting to play. Chapter 1 tells you all about the different parts of the bass guitar (and explains why playing bass is such a brilliant idea). Chapter 2 talks about how to hold your bass, where your hands belong, and how to tune your instrument. Chapter 3 shows you how to read the various notational systems used in this book (and all over the world).

Part II: The Bass-ics of Playing

Part II contains two chapters that are crucial to your bass-playing career. Chapter 4 gives you exercises for strengthening and coordinating your hands, and Chapter 5 introduces you to the world of chords and modes. In Chapter 5, you start playing real bass lines, and you find out what makes them sound "right" or "wrong."

Part III: Making the Moves, Creating the Grooves

Part III moves you into some intermediate-level material (and even some advanced-level material, but made easy). Chapter 6 tells you how to navigate out of the lower notes and into the higher notes of the bass. Chapter 7 is a cornerstone of this book, because it shows you how to create a groove step by step. Chapter 8 introduces you to soloing and fills.

Part IV: Using the Correct Accompaniment for Each Style

Part IV takes you on a journey of discovery through the different musical styles for bass guitar. Chapter 9 shows you how to play rock styles, and Chapter 10 introduces you to swing styles. Chapter 11 has some funky funk for you, and Chapter 12 takes you around the world with some exotic styles that you can add to your bass repertoire. Finally, Chapter 13 explains in detail how to play grooves in odd meter.

Part V: Taking Care of the One You Love: TLC for Your Bass Guitar

Part V gives you all the information you need to properly care for your bass. Chapter 14 leads you through the changing of the strings, and Chapter 15 explains how to set up your bass guitar and perform basic maintenance.

Part VI: A Buyer's Guide: The Where and How of Buying a Bass

The two chapters in Part VI give you information on choosing and buying a bass and the accessories that go along with it. Chapter 16 deals with selecting the right bass for your needs. Chapter 17 tells you what accessories will make your bass sound good (or sound at all).

Part VII: The Part of Tens

Part VII contains the *For Dummies* trademark section — the Part of Tens. In Chapter 18, I provide you with a selection of ten great bass players, and in Chapter 19, I give you ten great rhythm sections (and you get to hear their style on the CD).

Part VIII: Appendixes

Appendix A introduces the CD in the back of this book and explains how to use it. In the examples on the CD, a drummer accompanies the bassist; so, instead of playing with a drum machine, you get to play with a real drummer — a very cool experience. Appendix B provides a selection of really useful pages. It has blank music paper and grids, which you can copy and use for keeping track of your own music.

Icons Used in This Book

In the margins of *Bass Guitar For Dummies* (as in all *For Dummies* books), you find icons to help you maneuver through the text. Here's what the icons mean:

This icon points out expert advice to help you become a better bassist.

Be careful! This icon helps you avoid doing damage to the instrument, yourself, or someone's ears.

Brace yourself for some useless facts and information that may come in handy some day. If you want, you can skip over this stuff — and still not miss a beat.

Certain techniques are worth repeating. Take note of the techniques that are highlighted with this icon.

This icon helps you better understand what you're hearing when you listen to the audio samples of the different techniques on the CD.

Where to Go from Here

Well, to Hollywood Bowl, of course! Maybe not right away . . . but hey, never give up your dream. If you don't have a bass guitar yet, skip to Chapters 16 and 17 to see what's in store for you. If you're a beginner, you have a bass guitar, and you're ready to play, skip to Chapter 2 and start getting your instrument in tune (followed by getting your hands into shape). If you're already playing bass guitar, start reading Chapter 5 with your bass guitar in hand and enjoy playing your way through the rest of this book.

Whatever your current status as a bass player, *Bass Guitar For Dummies* will help make you better. Remember, bringing music into your life may well be the first step in a lifelong journey of musical enrichment.

Part I
The World
According to Bass

In this part . . .

Hop on board the bass train — you're in for a wild ride. This part gets you on the right track. Chapter 1 introduces you to the nuts and bolts of the bass and what each part does, and Chapter 2 shows you how to attach *your* anatomy (mostly your hands) to the bass. And finally, Chapter 3 explains the various forms of notation used in this book. So buckle your seat belt.

Chapter 1

Bass Bass-ics: What Is the Meaning of Bass?

*B*ass . . . the glue of rhythm and harmony . . . the heartbeat of the band!

The bass has unique qualities that draw you to play it — perhaps it's the rich, deep, mellow sound or the hypnotic rhythms. In the right hands, the bass is a tremendously powerful tool, because it gives a band its feel and attitude. The bass is at the heart of much of the music you hear today. But what exactly is the bass? What makes the bass so powerful? And how does it help give music that irresistible feel? Whether you're a raw bass recruit or a seasoned veteran, this chapter can help you answer these questions.

Discovering the Difference between Bass and Its High-Strung Cousins

Bass guitars differ from their high-strung cousins (otherwise known as the other guitars) in several significant ways:

- ✔ **Basses normally have four strings, while guitars have six.** In the 1970s, some bassists started adding strings. Nowadays you find five- and six-string basses (and beyond), but four-stringers are still the norm.

- ✔ **Nearly all bass guitars are electric.** Other guitars come in all flavors: electric, acoustic, or a combination of the two.

- ✔ **The bass strings are an equal distance musically from each other.** The sound of each bass string is tuned an equal distance from the string above it, making the instrument perfectly symmetrical. So if you play a scale starting on one string, you can use the same fingering to play that same scale starting on a different string. This type of tuning makes playing the bass much easier than playing the guitar, where the second-highest string is tuned differently from the others.

- ✔ **The bass has a lower pitch than the guitar.** The deep notes of the bass fill the lower end of the sound spectrum. Think of these notes as the "bass-ment," or foundation, of music.

- ✔ **The bass is longer than the guitar, thus making its strings longer.** The longer the string, the lower the pitch; the shorter the string, the higher the pitch. Think of a Chihuahua and a Saint Bernard: The Chihuahua has short vocal chords, and a rather high-pitched bark; the Saint Bernard . . . well . . . you get the idea.

- ✔ **The bass player and the guitarist serve different functions.** I won't bore you with the guitarist's job description, but the bass player's makes for fascinating reading, as the next section shows. (By the way, if you *do* happen to want to know more about the guitarist's job description, you can check out Wiley Publishing's *Guitar For Dummies,* by Mark Phillips and Jon Chappell.)

Understanding the Bass Player's Function in a Band

As a bass player, you play the most crucial role in the band (at least in my opinion). Everyone in the group depends on your subtle (and sometimes not-so-subtle) lead. If the guitarist or saxophonist makes a mistake, hardly anyone will notice, but if the bassist makes a mistake, everyone in the band and the audience will instantly know that something is wrong.

Making the link between harmony and rhythm

You're responsible for linking the harmony (chords) of a song with a distinctive rhythm (groove). This link contributes to the *feel,* or *style,* of the music.

Feel or style determines whether a song is rock, jazz, Latin, or anything else. Chapter 7 tells you exactly what you need to do to establish excellent grooves, and Part IV discusses the different musical styles you're likely to play. You want to be able to emulate any bassist in any style and, at the same time, be creative — using your own notes and ideas!

Moving the song along

Every song is made up of chords that are special to that tune, and all the notes in the tune relate to the sounds of those chords (see Chapter 5 for more information about chords). In some songs, all the chords are the same, and so all the notes relate to that one chord sound, making such songs easy to play. Most songs, however, have different kinds of chords in them; in these, the first group of notes in the tune relates to the first chord and has one kind of sound; the next group of notes relates to another chord sound; and so on throughout the song.

By playing one note at a time in a rhythmic fashion, you propel the music along. You set up each chord for the other players in your band by choosing notes that lead smoothly from one chord sound to the next.

Good music creates a little tension, which then leads to a satisfying release of that tension (a resolution). For example, you can feel the tension and release in as simple a tune as "Twinkle, Twinkle, Little Star." The tension builds as you sing the first line: "Twinkle, twinkle, little star." Can you end the song right there? No, because you want to hear how it ends. That's the tension. When you get through singing "How I wonder what you are," you feel a resolution to the tension, a sense of coming home. You can end the song there; in fact, that's how it does end. The bassist plays an important role in creating and releasing tension. You're pretty much in the driver's seat!

Keeping time

Keeping a steady rhythm, or a *pulse,* is one of the bassist's primary functions. I refer to this function as *locking in with the drummer,* because you work very closely with the drummer to establish the rhythm. So be nice to your drummers. Listen to them carefully and know them well. And while the two of you are on such cozy terms, you may want to spend some time together reading what Chapter 3 has to say about rhythm.

Nothing works better than a *metronome* at helping you develop an unfailing sense of time. The steady (and sometimes infuriating) click that emanates from it provides an ideal backdrop for your own note placement, be it on or off the beat. You can find out more about the metronome in Chapter 3.

Establishing rhythms

As a bassist, you need to have a very clear understanding of exactly how the rhythm relates to the beat. You need to know where to place the notes for the groove in relation to the beat. And you want to make your grooves memorable (see Chapter 7 for more about how to create memorable grooves). If you can't remember them, no one else will be able to either — including the listener (who, of course, makes the trip to hear you play).

Looking cool

While the guitarists move through their aerobic exercises, dripping with sweat and smashing their guitars, you get to be cool. You can join in with their antics if you want. But have you ever seen footage of The Who? John Entwistle was cool. And, if you ever get a chance to see U2, check out their bassist Adam Clayton. He's one cool cucumber, too. Great bassists are just too busy creating fabulous bass lines to join in the antics of their band mates.

Whew! A bassist has important responsibilities. Good thing you picked up this book.

Dissecting the Anatomy of a Bass Guitar

You can call it a bass guitar, an electric bass, an electric bass guitar, or just a bass. You hear all these labels when you discuss music and musical instruments — and you may encounter individuals who believe that only one of these labels is correct. But it really doesn't matter which term you choose, because they all refer to the same instrument.

Figure 1-1 shows you a picture of the bass guitar (or whatever you prefer to call it) with all of its main parts labeled.

You can divide the bass into three sections: The neck, the body, and the innards. The different parts of the neck and the body are easy to see, while the innards aren't so obvious. You have to remove the cover (or covers) to get at the innards, but knowing what they're there for is important.

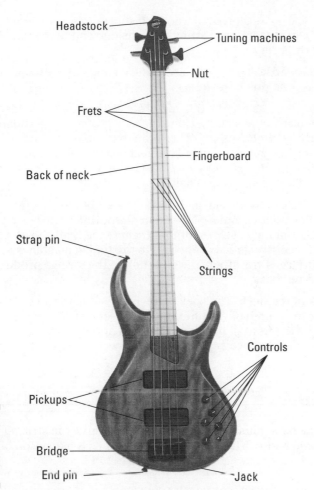

Headstock

Tuning machines

Nut

Frets

Fingerboard

Back of neck

Strap pin

Strings

Controls

Pickups

Figure 1-1:
The bass
guitar in all
its glory.

Bridge

End pin

Jack

The neck

The neck of the bass guitar falls under the dominion of the fretting hand (usually the left hand). The following list describes the function of each part.

- ✔ **The headstock:** The headstock is the top of the neck. It holds the tuning machines for the strings.

- ✔ **The tuning machines:** The tuning machines (also called *tuners* or *tuning heads*) hold the ends of the strings. (The other ends are anchored at the bridge on the body; see the next section for more info about the body of the bass.) By turning the individual tuning heads, you can increase or decrease the tension of the strings (which raises or lowers the pitch).

- ✔ **The nut:** The nut is a piece of wood, plastic, graphite, or brass that provides a groove for each string. It forms one end of the vibrating length of the string.

- ✔ **The fingerboard:** The fingerboard is the flat side of the neck, beneath the strings, that holds the frets.

- ✔ **The frets:** The frets are the thin metal strips that are embedded, perpendicular to the strings, along the length of the fingerboard. They determine the pitch (sound) of the note that's played. Frets are arranged in *half steps* (the smallest unit of musical distance from one note to the next). When a string is pressed against a fret, the string's vibrating length, and thus its pitch, is changed.

- ✔ **The strings:** Strictly speaking, the strings are not part of your bass, because you remove and replace them periodically. However, your bass would be absolutely useless without them (except maybe as a "bass-ball" bat). The strings are connected to the tuning machines at one end and the bridge at the other. The vibration of the strings produces the sound of your bass.

- ✔ **The back of the neck:** The back of the neck refers to the part of the neck that the thumb of your fretting hand rests on. The fingerboard is attached to the front of the neck. The neck and the fingerboard are usually made up of two separate pieces of wood, but not always.

The body

The body of the bass guitar falls under the dominion of the striking hand (usually the right hand). The following list describes the function of each part of the body:

- ✔ **The pickups:** The pickups consist of magnets that are embedded in a plastic bar that lies underneath and perpendicular to the strings. You can have two magnets for each string, or one long magnet for all the strings. The magnets form a magnetic field, and the vibration of the string disturbs (or *modulates*) that field. This modulation is then translated into an electric signal, which in turn is converted into sound by the amplifier and speaker.

- ✔ **The controls:** The controls are the knobs used for adjusting the volume (loudness) and tone (bass and treble) of the pickups. They are located toward the lower side of your bass (when you have it strapped on).

✔ **The bridge:** The strings are attached to the body at the bridge. The bridge holds one end of each string and is located at the end of the body. Modern pickups, such as piezo pickups or lightwave pickups, are sometimes installed inside the bridge. These pickups read the vibration of the string at the bridge.

✔ **The strap pin:** The strap pin is the metal knob on the neck end of the body where you attach one end of your shoulder strap (usually the thick end).

✔ **The end pin:** The end pin is the metal knob on the bottom end of the body (by the bridge) where you attach the thin end of your shoulder strap.

✔ **The jack:** The jack (also called the *input jack*) is the socket used for connecting the cord from your bass to the amplifier (for more on amplifiers, see Chapter 17).

The innards

The innards aren't obvious to the eye (they're hidden in the cavity of the instrument and covered with plates), but they are essential to the sound and feel of the bass guitar. The following list describes the innards of the bass guitar.

✔ **The truss rod:** The truss rod is an adjustable metal rod that runs the length of your bass guitar's neck. The truss rod controls the curvature of the neck and fingerboard and keeps them stable. The truss rod is usually accessed through the top or bottom of the neck if you need to make adjustments.

✔ **The electronics:** The electronics is a collection of wires, pots (pots are electronic capacitors, the round devices connected to the other side of a volume knob), and other important-looking electronic items that help convert the vibration of the string into sound. The cavity for the electronics is usually located under a plate on the back of your bass guitar's body. It may also be located under the control knobs on the front of your bass.

✔ **The batteries:** If your bass has *active electronics* (electronics with their own power source), you have one or two nine-volt batteries attached to the electronics (via some wires). These batteries are located in the same cavity as the electronics or in an adjacent cavity on the back of the body. If your bass has *passive electronics* (electronics with no batteries), you don't have to worry about replacing batteries.

On a Need-to-Know "Basses": Gearing Up to Play Bass

Getting yourself ready to play both physically (with exercises) and mentally (with theory) is essential to being a good bass player. You also have to prepare your instrument by tuning it and by playing it correctly. When you play the bass guitar correctly, your fingers can move with ease from note to note.

Coordinating your right and left hands

Because you play the bass with two hands (one hand striking and the other fretting; no, it's not worried!), both hands have to be well coordinated with each other. With the exercises in Chapter 4, you can warm up your hands on a daily basis (just like an athlete warms up before a sporting event).

Mastering major and minor chord structures

Two basic tonalities prevail in music: major and minor. Each tonality has a distinctive sound. Major sounds somewhat *happy* or *bright,* whereas minor sounds *sad* or *dark.* Musicians use these sounds to express the mood of the song (or themselves, for that matter).

As a bassist, you have a great advantage: Your major or minor chord will always *feel* the same to your fingers no matter where you play it on the neck, because the pattern of notes doesn't change. Each fret on the neck equals one half step, the smallest *musical interval* (distance between two notes). The sound of each string is exactly five half steps from the sound of the previous (lower) string . . . no exceptions! The bass is perfectly symmetrical, and all patterns remain intact no matter where you play them on the neck. Chapter 5 tells you all about these patterns.

Tuning your bass

Tuner and *bass* . . . sounds almost like a fishing expedition, but fishing for the right note is the last thing you want to do when you tune your bass. Your bass needs to be in tune with the other instruments as well as with itself. Chapter 2 explains several different methods for tuning your bass just right.

Combining scales and chords

Scales and chords form the backbone of music.

- ✔ *Scales* are groups of notes (usually seven) used to create tunes
- ✔ *Chords* are three or four notes, taken from the scale, that form the harmonic (musical) content

As a bassist, you use scales together with chords to form your bass lines (or grooves). This method gives you a certain degree of flexibility to express your individuality (see Chapter 5 for details). You can often spice up your bass lines by choosing from several corresponding scales.

Scaling the Bass Range: Expanding into the Second Octave

When you discover how to play two-octave scales (see Chapter 2 for more about octaves), you take a big step toward elevating your playing to the next level. You can cast off the limitations of the single octave and access the entire range of the instrument.

With access to the whole neck, you can make your chords more interesting by inverting the notes of the chords (switching the notes around), a technique that uses two octaves. You also use both octaves to play cool grooves and *riffs* (musical phrases used in creating solos). For the coolest and easiest solos, use notes from the blues and pentatonic scales. Whatever you play, the transition between the two octaves needs to be absolutely seamless and effortless.

Turning things upside down and inside out: Inversions

No, I don't mean that you have to stand on your head to play bass! Chords consist of notes taken from a scale and played in a traditional order: 1 (called the *root*) 3, and 5, meaning that the chord consists of the first, third, and fifth notes of the scale. An *inversion* is a chord in which the normal order of notes is scrambled; for example, 1, 3, 5 can become 5, 1, 3 or 3, 5, 1. The higher notes of an inverted chord reach into the second octave. Chapter 6 leads you through the inversion process rather painlessly.

Finding the right note

All your chords and scales fall into consistent patterns that you can play any-where on the neck. Here's the big question: "Where do you start the pattern?" Chapter 6 guides you through this process with ease.

Creating grooves and riffs

Certain elements are essential for the creation of grooves and riffs (Chapters 7 and 8 tell you all about these elements). Grooves have a rhythmic content (groove skeleton) and a harmonic content (chord and scale). Riffs are a short melody, usually played fast, that you can play to fill a space in the music. In fact, a bassist often plays a groove in the lower octave and then adds a riff in the higher octave to give the bass line variety and to keep the listener inter-ested. Creating grooves and riffs isn't just a matter of divine inspiration (although that never hurts); it's actually dictated by science!

Using the ultimate solo scales: Blues and pentatonic

When you need a very cool solo, or you need to fill some space with bass *flash* (a fancy mini-solo to show off your skills), the blues scales and penta-tonic scales are hard to beat, especially if you play them in the higher octave. Whether you're playing blues, rock, jazz, or anything in between, these scales, when properly applied, will never let you down. Once again, you benefit from the symmetry of the bass (and from Chapter 8, which gives you the lowdown on the blues and pentatonic scales): One fingering fits all!

Playing fills and solos

As a bassist, your job is to play the groove. You don't have to restrain your-self from playing tasty solos and fast-fingered fills, as long as your solo or *fill* (a miniature solo) relates to the groove and is indeed part of it. Chapter 8 tells you all about fills and solos and how to create them.

Experimenting with Different Musical Styles

Defining the *style* of a tune is your primary function as a bassist. You define a style by the notes and rhythms you choose — and you have to do this while locking in with the drums!

The following list defines some of the styles you'll encounter most often:

✔ **Rock.** A lot of styles are really part of one big overall style, such as rock. The rock styles are generally played with a steady eighth-note pulse, tightly locked with the drums, that drives the song. I have a broad selection of templates (note and rhythm choices for each style) for you to choose from, and I hope that you expand them for your own playing — just take a peek at Chapter 9 and rock on!

✔ **Swing.** Swing styles are based on the triplet feel. With the *triplet,* the beat is subdivided into three equal units, not the usual two. This style is somewhat lighter than the rock styles, and it includes the shuffle as well as jazz walking lines. Shuffle off to Chapter 10 to find out more about swing.

✔ **Funk.** The funk styles rely heavily on the sixteenth note, the smallest rhythmic subdivision commonly used in music. For bassists, this is the busiest style: You have lots of notes to play. You need to lock in very firmly with the drums and keep the groove tight. This style focuses a lot of attention on the bass and is usually a technical challenge. So check out Chapter 11 and get your fingers ready to play some intricate stuff.

✔ **World beat.** World beat is a widely recognized category in almost any record store. I use this term to describe styles that are not native to North American music but are relatively common, such as South American, African, and Caribbean styles. This book prepares you for the most-common world-beat styles, but bear in mind that many more international styles are out there, waiting to be explored. For more on international styles, see Chapter 12.

✔ **Odd meters.** Styles using odd meters aren't part of the regular four-beat patterns you may be used to, but meters that use five, six, or seven beats and beyond are definitely part of the odd meter family. Although unusual, these odd meters can sound quite natural when played correctly. In fact, the waltz (three beats to the measure) is an odd meter style that arguably feels very natural because it's so common. Chapter 13 tells you how to play odd meters smoothly.

Giving Your Bass Some Good Old TLC

Even though your bass requires very little maintenance, certain parts need an occasional adjustment or periodic replacement. You can do a lot of maintenance yourself, with a minimal complement of basic tools.

Certain repairs, however, should be left to the professionals, so don't get too carried away.

Changing the strings

Changing the strings is the most common bass maintenance. How often you change the strings depends on how clear you want your sound to be . . . and *please* don't listen to the stories about bassists who change their strings every 25 years (and then only if they need it).

Change your strings *at least* every three to six months (more often if you play a lot), and wash your hands before you play (sounds funny, doesn't it?) to keep dirt from your hands off your strings. For more info on changing your strings, see Chapter 14.

Cleaning your bass

Obviously, you can't just take a garden hose and power-wash your bass. Your bass, just like any other musical instrument, is very delicate. You need to handle it delicately when removing the soda stains from your last performance (cigarette burns are even more difficult). Cotton swabs and fine cloths are in order. See Chapter 15 for the complete lowdown on cleaning.

Buying Bass Gear

So many basses, so little time. Well, maybe you have a lot of time, but the fact remains: You have a lot of different basses to choose from, and new ones are coming on the market all the time. You need to know what to look and listen for. You also need to know what other gear you need to fulfill your *bass* desires.

Buying a bass

Some basses have a very specific sound, and some have an array of different sounds suitable for many different styles of music. Of course, you also want to choose a bass that you can play comfortably. Okay, your bass should also look cool, but remember: Looks are only varnish deep. Chapter 16 helps you with the entire bass-buying (or is it *bass-adoption?*) process.

Getting an amplifier

How much power do you need? How is the sound? Can you carry everything yourself, or will you need half a dozen burly roadies to budge the amp and speaker? Check out Chapter 17 for help with these questions. Oh, and speaking of "budge" . . . how big is your budget? How much money you have to spend is another thing you need to consider when thinking about purchasing an amp.

Accessorizing your bass

You need to carry some items in your bass bag at all times, such as a strap, tuner, and cables. Other items are optional, such as a chorus pedal or fancy stickers for the fans. Chapter 18 helps you determine which accessories you need and which you don't. Think about whether you can perform without an item: If you can, it's optional, and if you can't, it's a necessity.

Chapter 2

Getting the Tools and Skills to Play

In This Chapter

▶ Holding your bass properly

▶ Positioning your right and left hands

▶ Finding out how to read a fingerboard diagram

▶ Tuning your bass

*I*n this chapter, you tackle the bass-ics of playing the bass: how to hold your instrument, how to position your hands, how to read a fingerboard diagram, and how to tune your bass. So roll up your sleeves and get ready to dive in.

Getting a Hand-le on Your Bass

Before getting started, let me clarify some terminology. I refer to *right hand* and *left hand* in this book, but what really matters is what each hand does:

- ✔ The right hand is your *striking* hand; that is, it strikes (or plucks) each string and puts it into motion to produce a sound.

- ✔ Your left hand is your *fretting* hand; it pushes the strings onto the fret to settle on a pitch.

Frets are small metal strips that are embedded in the neck of the bass, underneath the strings. You usually have between 20 and 24 frets on your bass. To fret a note, you press the string onto the neck between two frets. For instance, to play a string at the 5th fret, press your finger between the 4th and 5th frets, closer to the 5th. Take a look at Figure 2-1 to see the proper way to fret a note.

If you're left-handed, and you decide to play your bass as a lefty, apply the instructions for your right hand to your left hand, and vice versa.

Figure 2-1:
Fretting
a note.

Holding Your Bass

In this chapter, you finally get to wear your bass, which, if you waded through the preliminaries in Chapter 1, is a welcome change.

If you watch other bass players, either live or on television, you may notice an array of different ways to hold a bass. Some definitely look cooler than others, but you may have difficulty playing with a proper hand position when the instrument is scraping along your ankles. Compromise is the name of the game here.

Strapping on your bass: Strings to the outside

When you strap on your bass for the first time, I recommend that you sit down to do it. Adjusting the strap is easier this way. Ideally, the strings of the bass cross between your belt line and your belly button at a slight angle upwards (up on the neck end). This position ensures optimum right- and left-hand coverage, and it works well regardless of whether you're standing or sitting. Oh, and yes, the strings should face the outside!

Strapping on a bass eventually becomes as natural as riding a bike or walking, but when you first start out, you have to follow some basic instructions to get it right. If your left hand is strained when playing, try raising the height of the bass. If your right hand feels uncomfortable, try lowering the bass.

You can achieve the ideal compromise position for both your left and right hands when you follow these steps:

1. **Attach the thick end of your strap to the *strap pin* (the little metal knob) on the body at the neck end of the bass.**

2. **Attach the thin end of your strap to the bottom strap pin (also called the *end pin*) of the bass.**

3. **Hold your bass solidly by the body or the neck with your left hand, and pull the strap over your head and right shoulder, putting your right arm through as well.**

   Allow the strap (with the bass attached) to rest on your left shoulder and continue across your back until it connects with the bottom strap pin of the bass just below the right side of your rib cage.

4. **Adjust your strap in length until the strings are in the area between your belly button and belt buckle, and then fine-tune it from there.**

   You can find your own personal preference, but you want your bass to rest in this general area. Take a look at Figures 2-2 and 2-3 and note that the general position of the bass is the same whether you're standing or sitting.

Voilà! Standing with your bass

And now, get on your feet! The time has come to take a stand with your bass. Here's how:

1. **Make sure that your strap is securely attached to the strap pins.**

   Also, make sure that your strap is straight, not twisted, from one end to the other.

2. **Let your bass hang loosely from your shoulder.**

   Keep your left hand underneath the neck, but don't clutch it. Some basses are a little neck-heavy, while others are perfectly balanced. No matter what type of bass you have, you need to get used to the feeling of it.

3. **Position your hands on the bass.**

    Your left hand should be free to roam the neck from top to bottom without having to hold the bass. Your right hand should be able to reach all of the strings comfortably.

The standing position will most likely be your *live* or *performance position* (see Figure 2-2).

Figure 2-2:
Standing
with your
bass.

Sitting with your bass

During those endless hours of practice, you may want to sit down to play (see Figure 2-3). I recommend using a stool or a tall chair without armrests. That way, the position of your bass is similar whether you're standing or sitting. In addition, you want your thighs to be at least parallel to the floor; try to sit so that they are higher than your knees, if possible.

After you sit down, keep the strap on. You may feel a slight slack in the strap when the bass touches your thighs, but it should still hold the bass in place. Your left hand is free to roam across the neck without your having to worry about holding the bass in place, and your right hand can reach all of the strings comfortably.

Figure 2-3:
Sitting with
your bass.

Getting Your Hands into Position

The secret to getting your hands into position is simple: Keep them loose and relaxed. You want to strike and fret the strings with the least amount of effort possible. The proper position enables you to play at great speed and with great accuracy. It also helps you to get the most control of your tone.

Positioning your left hand

You want your left hand to cover one fret per finger without causing any undue stress in your hand. By using one finger per fret, you set up your hand to execute almost any musical figure without *shifting,* or moving your hand position to reach a note. (A figure is an independent and self-contained musical phrase, sort of like a sentence when you're speaking.)

When you do have to shift, a move of one fret in either direction usually suffices. Check out Figure 2-4 for the proper left-hand position, and follow these steps to accomplish it:

1. **Hold out your left hand with your outstretched arm in front of you.**

   Keep your wrist and hand limp.

2. **Without changing the angle on your wrist, turn your hand over so that your palm faces up and your fingers are slightly curved.**

   Position your thumb so that it faces your index finger (or the area between your index and middle fingers).

3. **Bring in your elbow to the side of your rib cage (without moving your hand) until the neck of your bass is in the palm of your hand.**

   Remember: Don't close your hand!

4. **Place the tip of your thumb on the middle of the back of the neck (of the bass, not of your body).**

   Make sure that your fingertips are pointing upward.

5. **Gently spread your fingers onto the strings, with each finger close to an adjacent fret.**

6. **Curl your fingers until your fingertips are on one of the strings.**

   Be sure to keep the tips of your fingers close to the frets.

Now you're just about ready to press the string to the fret to play a note. Even though you can now fret the desired note, something still has to set the string in motion to produce the actual sound. This is where your right hand comes in.

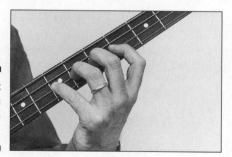 

Figure 2-4:
Position
of the
left hand.

Positioning your right hand

You may see several popular right-hand techniques; so many, in fact, that they could fill a book all on their own. In this book, I concentrate on the *finger-style* technique, which is the most flexible and widely used technique, covering virtually all styles of music. This technique also allows you to work more efficiently with *dynamics* (accenting certain notes). In this section, I show you the proper positions for the pick technique and *slap* (thumb) technique.

I refer to the right hand as the striking hand (and I don't mean that it's in a labor dispute) rather than as the plucking or pulling hand. The other terms are technically correct, but I prefer the term *striking* because *plucking* and *pulling* imply that you should pull the strings away from the body of the bass, which produces a thin sound. Instead, you need to strike the string *into* the body of the bass, not *away from* it.

Positioning your right hand for finger-style playing

The name *finger-style* refers to the use of the index and middle fingers. You can hear this style in country, rock, jazz, and funk — and just about any other type of music. Jaco Pastorius, James Jamerson, and Francis Rocco Prestia are only three of the multitude of bassists who use this technique. Use the following steps to set up your hand properly. Then you can compare the position of your hand to Figure 2-5.

Figure 2-5:
Right hand
in the
proper
position.

1. **Bring your right arm up, as though you're pointing to something in the distance, while keeping your wrist, hand, and fingers relaxed.**

   Keep your wrist at a 45-degree angle (approximately), keep your thumb facing your index finger, and keep your fingers gently curved, with your fingertips pointing to the floor.

2. **Start bending your elbow slowly, keeping it just slightly away from your rib cage.**

3. **Let your hand approach the instrument until your thumb settles onto the *thumb rest* (a plastic or wood bar for resting your thumb on) or the *pickup* (the magnetic bars that pick up the string vibration).**

   Keep your elbow next to your body, not behind it.

4. **Settle the weight of your arm onto your thumb.**

   This position may take some time to get used to, but it keeps your hand and shoulder in their most relaxed state. The thumb acts as a measuring device for your fingers and the individual strings. With this position, you can feel which string you're playing instead of having to look to see where you are.

5. **Reach for your high string with your index or middle finger (see Figure 2-6).**

Figure 2-6:
Hand
reaching
for the
high string.

Your thumb has to bend a little more, and your hand must pivot out on it to reach the highest string.

The terms *high string* and *low string* refer to the sound of the strings, not to the position of your hand. Your high string is actually the string closest to your feet, whereas your low string is closest to your head.

6. **Reach for your lowest string.**

   Your thumb is now straighter. Your hand pivots on the resting thumb, toward your body, and your palm is closer to the body of the bass, as shown in Figure 2-7.

Figure 2-7:
Hand
reaching
for the
low string.

Positioning your right hand for pick-style playing

Some players prefer to use a pick (a small triangular plastic piece, about the size of a quarter) to produce a note instead of using their fingers. Because the strings on a bass are much heavier than on a guitar, your bass pick needs to be heavier, as well.

You can hold the pick in one of two ways: closed or open. You can set your hand properly for closed-hand pick playing by following these steps:

1. **Hold your pick between your index finger and thumb.**

2. **Make a light fist and rest your thumb on top of your index finger.**

3. **Slide your index finger along the bottom of your thumb until it reaches the first knuckle of your thumb.**

   This is where the pick goes, with only the tip of it showing. See Figure 2-8.

From Carol Kaye to Paul McCartney: A brief primer on famous pick players

Pick-style playing was a popular technique in the early days of the bass guitar (the 1950s and '60s, which is, perhaps, not so early for you). Many first-generation players switched from guitar to bass and brought the pick along with them. Joe Osborn and Carol Kaye, two Los Angeles studio musicians, are examples of former guitarists who continued to use a pick to play their bass guitars. The sharp attack of the pick brought new levels of clarity and definition to the notes they played. In the process, it also shattered the belief (previously held by producers and engineers, who were used to the upright bass) that the bass should be felt and not heard. This helped the bass guitar gain worldwide acceptance. Joe Osborn can be heard on many of The Fifth Dimension's hits, such as "Aquarius/Let The Sunshine In." Carol Kaye played on a lot of the Beach Boys' hits, such as "Good Vibrations."

If you search the Internet for info on these two famous bassists, you'll find that they both played some great bass lines on a lot of famous tunes. A *great bass line* is a bass part that propels and builds the tune, has a unique quality that defines the tune (think about "Come Together" by the Beatles), and doesn't get in the way of the melody and vocals. Of course, one of the most famous pick players is Paul McCartney, the former bass player of the Beatles. Paul single-handedly (actually, he used both hands) brought the bass to the foreground in popular music, inventing some of the most memorable bass lines along the way. When you listen to his bass lines in "Penny Lane," or "Day Tripper," or the incredible "Something," you become more aware of the crucial role the bass plays in modern music.

You can also try playing with an open hand (see Figure 2-9). The pick still goes between your thumb and index finger, but you leave a space between your fingers and your palm. You may like the increased control you get when you rest your ring finger and pinkie against the body of the bass. Both styles require you to make a twisting wrist movement with your picking hand.

With a pick, you can strike the string from either above or below. Some players prefer only downstrokes; others use only upstrokes. Still other players combine the two strokes for an even faster technique. Feel free to experiment and find out which technique suits your musical style.

Pick playing is not an aural (or acoustic) necessity anymore. Technology has caught up, and I assure you that your bass will be heard equally well without a pick.

Figure 2-8:
Holding the pick in a closed-hand position.

Figure 2-9:
A pick in the open-hand style.

Slappers and thumbers

Slap style became popular in the 1970s and '80s. Larry Graham (Sly and the Family Stone, and Graham Central Station) was one of the first slappers, and players such as Stanley Clarke continued to expand the technique. Marcus Miller, Flea (Red Hot Chili Peppers), and Victor Wooten (Béla Fleck and the Flecktones) are some of today's popular thumbers.

Positioning your right hand for slap-style playing

The idea behind *slap style* or *thumb style* is to strike a low string with the side of your thumb, giving it a *percussive sound* (a sharp attack and decay of the note, like a drum), and then to *snap* (or pop) a high string with your index finger. Here's how you do it:

1. **Make a light fist with your right hand.**

   Lift your thumb away from your fist, as though you were hitch-hiking.

2. **Loosen up on your index finger and create a hook.**

   Your index finger should look like it's pulling the trigger of a gun.

3. **Rest your forearm on the body of the bass so that your right hand hovers above the strings.**

4. **With a sharp twist of your wrist, flick your thumb against one of the low strings, striking it at the very end of the fingerboard.**

   Lots of wrist movement is required for this style. Figure 2-10 (see left side of figure) shows you how to do it correctly.

5. **Hook your index finger under a high string, and with an opposing twist of your wrist, snap the string against the fret board.**

   Figure 2-10 (see right side of figure) shows you how to do it.

   Make sure that you lift your thumb off the string immediately so that the note rings.

   Don't pull too hard on the high string, or you may break it. Only a small amount of force is required.

Figure 2-10: Thumb striking the string (right), and index finger snapping the string (left).

Reading a Fingerboard Diagram

In some situations, musicians are required to read music and even play the exact note written on a chart, or page of music. (I give you the basics of reading music in Chapter 3.) However, most bassists prefer to create their own accompaniment for a given tune. They think of the selection of notes as a picture. Using a fingerboard diagram (or grid) is a great way to see such pictures.

Scales and chords

Musicians use a *scale,* an orderly ascending or descending sequence of notes, to create their music. The most commonly used scales have seven notes, beginning with the *root* (the first note). The eighth note in the sequence sounds similar to the root, but it's actually an *octave* (a higher root). A *chord* is a combination of three or more notes taken from a scale. I cover both scales and chords in more detail in Chapter 5.

You don't have to read music to play bass; music isn't a visual art, it's an aural art. In other words, you hear it. Some of my favorite bassists can't read a note. Most bass players, however, find that reading music is a useful skill when playing with other people. Some band leaders require you to read music.

Music is often written on paper so that it can be communicated to others. It can be communicated on paper in several different ways. For example, I often use the *fingerboard diagram,* or *grid,* to show you the positions of the different scales and chords on the bass neck. The grid is simply a picture of the bass neck on paper. Check out Figure 2-11 for a picture of the grid.

The grid is composed of the following elements:

- ✔ **The vertical lines represent the strings, from low (left) to high (right).** Because you can often play one complete scale (one octave) or chord with only three strings, the grid has only three strings, even though your bass has at least four strings. The beauty of this system is that you can apply the grid to any part of the bass, as long as you have enough strings and frets to work with.
- ✔ **The horizontal lines in the grid represent the frets.**
- ✔ **The solid black dots and the open circle represent notes to be played.** The open circle is the *root,* or *tonal center.* The root is the most important note in a scale or chord, and it's usually the first note you play. (I cover these terms and concepts in detail in Chapter 5.)

✔ **The numbers next to the dots tell you which finger to use to play the note, as follows:**

    1 = index finger

    2 = middle finger

    3 = ring finger

    4 = pinkie (little finger)

✔ **The arrows from dot to dot indicate the sequence of the notes to be played (if there is a specific sequence).** On the bass, you almost always play one note at a time.

The four-finger technique I describe in the preceding list can help you play everything with the least amount of effort, the fewest shifts, and the greatest level of consistency. Using the same fingering time after time when playing the same scale or chord is essential for speed and accuracy and for playing smoothly. The major scale starting on the root C, called the *C-major* scale or *the key of C,* looks and feels exactly like the major scales that begin on any other root. For instance, it looks exactly like the major scale starting on D (which, you guessed it, is called the *D-major* scale). Both scales have the same structure and are played with the same fingers in the same sequence; the D scale just starts two frets above the C scale.

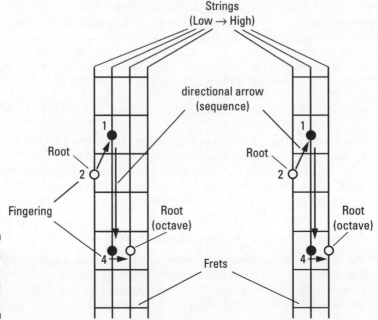

Figure 2-11:
Description of the parts of a grid.

When you memorize a pattern for playing a scale or chord in one key, you can play the same pattern for that scale or chord in every key, anywhere on the neck of the bass.

Viewing a diagram of the major and minor scales

The major and minor scales are the two primary scales in music. Both are constructed in half-step and whole-step combinations. A *half step* is the distance from one fret to the next on the bass. A *whole step* skips one fret. I cover the exact construction of major and minor scales in Chapter 5.

In Figure 2-12, you see grids that indicate the notes of two scales.

- ✔ The one on the left is a major scale.
- ✔ The one on the right is a minor scale.

To play one complete scale, you start on one note (C, for instance) and play an ascending scale up to the same note (C), but higher, as you can see on the grids in Figure 2-12. The notes of the scales fit on three strings, and you can play them without shifting your left hand. One complete scale is an octave.

TRACK 2, 0:00   TRACK 2, 0:18

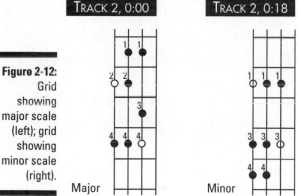

Figure 2-12:
Grid
showing
major scale
(left); grid
showing
minor scale
(right).

Major

Minor

You can play any of the major and minor scales without shifting the position of your hand.

You hear the scales from Figure 2-12 played one at a time. The first sample is a major scale in G, which means that it starts on the note G. (Keep in mind that the structure of the scale doesn't change if you play it in any other key. Try playing the same major scale in D, or in any other note on your bass's neck.) The second sample is a minor scale in G; again, it starts on the root G. (You can play the minor scale in any key without changing the structure.)

Open string scales

Playing open string scales involves a slightly different pattern. Open strings are played without pressing down on a fret. The open string itself is the root. In two keys, E and A, you can use *open* (nonfretted) strings to play a major or a minor scale. See Figure 2-13.

Figure 2-13: Grid #1: open E major scale, grid #2: open A major scale, grid #3: open E minor scale, and grid #4: open A minor scale.

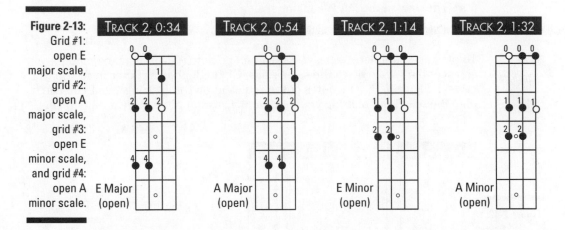

Finding the notes on the neck

Any of your patterns (except for the *open* E and A scales) will work in all keys, so only one question remains: How do you find a certain key when someone asks you, for example, to play in C? Because your patterns can be transposed to any key, all you have to do is nail the root (in this case, C) with the proper finger of the left hand (usually the middle finger for the major patterns, and the index finger for the minor patterns), and you're in position.

The sides, and sometimes the top, of your bass's neck are marked by dots. These dots are your landmarks for determining where a note is located. The notes are organized in a sequence of *half steps,* the smallest step in music (at least in music of the Western Hemisphere). Each half step is one fret. The order of notes in half steps is: C, C♯ (C *sharp*) or D♭ (D *flat*), D, D♯ or E♭, E, F, F♯

or G♭, G, G♯ or A♭, A, A♯ or B♭, B, and C. Notice that some of the notes have two names. For example, C♯ and D♭ are the same note. (It's a half step above C or a half step below D.)

If a note is raised by a half step (one fret), it has a ♯ next to it. For instance, if you take the C that's played on the third fret of the A string (the second thickest string) and raise it a half step to the fourth fret, it becomes C♯. If a note is lowered by a half step, it has a ♭ next to it. For instance, if you lower the B that's on the second fret of the A string by a half step (to the first fret), it becomes B♭.

The notes on the open strings of your bass are tuned (from low to high) E, A, D, and G. You can start from any open string and can count the half steps to find your note. For example, to find C on the A string (see Figure 2-14), your first fret on the A string is A♯ or B♭, the next fret is B, and the one after that is C (the fret with the first dot).

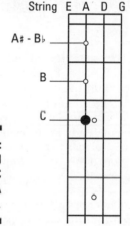

Figure 2-14:
Grid
showing C
on an A
string.

Your bass has two dots on the 12th fret. These dots are your octave marker. By pressing down any string at the 12th fret and striking it, you produce the same note you get when playing the open string, but the note is an octave higher. If you want to find C on the E string (see Figure 2-15), you can start on the E-string octave marker and go backward: E, E♭ or D♯, D, D♭ or C♯, and C. C is four frets below the octave marker, between the third and fourth dots of the E string.

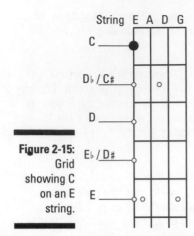

Figure 2-15:
Grid
showing C
on an E
string.

Identifying intervals: They're always in the same place

An *interval* is the distance between two notes. For example, in the scale of C, the distance from the root C up to F is four notes (C, D, E, F), so the interval is called a 4th. When you identify an interval, you count the original note (C in this example) as well as the final note (F). Musicians communicate with interval terminology: "Hey, try a 4th instead of the 5th on the G chord," which means "play the G with a C (an interval of a 4th) instead of the G with a D (an interval of a 5th)." Therefore, knowing what intervals are is important. The intervals are always in the same configuration; a 4th, for example, always looks and feels the same, regardless of what key it's in.

Figure 2-16 shows the names and configurations of each interval. The open circle is the note you're measuring the distance from; the small black dot is the interval. You can find them on your own by feeling them with your hand (again covering one finger per fret). When you get comfortable with how they feel, you'll have an easier time applying them in a playing situation.

Tuning Your Bass Guitar

After you strap on your bass, tuning it is the first item on your to-do list. Tuning can be achieved in several ways. The following sections lead you through the different tuning techniques step by step. It may take you a little time to get used to hearing the low frequencies of the bass notes, but with practice and a few tricks (which I show you), you'll be able to tune a bass in no time.

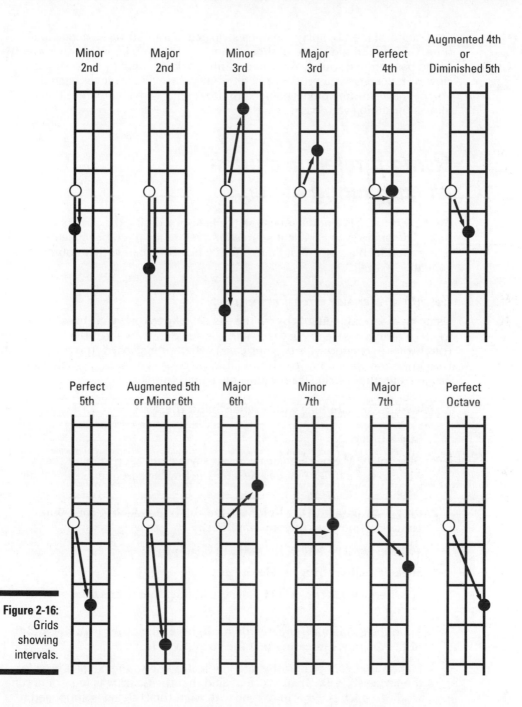

Figure 2-16: Grids showing intervals.

On Track 1 of the CD, I play the open strings of a four-string bass one at a time. Get used to the sound of those strings so that you know how a correctly tuned bass should sound. You can use this track for tuning your own bass. However, because you probably won't want to bring a CD player each time you play away from home, you need to be familiar with some other techniques for tuning your bass, as well.

Using a reference pitch when playing alone

A *reference pitch* is a note you use as the basis for tuning the strings on your bass. The piano is an excellent source for a reference pitch because its tuning is very stable. But you're not limited to the piano — many other sources are available, as well.

Getting a reference pitch from a tuner

Using an electronic tuner is by far the easiest way to tune your bass. The modern tuners have a display that lets you see exactly where your string is (pitchwise — of course it's *on* your bass), whether it's sharp (too high) or flat (too low), and what note you're closest to (in case your bass gets knocked around, and the G string is now closer in sound to F than G).

To get your bass into tune with a tuner, follow these steps:

1. **Buy a tuner.**

   Okay, okay! Maybe that goes without saying, but keep in mind that you want to use a tuner that can register the low bass frequencies. Not all tuners can hear bass notes.

2. **Plug your bass into the tuner via the cable (an electric cord that connects your bass to your amplifier).**

   You can see a picture of the cable in Chapter 17.

3. **Strike an open string and let it ring.**

   Low frequencies travel very slowly, and the tuner needs time to read the note.

4. **Tune the string until the needle (or light) of the tuner is in the middle of the display, indicating that the string is in tune.**

   Make sure to check that the pitch indicator shows the correct note for the string (E, A, D, G), or you may find that the G string is in perfect tune with G♯, which is way out of tune with what the G string is supposed to sound like.

Tuning with a tuner works even when you're in a noisy environment. Make sure that you have a spare battery for your tuner, though. Otherwise, the only way you can see motion in the tuner's needle is by watching it jump as you fling it against the wall in frustration.

You don't want to depend entirely on a mechanical device. You need to know how to tune the bass by yourself in case a garbage truck backs up and crushes your tuner as you're loading your gear into your car.

Getting a reference pitch from one of your own strings

When you play alone, you can tune your bass relative to itself, which is referred to as *relative tuning*. With relative tuning, you use one string, usually the low E, as a reference pitch and adjust the other three so that they are in tune with it. (I explain how to do this in the section "Tuning the bass guitar to itself," later in this chapter.)

When you use relative tuning, you may not be in tune with anyone else's instrument because the E string you used as a reference for tuning the other strings may not be a perfectly tuned E.

Getting a reference pitch from a tuning fork

The tuning fork gives you one reference pitch only. It corresponds to the A, the second-thickest string (although, several octaves apart), or the second string from the top (closest to your head). The tuning fork gives you an excellent way to tune your bass, provided you follow these steps:

1. **Strike the tuning fork against a hard surface and place the handle of it (without touching the two prongs) between your teeth.**

   You can now hear the note A resonating in your head. ***Note:*** You may not want to share your tuning fork (other than with that special someone), and you may want to keep it reasonably clean.

2. **Tune your A string, either open or with harmonics (see "Using harmonics in tuning," later in this chapter, for complete details), to the A of the tuning fork.**

3. **Tune the other strings to the A string.**

   The section "Tuning the bass guitar to itself," later in this chapter, explains the basics of the tuning process.

When you play alone, you can use an electronic tuner or a tuning fork to tune your bass guitar, or you can tune to your own E string. But if your guitar- and piano-playing friends come over to jam, stop what you're doing and get your bass in tune with everyone else.

Using a reference pitch when playing with others

When you play with other musicians, you need to get your bass in tune with their instruments. You can tune all your strings by comparing them individually with the appropriate note of the same pitch from an instrument that is already in tune, such as a piano.

However, I strongly urge you to get one string in tune with the reference pitch (using regular notes or a harmonic; see "Using harmonics in tuning," later in this chapter) and then use your tuned string as a reference pitch for tuning your other strings.

Getting a reference pitch from a piano

Because the tuning on a piano is very stable, it serves as an excellent source for a reference pitch. Figure 2-17 shows the keys on the piano that match your open strings. You may find it easiest to use a reference pitch (on the piano) that is an octave higher than the note you want to tune on your string.

Getting a reference pitch from a guitar

The lowest (thickest) four strings of the guitar correspond to the four strings of your bass: Going from low to high (thick to thin), the strings are E, A, D, and G. Bear in mind that the guitar strings sound one octave higher than your bass strings. They are the same note, only higher.

Figure 2-18 shows which guitar strings correspond to your bass strings.

Using harmonics in tuning

Most of the notes that are offered to you as reference pitches (such as from a guitar) are in a higher octave. If you tried to match the higher note, the string you're tuning would snap and whip around your ears. Comparing notes that are an octave (or two) apart is easier with harmonics.

Harmonics are notes that sound naturally on a string when you lightly touch it at certain points and then strike it with your right hand. Because the bass strings sound so low, the higher harmonics are much easier to hear. The strongest and clearest harmonics can be found at the 12th fret, the 7th fret, and the 5th fret.

Take a look at Figure 2-19 for the main harmonics.

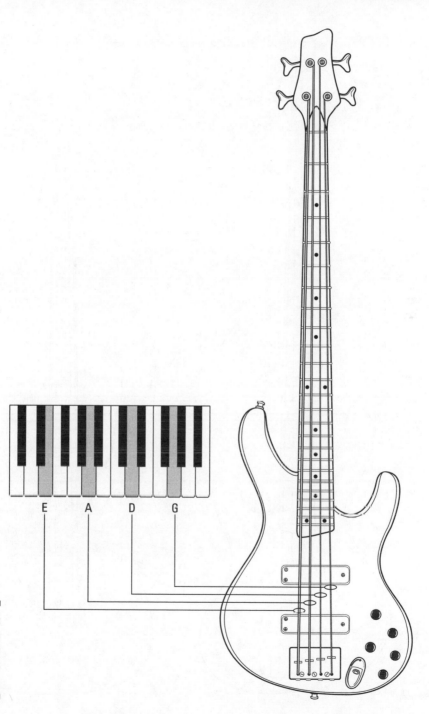

E   A   D   G

Figure 2-17:
Piano keys
that match
open strings
on the bass.

Figure 2-18:
Guitar
strings that
match open
strings on
the bass.

G
D
A
E

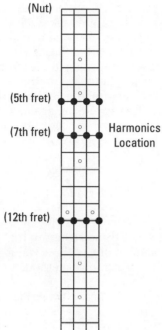

(Nut)

(5th fret)

(7th fret) — Harmonics Location

(12th fret)

Figure 2-19:
The main
harmonics.

The sounds of the harmonics are crystal clear, which makes them a great tuning tool, but to use the harmonics, you must first develop a solid technique for playing them. To play harmonics, follow these steps:

1. **Lightly touch the desired string at the 12th, 7th, or 5th fret with one of the fingers on your left hand (the middle or index finger is best, but any will do).**

   Don't press the string to the fret. Leave your left-hand finger at the contact point (12th, 7th, or 5th fret) when you strike the string with your right hand.

2. **Place your right hand close to the bridge, and strike the string (that you're touching with your left hand) with either the index or middle finger of your right hand.**

   The closer your striking (right hand) finger is to the bridge, the clearer your harmonic will be.

3. **When the harmonic rings out, you can remove your left-hand finger from the string.**

   The harmonic will continue to ring out as long as you don't touch the string.

When you strike a harmonic on a string that isn't in perfect tune, you can hear a *beating* or *wavering* sound. This wavering sound takes a little getting used to, but Track 3 of the CD can help you figure out what to listen for. Let the harmonics ring, and slowly turn the tuning head of the string you're trying to tune. If the wavering gets faster, you're turning in the wrong direction. If the wavering gets slower, you're turning in the right direction. Turn the tuning head until the wavering stops. When the tone is even, your string is in tune. If the wavering gets slower and then speeds up again, you're turning the tuning head past the point where it needs to be. Slowly turn the tuning head in the other direction until the wavering stops.

Tuning the bass guitar to itself

Eventually it always comes down to this: You tune one string of your bass to a reference pitch, and then you tune the other three strings to that tuned string. You can tune your bass guitar to itself in one of three ways: with the 5th-fret method, the 7th-fret method, or the harmonics method.

In all cases, if the notes don't match exactly, you hear a wavering sound. When you turn the tuning head for each string, the wavers occur at wider intervals as they approach an exact match. When you find the exact match, the wavering stops.

The 5th-fret tuning method

The following steps explain how to tune your bass using the 5th-fret method (see Figure 2-20). If you're playing with other people, be sure to get a reference pitch for the E string (the lowest and thickest string) from one of the other tuned instruments before starting.

1. **Using one of the fingers on your left hand, press the E string down at the 5th fret.**

   Touch only the E string, because the open A string needs to vibrate freely. The place to press is actually between the 4th and 5th frets, slightly behind the 5th fret.

2. **Strike the E and the A strings together with your right hand and let them ring.**

   While you're comparing the sounds of the two strings, keep your left-hand finger at the 5th fret of the lower string. Get used to turning your tuning heads with your right hand (by reaching over your left hand) when using this method. The notes should be a perfect match. If they're not (which is usually the case), follow these steps:

   a. **Listen to whether the A string is lower (flat) or higher (sharp) than the E string.**

      You hear a wavering sound if the strings aren't in tune.

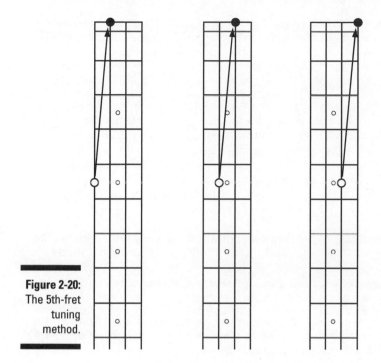

Figure 2-20:
The 5th-fret
tuning
method.

    b. If you're not sure whether the A string is sharp or flat, lower the pitch of the A string until you can hear that it's flat.

    c. Restrike both strings, and then slowly raise the pitch of the A string by turning its tuning head with your right hand until it matches the pitch of the 5th fret of the E string.

    If you go too far, you hear that the A string is sharp (too high). In that case, lower the pitch of the A string by turning the tuning head in the other direction. When the A string is in tune with the E string, continue with the next step.

3. Press the A string down at the 5th fret (touching only the A string).

4. Strike the A and open D strings together and let them ring.

    Listen to whether the D string is sharp or flat, and turn the tuning head for the D string accordingly until the pitch of both strings matches perfectly. When the D string is in tune with the fifth fret of the A string, proceed to the next step.

5. Press the D string down at the 5th fret (touching only the D string).

6. Strike the D and open G strings together and let them ring.

    Listen to whether the G string is sharp or flat, and turn the tuning head for the G string accordingly until the pitch of the fifth fret of the D string matches the open G string perfectly.

Your bass is now in tune with itself. If you tuned the E string to a reference pitch, you're now ready to play with anybody who's in tune with that same reference pitch.

The 7th-fret tuning method

The 7th-fret method is similar to the 5th-fret method, but it works in reverse (from high to low). You need to tune your G string (not your bathing suit, but the highest or skinniest string on your bass) to a reference pitch from a tuned instrument (if you're playing with others). When you have the G string in tune, press down on it at the 7th fret. The note you get when you strike the string with the 7th fret pressed is D, although it's an octave higher than the next lowest (thicker) string. (See Figure 2-21 for a picture of the 7th-fret tuning method.)

Following is a step-by-step description of how to tune your bass with the 7th-fret method:

1. **Using a finger on your left hand, press the G string down at the 7th fret.**

   This brings a whole new meaning to the expression of fretting about the G string, doesn't it? Make sure that you don't touch the adjacent (lower) D string; both strings should vibrate freely.

2. **Strike the G and (open) D strings with your right hand and let them ring together.**

   The pitch is an octave apart, but it's the same note. Listen to whether the D string is sharp or flat, and turn the tuning head for the D string accordingly until the strings are in tune with each other.

3. **Press the D string down at the 7th fret without touching the next lowest string (the A string).**

4. **Strike the D and (open) A strings and let them ring together.**

   The pitch is an octave apart, but it's the same note. Again, listen to whether the A string is sharp or flat, and turn the tuning head for the A string accordingly until the A string is in tune.

5. **Press the A string down at the 7th fret, making sure that you don't touch the E string.**

6. **Strike the A and (open) E strings together and let them ring.**

   As with the other strings, the pitch is an octave apart, but it's the same note. Listen to whether the E string is sharp or flat, and turn the tuning head for the E string accordingly. When the E string is in tune, your entire bass will be in tune.

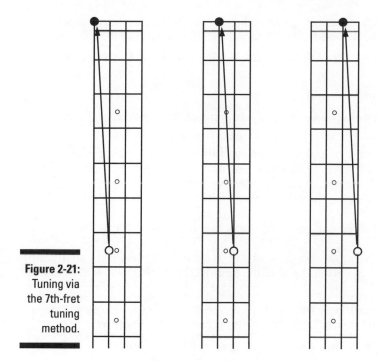

Figure 2-21:
Tuning via
the 7th-fret
tuning
method.

The harmonics tuning method

The harmonics tuning method is the most difficult and most precise tuning method you can use to tune your bass without a tuner. But if you follow these steps, you'll get the hang of tuning your bass to itself using harmonics in no time.

1. **Using the pinkie of your left hand, lightly touch the G string at the 7th fret.**

   Strike the harmonic and let it ring. (If you need help playing the harmonics, check out the section, "Using harmonics in tuning," earlier in this chapter.)

2. **Using the middle finger of your left hand, lightly touch the D string at the 5th fret.**

   Strike the harmonic and let it ring *together* with the previous harmonic. Adjust the tuning head of the D string until the wavering stops.

3. **Using the pinkie of your left hand, lightly touch the D string at the 7th fret.**

   Strike the harmonic and let it ring.

4. **Using the middle finger of your left hand, lightly touch the A string at the 5th fret.**

Strike the harmonic and let it ring *together* with the previous harmonic. Adjust the tuning head of the A string until the wavering stops.

5. **Using the pinkie of your left hand, lightly touch the A string at the 7th fret.**

   Strike the harmonic and let it ring.

6. **Using the middle finger of your left hand, lightly touch the E string at the 5th fret.**

   Strike the harmonic and let it ring *together* with the previous harmonic. Adjust the tuning head of the A string until the wavering stops.

Check out Figure 2-22 for the relationships between the harmonics.

The following list gives you the most important harmonics for tuning:

✔ The 7th-fret harmonic on the G string (the thinnest string) is exactly the same note as the 5th-fret harmonic on the D string (the second-skinniest string).

✔ The 7th-fret harmonic on the D string is exactly the same note as the 5th-fret harmonic on the A string (the second-thickest string).

✔ The 7th-fret harmonic on the A string is exactly the same note as the 5th-fret harmonic on the E string (the thickest string).

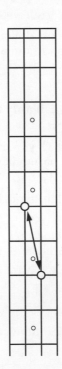
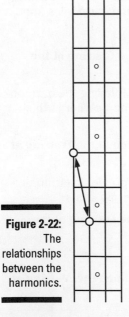
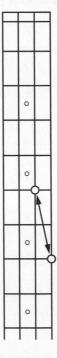

Figure 2-22:
The relationships between the harmonics.

On Track 3 of the CD, you can listen to the wavering and how it can be used to bring your strings into tune when you're tuning with harmonics. Then listen to the wavering and tuning when using the 5th-fret method. Finally, listen to the wavering and tuning when using the 7th-fret method.

Here's a common tuning scenario: You're in a playing situation, be it a rehearsal or performance, and everyone needs to tune. Someone (usually the piano player) strikes a note, and everyone is expected to use it as a reference pitch for tuning their instrument. Ask for either an E or G as a reference pitch, and use one of the tuning methods from this chapter. Happy playing!

Chapter 3

Reading, 'Riting, and Rhythm

Reading music is not nearly as important to bass players as it is for classical musicians (who re-create someone else's music when they read it). A bassist is much more likely to create his or her own bass lines for a tune by incorporating chords and scales (see Chapter 5), or just by listening. However, sometimes you come up with an idea for a bass part that's just perfect for a tune, and you don't want to forget it. What do you do? You write it down. How do you remember it when you need it? You read what you wrote. In this chapter, I introduce you to some fast and easy ways for tackling the dilemma of reading. And by the time you're finished with this chapter, you'll probably agree that reading is really pretty easy . . . and useful.

Reading Notation: Relax, It Won't Hurt a Bit

The phrase "reading music" is nothing to be afraid of. You don't have to read music to be a good (or great) bass player, but it certainly enriches your musical experience and opens doors that may otherwise remain shut.

When you solve the mystery of reading music and discover the joy in it, you may well find yourself reading Bach preludes instead of a novel before going to bed. In this section, I introduce three types of musical notation: chord notation, musical notation, and tablature (or tab). For bassists, these are the most important notational systems.

Chords as mood-makers

Chords can evoke certain moods. For instance, a major chord usually sounds happy and bright, whereas a minor chord sounds sad and dark. Just as a color on canvas may evoke a certain feeling, a chord works on the same principle, only acoustically instead of visually.

Chord notation: The chord chart

The first form of musical notation, the *chord chart,* tells you (in *chord symbols*) what notes you can choose and how many beats each chord lasts. Chord symbols state the *root* of a chord (E, for example; see Chapters 2 and 5 for more info on the root) and the *color* of that chord (*m* for minor or *Maj* for major, for example; see the sidebar "Chords as mood-makers" for more info about the color of chords). You can play the notes from the chord or scale that relates to the chord symbol. For more details on the happy mating of chord symbol, chord, and scale, check out Chapter 5.

A chord chart doesn't tell you exactly which notes to play. The style of the music (and your or your bandleader's taste) influences the sequence and rhythm of the notes you choose from the chord. Part of the fun of playing is choosing your own notes and developing your own creative style. Just keep an open mind . . . and open ears. If it sounds good, it usually is. For more information about which notes are best, look at Part IV of this book, which discusses the different styles of music and tells you how to play different chords within the styles. Figure 3-1 shows you how to play four beats of music for the E minor chord in a rock style.

Music notation: Indicating rhythm and notes

The second form of notation spells out both the rhythm and the notes; it is what is known as regular *music notation.* Regular music notation is written on a musical staff. The *musical staff* consists of five lines and four spaces on which the notes are written. The *clef* (the first symbol you see at the beginning of the musical staff) shows whether the notes on the staff are low (bass) or high (treble). For bass players, the bass clef is the clef of choice. (We try to stay out of treble if we can.)

Figure 3-1:
Measure of
E minor from
a chord
chart in
chord
notation.

Music notation is much more exact than the chord chart. Not only does it tell you what note to play, it also tells you which octave to play the note in, how long to hold the note, which note to accent, and so on. In short, this method doesn't leave much room for creativity, but it does leave the embellishments up to you. Figure 3-2 shows the measure of E minor in music notation; it also shows the different parts of the staff.

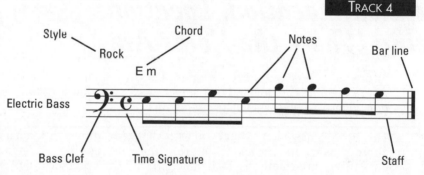

Figure 3-2:
Measure of
E minor in
music
notation
with a
description
of the staff.

The bass sounds one octave lower than the written note. Piano players, when reading from the same sheet as the bass player, play the same notes an octave higher (see Chapter 2 for a discussion of octaves).

Tablature notation: Showing strings, frets, and sequence

The third notational device, *tablature* (or *tab*), shows you which strings to press on which frets for the correct notes. Using this method, you can see the exact notes and their sequence, but you generally can't see the rhythm, which is why tablature is usually accompanied by music notation (see previous section).

When you rely on tab notation, bear in mind that the frets indicated may not be the only places on the neck where you can find those notes. For example, the G on the open G string can also be found on

- The 5th fret of the D string
- The 10th fret of the A string
- The 15th fret of the E string

See Figure 3-3 for the different locations of the same note G.

The best choice for a note is determined by the position of the other notes in the pattern you're playing. Keep in mind that you want to avoid any unnecessary shifts in your left hand; whenever possible, play the notes of the chord in one area of the bass neck.

Location, Location, Location: Seeing Where the Notes Are

After you understand the three types of musical notation, you need to know where the notes are located on the bass neck and what they look like in notation. Figure 3-4 gives an illustration of this.

This book is designed to help you with all three of the notational methods — chord, music notation, and tablature — that I discuss in the previous section. I use these three methods in conjunction with the grid (see Chapter 2), which shows you how to position your notes and patterns on the bass. In addition, I provide you with a great number of notational figures throughout this book, especially in Part IV. You can use the CD (included with the book) to listen to the music shown in the figures.

Later in this chapter, I show you how to put musical notation into practice, but first you need to understand rhythm.

Using the Metronome: You Know, That Tick-Tock Thing

A *metronome* is a device that helps you develop good rhythm. Metronomes come in many shapes and colors, but they all have one thing in common: They give you a steady clicking sound to base your timing on. Like a very loud clock tick, the metronome produces a steady beat. You can adjust the speed of the click to suit your needs.

The old-fashioned acoustic metronomes have a small weight that swings back and forth. They need to be used on a level surface, and they must be wound up periodically. Electric metronomes need to be plugged into a wall outlet. The small battery-powered metronomes, however, are the most common and the most user-friendly.

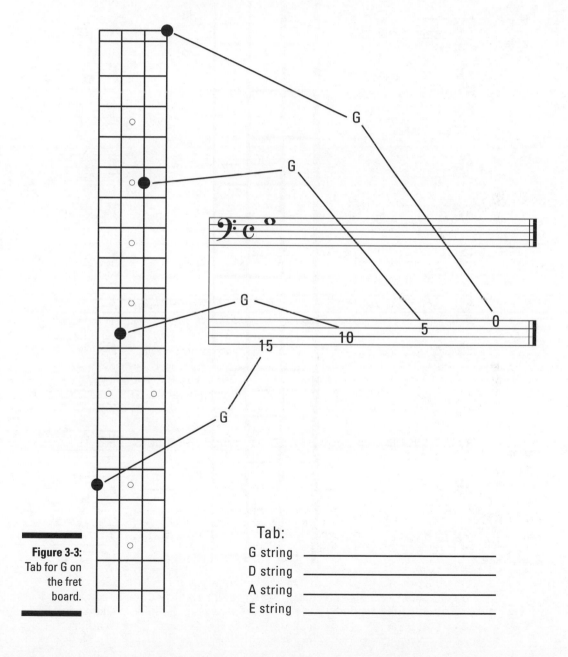

Figure 3-3: Tab for G on the fret board.

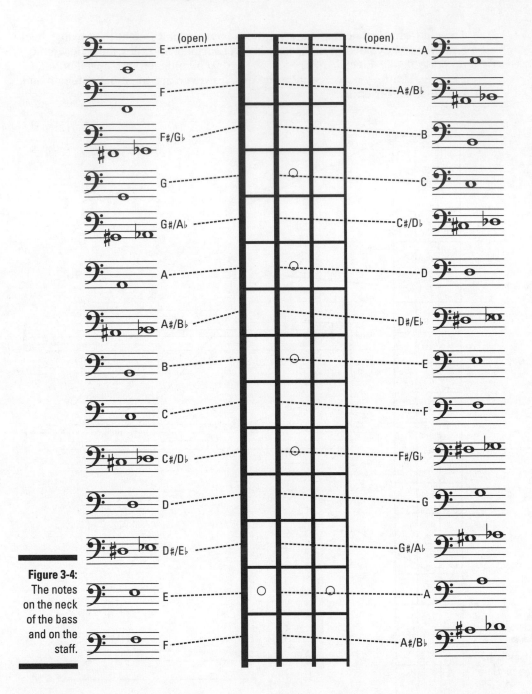

Figure 3-4:
The notes
on the neck
of the bass
and on the
staff.

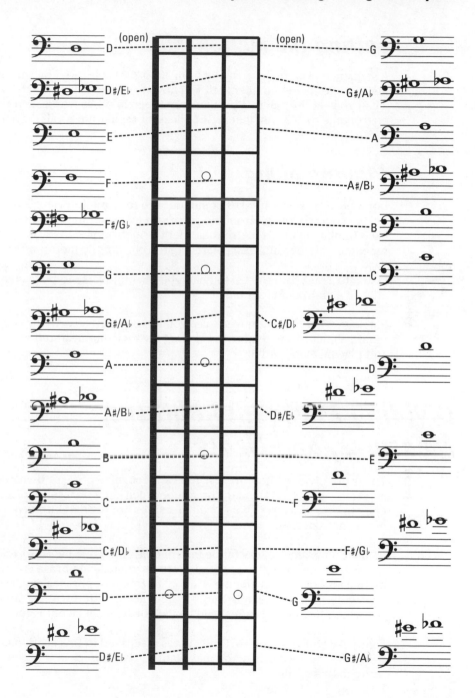

Setting the metronome

A sequence of numbers (usually from 40 to 208) is located on the face of the metronome. These numbers tell you how many clicks per minute you'll hear when you set the dial to a particular number. In other words, if you set your metronome to 162, you'll hear 162 clicks, at regular intervals, in one minute.

Playing along

Don't be surprised if it takes some practice to regulate your playing to the ticking sound of the metronome. Here's an exercise that may help you get used to playing with a metronome: Set the metronome to 80 and play a repeated note on your bass, matching the click of the metronome.

Listen to Track 5 on the CD to hear what it sounds like to play evenly to the click of a metronome set on 80.

Playing with a metronome enables you to keep a steady rhythm not just at tempo 80 but at any tempo. Try setting the metronome at different tempos and playing along with it.

Dividing Music into Phrases, Measures, and Beats

Tunes are divided into phrases. You can recognize phrases by listening to singers — they tend to take a breath between each phrase. Phrases are divided into measures (bars), and measures are divided into beats (or clicks of the metronome).

In most tunes, four clicks of the metronome equal one measure, and four measures equal one phrase. In other words, a musical phrase is 16 beats long, or 16 clicks of the metronome. The organization of phrases makes it easier to keep your place in the music and communicate with the other musicians. To see what phrases, measures, and beats look like, check out Figure 3-5.

Figure 3-6 shows all the rhythmic notes discussed in this section and how they relate to each other. You may want to glance back at it as you read through this section.

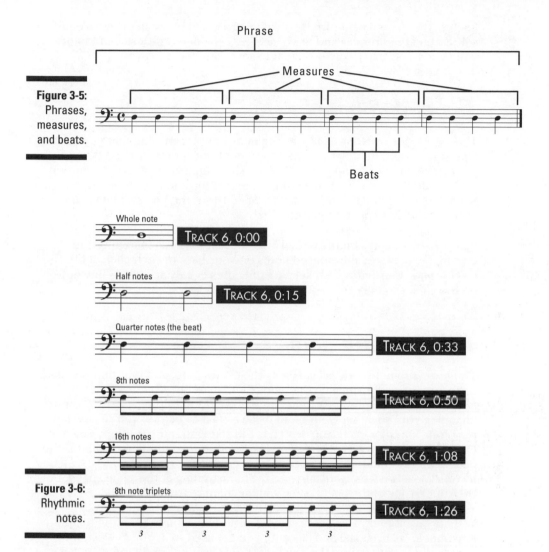

Figure 3-5: Phrases, measures, and beats.

Figure 3-6: Rhythmic notes.

The quarter note

The four beats (metronome clicks) in a measure (or bar) each equal a quarter note. These four beats make up the *1-2-3-4* of the musical count. Imagine that you're marching on the street. You walk at a steady, even speed, and your feet go in a regular rhythm: Left, right, left, right, and so on. This steady marching is what your quarter-note rhythm feels like — a regular pulse: *1-2-3-4, 1-2-3-4,* and so on.

Each of the beats can in turn be divided into equal parts. In order to come up with interesting grooves and bass parts (like the ones I describe in Chapter 7), you need to be able to divide a beat in several different ways.

The eighth note

The eighth note is twice as fast as the quarter note. Imagine that you're still marching — left, right, left, right. As you continue, tap your hand twice on your thigh, at regular intervals, for each step you take. Instead of counting *1-2-3-4,* subdivide the beat by adding an *and* at the end of each number, making it *1 and 2 and 3 and 4 and.* If you do this right, you still move at exactly the same speed as before.

Playing eighth notes on the bass works the same way as marching and tapping. Play two evenly spaced notes on your bass to each click of the metronome. Concentrate on keeping the notes evenly spaced — one note on the click and the other note between the clicks.

The sixteenth note

The sixteenth note is twice as fast as the eighth note, and four times as fast as the quarter note. Imagine that you're still marching (by this time you're probably miles from home) and counting *1 and 2 and 3 and 4 and.* Without changing your pace, tap your hand twice as fast as before. You're now tapping four times for each step, which is the sixteenth-note rhythm. Take your count of *1 and 2 and 3 and 4 and* and add *e* after the number and *a* after the *and.* Keep the count even, and count *1 e and a - 2 e and a - 3 e and a - 4 e and a.* Your pace is unchanged, and you're still marching at the same speed, but the subdivision of the beats gives you much more to "talk" about.

You may want to try this exercise with your metronome. Keep the tempo reasonable (between 60 and 80) until you get used to it. You may want to try marching your feet to the clicks of the metronome and tapping out the subdivisions for the eighth and sixteenth notes with your hand. When you're comfortable with this exercise, start doing it with your bass instead of with your hands and feet.

The half note

The half note is half as fast as the quarter note. In other words, two quarter notes fill the space of one half note. If you're still marching (by now you're probably halfway across the continent), tap your hand once for every two steps you take. You're still moving at the same speed, but your rhythm is now only half as fast.

The whole note

The whole note is half as fast as the half note, and four times slower than the quarter note. If you're still marching (and you haven't come to a large body of water yet), tap your hand *once* for every four steps you take. As always, your speed doesn't change; the rhythm of your hand is the only thing that changes.

All the subdivisions of the notes I describe in the previous sections are either double or half, and divisible by two. In many tunes, however, the beats are subdivided into three parts.

The triplet

A *triplet rhythm* subdivides the beat into three even rhythmic intervals. As you continue to march, tap your hand three times evenly for each step you take. Your step still represents the quarter note, but your hand is now tapping an eighth-note triplet.

The dot: Why not?

The *dot* is a notational device that allows you to extend the value (duration) of a note by half its original value. The quarter note has a value of two eighth notes; when you add a dot to a quarter note, you add an extra eighth note to its value, and you end up with a note that has a value of three eighth notes. Figure 3-7 shows you the most common dotted notes.

Figure 3-7: The most common dotted notes.

1/4 + 1/8   1/8 + 1/16

The tie: Very formal

The *tie* combines two notes. If you tie a quarter note to another quarter note, you increase the length of the original quarter note by another quarter note. (You don't restrike the second note.) The tie simply adds the two notes together. You can combine any two notes with a tie. Figure 3-8 shows common ties between notes.

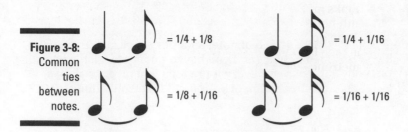

Figure 3-8:
Common ties between notes.

The rest: Don't take a nap

You don't have to play a note on every single beat. Many beats are silent. The *rest* tells you when to avoid playing a beat. It works exactly like the rhythmic notation (including the dot), except you don't make a sound.

Figure 3-9 shows you the rest equivalent to the note (a quarter-note rest takes the same amount of time as a quarter note, an eighth-note rest takes the same amount of time as an eighth note, and so on).

Figure 3-9:
The values of note and rest, and their typical application.

TRACK 7

Discovering How to Read Music

As you read this sentence, notice that you're not reading letter by letter; you're reading words. You read music the same way. Music notation is recognizable in chunks of notes (or musical words). Certain chunks tend to be repeated again and again. You just need to train your eyes to recognize these patterns. When you get used to seeing and hearing music in chunks, you can get a good idea of what the music on the page sounds (and feels) like just by scanning the page.

Reading music in chunks makes playing much easier. The chunks may be a group of four sixteenth notes or perhaps two eighth notes. Become familiar with the picture of these notes (or the way they look when grouped together) for faster recognition (see Figure 3-10), and practice playing and singing them to the click of your metronome.

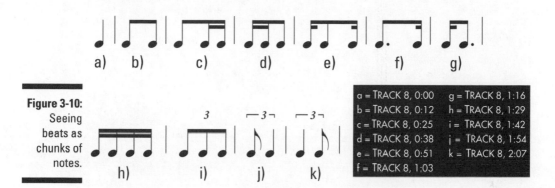

Figure 3-10:
Seeing beats as chunks of notes.

a = TRACK 8, 0:00	g = TRACK 8, 1:16
b = TRACK 8, 0:12	h = TRACK 8, 1:29
c = TRACK 8, 0:25	i = TRACK 8, 1:42
d = TRACK 8, 0:38	j = TRACK 8, 1:54
e = TRACK 8, 0:51	k = TRACK 8, 2:07
f = TRACK 8, 1:03	

Part II
The Bass-ics of Playing

In this part . . .

Put on your sweats and strap on your ankle weights — class is now in session. In this part, you discover how to get (and keep) yourself in perfect bass-playing shape. Chapter 4 shows you exercises to coordinate and strengthen your hands, and Chapter 5 helps you work out your brain muscle with some chords and modes.

Chapter 4

Warming Up: Getting Your Hands in Shape to Play

* *

In This Chapter

▶ Recognizing how your bass produces sound

▶ Conditioning your right hand for striking

▶ Conditioning your left hand for fretting

* *

*I*n this chapter, I help you understand how you produce sound on the bass, and how you can strengthen your hands and coordinate them to produce that sound. That's right: One hand needs to know what the other is doing. Ready? Strap your bass safely around your shoulder. Place it at the proper angle and height (see Chapter 2), put your hands in position (also in Chapter 2), and get ready to play your heart out.

Wait! Not quite so fast. Keep that bass strapped on, but before you start, you need to know what makes this thing (the bass) tick — or sound, actually.

Understanding the Sound

When you strike a bass string, the string vibrates. This sustained vibration is what you hear as the *pitch,* or *tone* (it's also referred to as a *note*). Each note vibrates at a different speed (called *frequency*). To give you an idea of how fast this vibration is, the open A string vibrates at a frequency of 110 times per second when properly tuned. The *pickup* (the magnet underneath your strings, see Chapter 1) on your bass translates this string vibration into an electrical charge, which in turn is converted to sound by the amplifier and speaker (see Chapter 17 for more about amplifiers and speakers).

Two things determine the pitch of a string:

 ✔ Tension
 ✔ Length

The more tension a string has, the higher its pitch; the less tension a string has, the lower the pitch. (Just think about how your voice gets higher and higher when you get tense.) The shorter a string is, the higher its pitch; the longer a string is, the lower its pitch.

When a string is tuned at the proper tension, all you need to do to change the pitch is to change its length. You change the length by fretting the string (no, you don't make it nervous). *Fretting the string* means that you place a "left-hand finger on the string and press it onto a fret on the fingerboard, thus shortening the length of the string. Voilà, the string is shorter and the pitch (or note) is higher.

To get the desired bass note, hold the string down on that fret, and strike the string (causing it to vibrate) with a right-hand finger.

Performing Right-Hand Warm-Ups

Just as with any other physical activity, you need to prepare your body for the task. Without proper exercise, your hands simply won't be strong enough or coordinated enough to endure long hours of bass playing. A few minutes a day with the proper exercises go a long way.

Start the exercises in this section by positioning your right hand on the bass. If you have any questions about your hand positions, check out Chapter 2 for a thorough description. To avoid any confusion, I use letters for the fingers of the right hand and numbers for the fingers of the left hand. The letters are as follows:

 ✔ Index finger = *i*
 ✔ Middle finger = *m*

For now, your left hand gets to take a break while your right hand is working out. Feel free to use it for scratching various body parts.

Right-hand same-string strokes

When you play notes on the same string, you need to be able to alternate between your index and middle fingers, so you can play notes in rapid succession and with an even tone. The following steps show you how to practice these same-string strokes.

1. **Using the index finger (*i*) or middle finger (*m*) of your right hand, strike the lowest string.**

   Alternate between your *i* and *m* fingers (striking the string with one finger at a time) and keep the sound even.

2. **Pull your fingertips across the string.**

   Don't lift your fingers really high and slap them down. When you slap the string, you create a lot of unwanted fret noise. Don't pluck the string up (like a classical guitar player), either. When you pluck the string up, it vibrates over the pickup in a way that produces a very thin sound. Your angle of attack (your strike) should be *into* the instrument, making the tone full and round.

   Take a look at Figure 4-1 for the proper strike angle for the right hand. This technique gives you an authoritative sound, which is exactly what you want as a bass player.

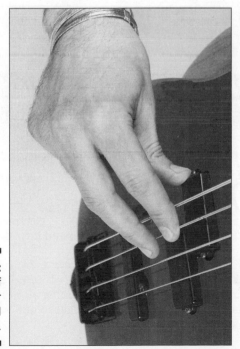

Figure 4-1:
Angle of attack for right-hand strike.

Listen to Track 9. First, you hear a clearly marked section of a wrong finger slap for eight beats and then a clearly marked, wrong guitarlike pluck for eight beats. Next, you hear a clearly marked, beautiful tone produced by — you guessed it — the correct strike for eight beats.

A word about terminology: I personally say *strike* rather than *pluck* because the word pluck is used extensively for guitar playing. Guitar players and bassists *attack* their strings differently, and I simply want to differentiate between the two. But don't be surprised to find pluck or similar terms in other books about bass playing.

Play evenly on each string, alternating between your *i* and *m* fingers. Aaaaaah, can you feel those calluses building up? You want those calluses, believe me. You better make your fingers tough and hard so that you can strike the string all day long without any pain (or blisters).

As you play, you probably realize that your striking fingers are coming to rest on the next lowest string when you play the adjacent higher string. This technique is correct; it helps mute the strings that are not being played. When you play the lowest string (the E string), your fingers should come to rest against your thumb (which, of course, is firmly anchored, right?). Check out Figure 4-2 for the proper striking sequence.

Figure 4-2:
Sequence
of fingers
striking the
string.

Getting control of the strength in your striking hand: Right-hand accents

This section takes you one step closer to creating music and introduces accents into your playing.

Accenting a note means making it slightly louder than the other notes. To accent a note, just strike the string slightly harder. Accenting allows you to control the volume of each note as you play it, which makes your bass line more interesting.

Don't accent a note too hard, though. If you strike a string too forcefully, the sound becomes distorted, and the tone leaves much to be desired. (It also tires out your hands very quickly.)

Follow these steps to accent a note correctly with either striking finger:

1. **Start playing the E string with alternating *i* and *m* fingers of your right hand.**

2. **Accent (that is, play it louder) each note that you strike with your *i* finger.**

3. **After you get comfortable using your *i* finger, accent each note that you strike with your *m* finger.**

4. **Repeat this exercise on the A string, and then move on to the D string and G string.**

    You want to familiarize yourself with all the strings, because each string has a slightly different feel.

When you're comfortable accenting with either finger, put the previous instructions into exercise form.

1. **Play evenly, alternating between your *i* and *m* fingers.**

    Think of this as a four-note sequence where you play *i m i m.*

2. **Accent the first note of each sequence (the underlined *i*), making it *i̲ m i m, i̲ m i m, i̲ m i m,* and so on.**

3. **When you have a handle on playing *i m i m,* start the sequence with *m,* making it *m i m i.***

4. **Accent the first note again (this time, the underlined *m*), making the sequence *m̲ i m i, m̲ i m i, m̲ i m i,* and so on.**

5. **Repeat this exercise on all the strings.**

Check out Figure 4-3 for the notation for this exercise.

Figure 4-3:
Right-hand
accents.

TRACK 10

Notice how the accented notes in Figure 4-3 are still within a certain range of volume; they don't distort. Your notes should always sound clear and controlled. This exercise sounds the same using either finger, which is, of course, the idea.

Getting across the strings smoothly: Right-hand string crossing

The final stage of the right-hand warm-up is called *string crossing.* How do you cross the strings? It's very straightforward. Just remember the following three rules:

✔ Alternate your middle and index fingers when you're striking the same string. (The "right-hand same-string strokes" exercises are covered in the previous section.)

✔ Alternate your middle and index fingers when you're crossing from a *lower* to a *higher* string.

✔ Rake with the same finger when you're crossing from a *higher* to a *lower* string. (*Raking* means striking a string with one finger and then striking the next lower string with the same finger.)

Take a look at your alternating fingers when you're crossing from a lower to a higher string. Remember, the lower string is the one on top (nearest your head). A regular four-string bass is tuned (from low to high) E, A, D, and G. Try the following exercise for right-hand coordination:

1. **Strike the E string with *i* (the index finger).**

2. **Strike the A string with *m* (the middle finger).**

3. **Strike the D string with *i*.**

4. **Strike the G string with *m*.**

Now strike the G string again, this time with *i* (alternating on the same string), and rake it all the way across the D, A, and E strings. Keep the rhythm and volume even.

After you play the E string with *i,* continue with the second half of the exercise:

1. **Strike the E string with *m* (the middle finger).**

2. **Strike the A string with *i* (the index finger).**

3. **Strike the D string with *m*.**

4. **Strike the G string with *i*.**

Now strike the G string again with *m* (alternating on the same string), and rake it all the way across the D, A, and E strings. Again, keep the rhythm and volume even in both directions.

Listen to this exercise on Track 11 of the CD. You won't hear a difference in the sound of the strings as the fingers alternate. Listen to the evenness of the volume of the notes, and to the timing between the notes. The timing is identical whether you're going up or down on the strings. Make sure that your fingers strike the strings evenly.

Coordinating Your Left Hand with Your Right Hand

The job of your left hand is to press down on the string at the appropriate fret, which gives you the desired pitch, while the right hand strikes the proper string at the same time and produces the sound. You see bass players use a variety of left-hand positions, but without a doubt, the most economical position is the one that uses all four fingers on the frets (the thumb is on the back of the neck). In this section, I show you how to train your left hand for some finger independence.

The left-hand fingers are numbered in the figures throughout this book as follows:

- Index finger = 1
- Middle finger = 2
- Ring finger = 3
- Pinkie (little finger) = 4

Doing finger permutations

Get ready for one of the best exercises you'll ever find for bassists: finger permutations. The *finger permutation* exercise gives you a workout for every possible combination of finger sequences on your left hand. Here's how it works:

1. **Position your hand on the neck of the bass so that your index finger (1) is on low G (the 3rd fret on the E string).**

2. **Spread your fingers so that each one covers one fret.**

3. **Press the notes that are under your fingers, one finger (fret) at a time, in order: 1 2 3 4 (the right hand strikes the string to sound each note).**

4. **Repeat the process on the A string (the next string), the D string, and the G string.**

5. **When you complete this finger combination on every string, go back to the E string and do the next combination.**

Table 4-1 shows you the complete list of left-hand permutations (all the fingerings starting with 1, and then 2, 3, and 4). Practice one column at a time, and repeat the process until you do all the combinations (and I mean *every* one). These exercises give your left hand the desired coordination (and strength) so that you can play all those hip bass lines I show you in Part IV.

Table 4-1	Left-Hand Permutations		
Index Finger	*Middle Finger*	*Ring Finger*	*Pinkie*
1 2 3 4	2 1 3 4	3 1 2 4	4 1 2 3
1 2 4 3	2 1 4 3	3 1 4 2	4 1 3 2
1 3 2 4	2 3 1 4	3 2 1 4	4 2 1 3
1 3 4 2	2 3 4 1	3 2 4 1	4 2 3 1
1 4 2 3	2 4 1 3	3 4 1 2	4 3 1 2
1 4 3 2	2 4 3 1	3 4 2 1	4 3 2 1

Take a look at an example of the *first line* (the first combination) of the left-hand permutations in Figure 4-4. You can try doing these exercises on any area of the neck of the bass. On the CD, the exercises start on low G (with the index finger on the third fret of the E string), but don't limit yourself to that area.

TRACK 12

Left Hand

Figure 4-4:
First line (1 2 3 4) of left-hand permu-tations.

Left Hand:
1 = index finger
2 = middle finger
3 = ring finger
4 = pinkie (little finger)

I highly recommend doing both the right- and left-hand exercises in this chapter every day before you play. The more familiar you become with these exercises, the quicker you can cruise through them. Nothing warms you up better.

What's that hum? Muting the strings

When you play, you may find that some strings vibrate even though you didn't strike them. *Sympathetic vibration* (the official name for this) is a natural phenomenon. You can silence, or *mute,* any string by touching it lightly with either your left hand (preferably with more than one finger) or your right hand, or even with both hands. As you refine your technique, sympathetic vibration will become less and less of a problem.

For example, if you strike a low G on the E string, the open G string vibrates as well. Just keep your left hand fingers in (light) touch with the strings, and you won't have a problem. Take a look at Figure 4-5 to see what muting with the left hand looks like. Notice how the undersides of the fingers touch the other strings, preventing them from vibrating.

Figure 4-5:
Left hand playing low G while muting the other strings.

Putting it together

Try the simple exercise in Figure 4-6 that coordinates the fingering of the left hand with the striking of the right hand.

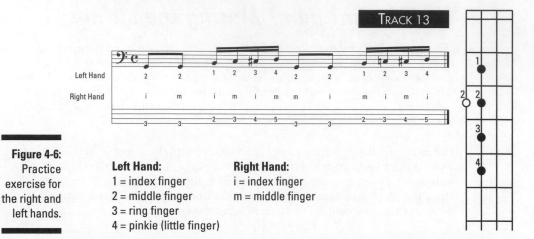

Figure 4-6:
Practice exercise for the right and left hands.

Left Hand:
1 = index finger
2 = middle finger
3 = ring finger
4 = pinkie (little finger)

Right Hand:
i = index finger
m = middle finger

The notation and the tab (tablature) show you where to place the notes. If you use the grid (see Chapter 2), you can transpose this pattern into any key.

Make sure that your right hand alternates properly. You start this exercise with a different finger on each repetition (alternating *i* and *m* fingers). As for your left hand, it doesn't have to shift for the entire exercise as long as you use all four left-hand fingers properly.

Chapter 5

Understanding Major and Minor Structures

Sing a note, any note. Go ahead. "Lah!" Now use this note to sing the first line of "Twinkle, Twinkle, Little Star." You have just established a tonal center. The *tonal center* is the most important note of a tune. The tonal center often begins the tune (as is the case when you sing "Twinkle, Twinkle, Little Star"), but not always (for example, "Happy Birthday" doesn't start on the tonal center). The tonal center, however, usually ends the tune. Just sing both tunes all the way through, and you end on the tonal center.

All the other notes in the tune relate to the tonal center and sound as though they're gravitating toward it. The other notes gravitate toward the center in two basic ways: via a major scale, or via a minor scale. These two *tonalities* (sounds) rule the world of music. Major has a happy, bright sound, while minor sounds dark and brooding. Without the contrast between major and minor tonalities, music would be about as interesting as a picture of white clouds on a white background.

Subtle variations exist within the major and minor tonalities, but the basics remain the same: In the first part of this chapter, I explain some technical stuff, such as scales (also called modes) and chords. Don't worry, I promise not to bore you to tears. You'll use all the information in this chapter again and again when you're playing bass. In the later part of the chapter, you get to apply scales and chords the way they're used in a real-life playing situation, when you're playing a song.

Building Major and Minor Scales

A *scale* is a combination of notes (usually seven different notes) starting with a tonal center (root) and ending with its octave. For example, you can play a scale from C to the octave above or below it. Check out Figure 5-1 for an example of a scale.

Musicians also refer to the group of notes between a root and its octave as an *octave.* Unfortunately it's the same term for both, just to confuse beginners.

An *interval* is the distance between any two notes you play. The notes of any interval — and an octave is an example of an interval — are always in the same relationship to each other on the bass; they're always positioned the same way on the fret board. You can finger an octave the same way, no matter where the first note occurs. Take a look at Chapter 2 for a listing of intervals and their positions.

Figure 5-1: Notation and placement of a scale.

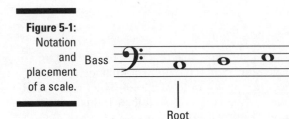

A half-step interval is the distance from one fret to the next on the bass neck. A whole-step interval is the distance between two frets on the bass neck (see Chapter 1 for more on frets). One octave equals 12 half steps.

Most scales are made up of sequences of notes in half-step and whole-step intervals. As is the case with intervals, the shapes of the scales remain constant in any position on the fingerboard of the bass guitar. If you know a scale in one position, you know it in all positions. Here's a little hint: Don't tell any of the other musicians that you don't have to think about each individual scale; they'll be jealous, and they may decide to pay you less.

Major scales

The major scale has seven notes arranged in whole- and half-step intervals within one octave.

✔ The starting note is the *root* (the tonal center). It's also called the *1,* for the first note of the scale.

✔ All the notes *(scale tones)* between the 1 and the octave are numbered in sequence. So the major scale consists of the root (or 1), 2, 3, 4, 5, 6, and 7.

✔ The note after the 7 is the *octave.* The octave is the same note as the 1 but higher. You can use this octave as a new 1 (root) for repeating the first scale an octave higher.

When you describe the notes of the major scale, you call them the root, 2nd, 3rd, 4th, 5th, 6th, 7th, and octave.

Here is the structure of the major scale. (I label the whole steps with "W" and the half steps with "H" to show you the distance from one note to the next in the major scale.)

Root <**W**> 2nd <**W**> 3rd <**H**> 4th <**W**> 5th <**W**> 6th <**W**> 7th <**H**> octave

Figure 5-2 shows you the structure of the major scale on a grid. (See Chapter 2 for a description of the grid.) The open circle represents the root, and the solid dots represent the other scale tones (notes).

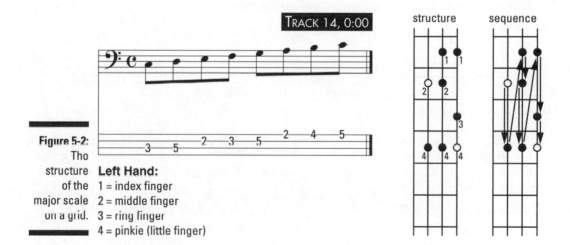

Figure 5-2: The structure of the major scale on a grid.

Left Hand:
1 = index finger
2 = middle finger
3 = ring finger
4 = pinkie (little finger)

You can play the major scale anywhere on the fingerboard as long as you have three strings and four frets at your disposal. Going up, if you start the scale with your middle finger, you can complete it without shifting your left hand. (For more on shifting, see "Chromatic tones outside the box," later in this chapter.) Going down, you start the scale with your pinkie.

The major scale structure forms the basis for all your other scales and their intervals, which means that the intervals of all the other scales are compared to the major scale intervals. When a note deviates from the notes in the major scale, it is specially marked with a ♭ or a ♯.

✔ When you lower any note by a half step, the note is *flatted* (shown with the symbol ♭ next to the note or number).

✔ When you raise any note by a half step, the note is *sharped* (shown with the symbol ♯ next to the note or number).

Minor scales

Like the major scale, minor scales have seven different notes within an octave, but the whole and half steps are arranged in a different order. The *natural minor scale* is the basis of all other minor scales. Here is the sequence of the notes in a natural minor scale:

Root, 2, ♭3, 4, 5, ♭6, ♭7, and octave

Notice that the 3rd, 6th, and 7th notes in the natural minor scale are each a half step lower than the 3rd, 6th, and 7th notes in the major scale. The ♭3 (flat 3) is the fundamental note in a scale that defines it as minor instead of major; this note is often referred to in music theory as a minor 3rd.

Here is the structure of the natural minor scale:

Root <**W**> 2nd <**H**> ♭3rd <**W**> 4th <**W**> 5th <**H**> ♭6th <**W**> ♭7th <**W**> Octave

Start playing this scale with your index finger. You can play the natural minor scale in one position (without having to shift your left hand). Figure 5-3 shows you the structure of the natural minor scale.

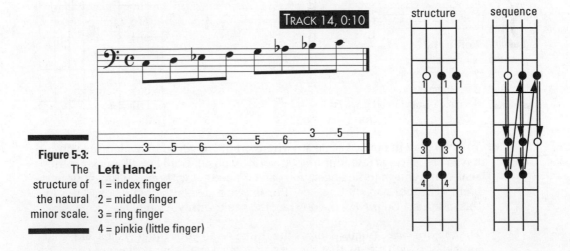

TRACK 14, 0:10

structure

sequence

Figure 5-3:
The structure of the natural minor scale.

Left Hand:
1 = index finger
2 = middle finger
3 = ring finger
4 = pinkie (little finger)

Building Chords: One Note at a Time, Please

A *chord* is a combination of three or more notes taken from a related scale. Piano players and guitarists often play the notes of a chord simultaneously. For example, a guitarist may play a three-note chord on the first beat of a measure and let the complex chord-sound (or harmony) ring out for the rest of the measure. But bassists take a different approach when playing the notes of a chord. When playing bass, you execute chords by playing the notes one at a time. You can combine the notes in any number of ways with any number of rhythmic patterns. (See Chapter 3 for different rhythmic patterns.)

Triads: The three most important notes of a chord

The *triad* is the basic chord form, consisting of the three most important notes of any scale: root, 3rd, and 5th. This structure is called a *triad* because it has three notes. You can find the notes for the triad by playing any scale up to the 5th note, skipping every other note: You play the root, skip the 2nd note, play the 3rd note, skip the 4th note, and play the 5th note.

You can tell if a scale is major or minor merely by listening to its triad. A major triad has a regular 3 (1, 3, 5) and produces a happy sound. A minor triad has a ♭3 (1, ♭3, 5) and produces a sad sound.

Musicians sometimes simply refer to triads as *chords*. For instance, a major triad may be referred to as a major chord. (Note that a more complex combination of notes in the major tonality may also be called a major chord.)

Major triads

The *major triad* is the chord that is related to the major scale. Just play the root, 3rd, and 5th notes of the major scale to get a major triad. You can easily play it in one position (with no shifts in your left hand). Make sure that you start the major triad with your middle finger.

To see the form of the major triad, check out Figure 5-4. The open circle represents the root, and the solid dots represent the other chord notes.

Take a look at Figure 5-5 for some examples of major triad *accompaniments* (bass lines you play to support soloists). The simple structure of the major chord (major triad) gives you enough notes to choose from to play some hip accompaniments.

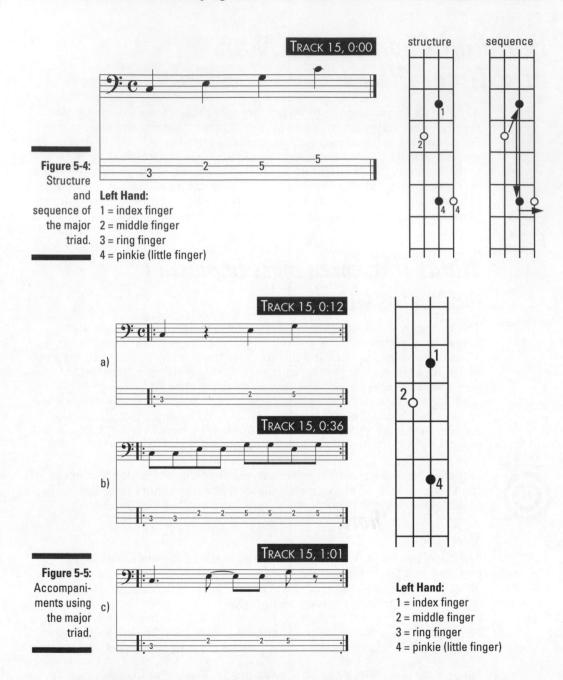

TRACK 15, 0:00

structure   sequence

Figure 5-4:
Structure
and   **Left Hand:**
sequence of 1 = index finger
the major   2 = middle finger
triad.   3 = ring finger
             4 = pinkie (little finger)

TRACK 15, 0:12

a)

TRACK 15, 0:36

b)

Figure 5-5:
Accompani-   TRACK 15, 1:01
ments using c)
the major
triad.   **Left Hand:**
             1 = index finger
             2 = middle finger
             3 = ring finger
             4 = pinkie (little finger)

Minor triads

The *minor triad* comes from the minor scale. You construct the minor triad by playing the root, 3rd, and 5th notes of the minor scale, which translates into root, ♭3, and 5. You play the minor triad in one position (no shifts with the left hand), and you start it with your index finger. Check out Figure 5-6 for the form of the minor triad.

Figure 5-6: Structure and sequence of the minor triad.

Left Hand:
1 = index finger
2 = middle finger
3 = ring finger
4 = pinkie (little finger)

Like the major triad, the minor triad gives you plenty of notes to choose from for some cool accompaniments over minor tonalities. See Figure 5-7 for some examples.

You can play any of the grooves from Figures 5-5 and 5-7 in any key (not just in C), without changing the *shape of the grooves* (the pattern of the notes in relation to each other). For example, try starting on a different note, such as on D, when you play the note patterns shown on the grids in these figures.

Seventh chords: Filling out the triad

The 7th chord has one more note than the triad: You guessed it, the 7. The sound of the 7th chord is a little more complex than the sound of a triad, though.

Contemporary music makes extensive use of the 7, and you frequently play the 7th chord in your accompaniments. As with triads, the 7th chord is based on a scale (usually the major or minor scale). You find the notes of any 7th chord by playing the scale and skipping every other note: You play the root, you skip the 2nd note, you play the 3rd note, you skip the 4th note, you play the 5th note, you skip the 6th note, and you play the 7th note. The notes in any chord are called *chord tones*.

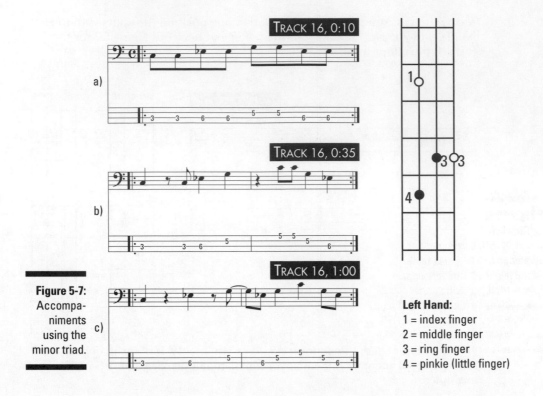

Figure 5-7:
Accompaniments using the minor triad.

Left Hand:
1 = index finger
2 = middle finger
3 = ring finger
4 = pinkie (little finger)

The four most commonly used 7th chords are the major, minor, dominant, and half-diminished chords. Table 5-1 gives you the structures of these four main 7th chords.

With contemporary music, the term *dominant* refers to the tonality of the chord and not just to the function of that chord.

Table 5-1	The Main 7th Chord Structures
Chord Name	*Chord Tones*
Major	Root - 3 - 5 - 7
Dominant	Root - 3 - 5 - ♭7
Minor	Root - ♭3 - 5 - ♭7
Half-Diminished	Root - ♭3 - ♭5 - ♭7

As Table 5-1 shows, the root, 3, and 5 follow either the basic major or basic minor structure. The *flatted 7* is what differentiates the dominant chord from the major chord. The *flatted 5* is what differentiates the half-diminished chord from the minor chord.

Figure 5-8 shows the chords with their related scales.

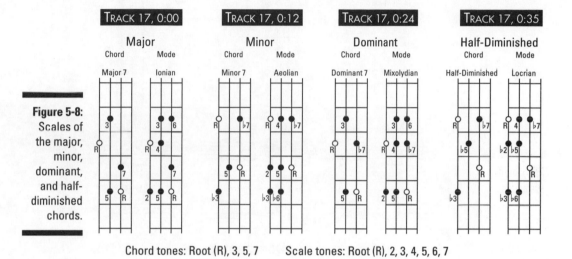

Figure 5-8: Scales of the major, minor, dominant, and half-diminished chords.

Chord tones: Root (R), 3, 5, 7   Scale tones: Root (R), 2, 3, 4, 5, 6, 7

Spicing Up Your Sound: The Seven Main Modes (Scales)

Seven more scales?! Don't panic. Four of them are from the previous section — the major, dominant, minor, and half-diminished scales — so playing three more is a piece of apple pie with ice cream. These new scales are closely related to the previous ones, and with all of these scales at your fingertips, you get more choices in terms of flavor, or *color* (it's like different shades of blue, for example). Think of starting with the same basic cooking recipe but adding different flavors (different sounds) to change it slightly.

In almost all songs, one *mode* (scale) predominates. *Mode* is simply a fancy word for scale. When you play with other musicians, the first song may be primarily dominant, the next minor, and the next major. Know the mode you're in, and you're well on your way to providing great bass lines for any song.

Figure 5-9 shows the seven main modes and how they relate to the four main chords (major, minor, dominant, and half-diminished).

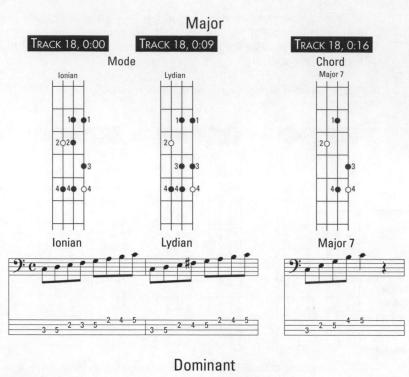

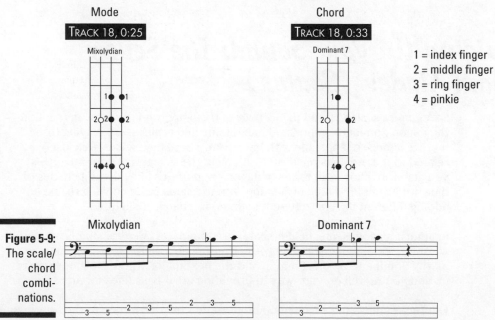

Figure 5-9: The scale/ chord combi- nations.

Minor

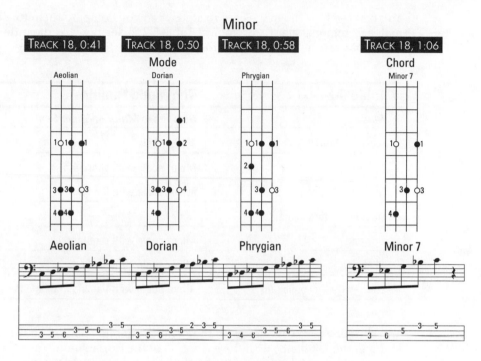

TRACK 18, 0:41 TRACK 18, 0:50 TRACK 18, 0:58 TRACK 18, 1:06

Half-Diminished

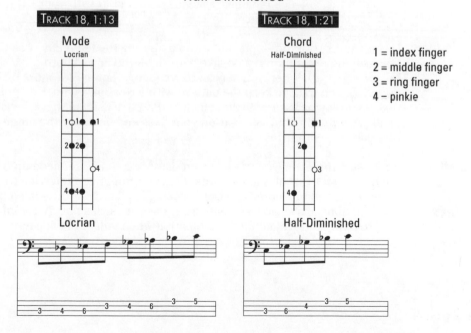

TRACK 18, 1:13 TRACK 18, 1:21

1 = index finger
2 = middle finger
3 = ring finger
4 = pinkie

You can see how the modes are related when you compare them to either the major or minor scale. Take a look at Table 5-2 to see how to adjust the major or minor scale to create each of the modes on the fingerboard.

Table 5-2	The Mode Families
Mode	*Relation to Major or Minor Scale*
Ionian (major)	Major scale
Lydian	Major scale with sharp 4th
Mixolydian (dominant)	Major scale with flat 7th
Aeolian (natural minor)	Minor scale
Dorian	Minor scale with regular 6th
Phrygian	Minor scale with flat 2nd
Locrian (half-diminished)	Minor scale with flat 2nd and flat 5th

You can play all the modes, with their chords, in one position on the bass (no shifts in the left hand) with the exception of the Dorian mode (see the sidebar "The alpha and omega of the modes" for more info). In the case of the Dorian mode, you need to make a small one-fret shift with your left hand in order to execute the mode.

I refer to this position — playing without shifting the left hand — as the *box* because the notes fit into a boxlike pattern on the fingerboard (or look like a box on the grid). When you play a groove (see Chapter 7 for more on creating grooves), you want to keep the pattern within the box as much as possible so that your playing is smooth and efficient. Practice each of these seven modes (scales) in the previous sidebar on your bass and listen for the unique sound that each one produces.

Bass lines (the notes you use in accompanying a tune) are made up primarily of notes from the scales and chords in this section. Keep referring to Tables 5-1 and 5-2, and to Figure 5-9, because being familiar with the scale/chord combinations allows you to create great bass lines. See Part IV for info on how to apply the scale/chord combination when you're playing music.

The alpha and omega of the modes

The modes are easy to understand when you know their origin.

The C-major scale (C, D, E, F, G, A, B, and C), which is also known as *C Ionian,* starts and ends on the 1 of the scale — the C. If you play the exact same C scale but start on its 2nd note (D), you end up with the *D-Dorian mode* (D, E, F, G, A, B, C, and D). Even though D Dorian has the same notes as C Ionian, it sounds different — somewhat sad. A tune based on D Dorian will also sound sad.

If you start and end on the 3rd note of the C-major scale (E), you end up with the *E-Phrygian mode* (E, F, G, A, B, C, D, and E). You hear a sound that is different from the Ionian and Dorian modes, even though the notes are the same. It sounds somewhat exotic.

If you start and end on the 4th note of the C-major scale (F), you get the *F-Lydian mode* (F, G, A, B, C, D, E, and F). This mode produces a sound that is somewhat similar to the sound made by the Ionian mode — major and happy.

If you start and end on the 5th note of the C-major scale (G), you get the *G-Mixolydian*

mode (G, A, B, C, D, E, F, and G). This mode is the dominant scale.

Start and end on the 6th note of the C-major scale (A) and you get the *A-Aeolian mode* (A, B, C, D, E, F, G, and A), which is also your natural minor scale.

If you start and end on the 7th note of the C-major scale (B), you get the *B-Locrian mode* (B, C, D, E, F, G, A, and B), which produces a somewhat harsh sound. As you can see, each mode starts on a different note of the C scale but uses the same notes.

Notice that each of these modes has its own 7th chord — the 1, 3, 5, and 7 — and each chord sounds uniquely like the mode it's related to. For instance, the 1, 3, 5, and 7 of C Ionian are C, E, G, and B. The 1, 3, 5, and 7 of D Dorian are D, F, A, and C.

The common order of these modes is: Ionian, Dorian, Phrygian, Lydian, Mixolydian, Aeolian, and Locrian. Sounds Greek to you? It actually is!

Using Chromatic Tones: All the Other Notes

When you play a bass line, you're not limited to the notes in the main modes; you can supplement them with notes outside the mode. The extra notes that fall within the box — the chromatic tones — are the most convenient notes for supplementing your modes.

Chromatic tones normally refer to any sequence of notes moving in half steps, either up or down, one fret at a time. For bass lines, however, *chromatic tones* refer to the notes outside the regular mode. These notes are a half step away from a scale tone.

Melodic and harmonic minor scales

The melodic and harmonic minor scales are special cases in the scale business. Both scales are a sort of hybrid of the minor and major tonalities. The *melodic minor scale* is a natural minor scale with a regular 7 instead of a ♭7 and also a regular 6 instead of a ♭6 (see related figure), and the *harmonic minor scale* is a natural minor scale with a regular 7 instead of a ♭7 (see related figure). You're likely to encounter the melodic and harmonic minor scales when playing melodies in a minor tonality.

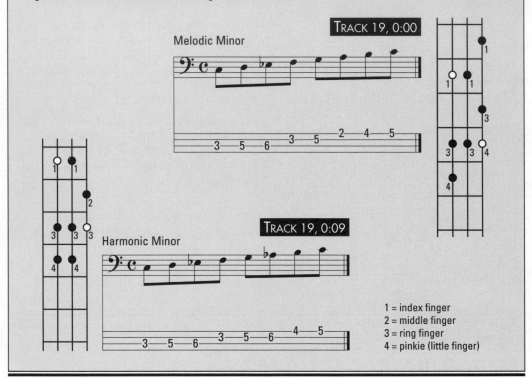

TRACK 19, 0:00

Melodic Minor

TRACK 19, 0:09

Harmonic Minor

1 = index finger
2 = middle finger
3 = ring finger
4 = pinkie (little finger)

Chromatic tones within the box

Figure 5-10 shows a bass line in a major tonality using a chromatic tone. You don't need to shift your left hand to reach these chromatic notes, because they're in the box. You can use these notes as quick links to one of the chord tones (root, 3, 5, 7).

Figure 5-11 shows you a bass line in a minor tonality using a chromatic tone.

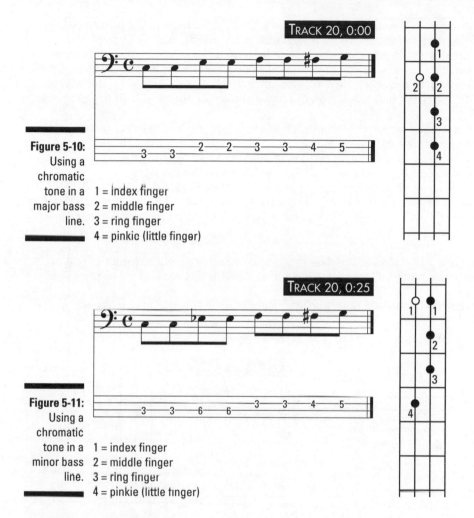

Figure 5-10:
Using a
chromatic
tone in a
major bass
line.

1 = index finger
2 = middle finger
3 = ring finger
4 = pinkie (little finger)

Figure 5-11:
Using a
chromatic
tone in a
minor bass
line.

1 = index finger
2 = middle finger
3 = ring finger
4 = pinkie (little finger)

The chromatic tone in Figures 5-10 and 5-11 adds a little tension to the bass lines — tension that is promptly released on the next note. Listen to how the chromatic tone *resolves* (leads) to the next note, making an interesting bass line.

Chromatic tones outside the box

Most tunes have a *shape*, or *form* — a certain way the melody moves up and down and repeats ideas (phrases). Tunes are arranged into measures and phrases; in the vast majority of cases, four measures equal a phrase (see Chapter 3 for details about how music is arranged). Just as horn players and singers pause at regular intervals to breathe, a tune also pauses between musical phrases. As the bassist, you're responsible for indicating the form of the tune to the other players. The notes you play tend to set up the beginning of each new phrase, and you often use chromatic tones to lead to the phrase.

You usually use chromatic tones that are inside the box to lead from one strong note to the next, but you may also use chromatic tones that fall outside the box (which means that you have to shift your left hand to reach them). Use them to lead to chord tones (root, 3, 5, 7), which identify the tonality.

As you experiment with chromatic tones, make sure that your overall tonality doesn't get obscured. You still want your sound to be recognizable as major or minor.

Figure 5-12 shows a bass line in a major tonality using a chromatic tone outside the box leading to a strong chord tone (in this case, the 3 of the chord).

Figure 5-13 shows a bass line in a minor tonality using a chromatic tone outside the box.

Figure 5-12:
Using a chromatic tone outside the box in a major bass line.

1 = index finger
2 = middle finger
3 = ring finger
4 = pinkie (little finger)

Listen to how the overall tonality in Figures 5-12 and 5-13 is preserved despite the addition of chromatic tones outside the box. The chromatic tones serve to make the groove more interesting. You reach outside the scale temporarily to give the music tension, but then you resolve it (lead to a chord tone).

TRACK 21, 0:23

Figure 5-13:
Using a
chromatic
tone outside
the box in a
minor bass
line.

1 = index finger
2 = middle finger
3 = ring finger
4 = pinkie (little finger)

Bringing a Groove to Life with Dead Notes (Weird but True)

You may need to enhance a simple groove rhythmically, but none of the notes, chromatic or modal (from the mode), seem to be quite right. You may feel that the bass line needs something more to really make the music happen. Enter the dead note.

A *dead note* is a note that's heard as a thud without any pitch. It gives the rhythm some attitude. Dead notes are favorites among many contemporary bassists. Playing a dead note is a cool way to boost a groove without getting into trouble.

To play a dead note, rest two or more fingers from your left hand on a string. (Be sure not to press the string to the fingerboard.) Then strike that string with your right-hand index or middle finger. The result is a nonpitched thud. Figure 5-14 shows an example of a groove using dead notes. Note (no pun intended) how the second measure just keeps the rhythm going.

Listen for the thud of the dead notes in Figure 5-14. Dead notes are completely devoid of pitch, but they sound as if they belong to the tonality.

Figure 5-14:
Using dead
notes in a
groove.

1 = index finger
2 = middle finger
3 = ring finger
4 = pinkie (little finger)

Sampling Accompaniments

If you've read through the previous sections of this chapter, you may be feeling anxious to put some of this knowledge to good use. So strap on your bass and let me guide you through a few bass lines.

The word *groove* is used in two ways: It can refer to a *bass line,* which is the overall accompaniment to a tune, or it can refer to a *phrase* (usually one, two, or four measures long) that a bassist repeats throughout a tune, which establishes the rhythm and the harmony.

The following grooves are based on a chord tonality that is dominant (root, 3, 5, ♭7) and thus related to the Mixolydian mode (root, 2, 3, 4, 5, 6, ♭7). The tonal center (or root) is the same for all these grooves, so you can compare one groove with the next. In each of the following examples, the basic groove uses the same chord. When you embellish a groove with other chord and scale tones, chromatic tones, and dead notes, it develops into a much more interesting and intricate bass line.

Figure 5-15 shows a groove based solely on a chord — a triad (root, 3, 5). This groove isn't very interesting, but it does the job of outlining the harmony with some rhythm.

Figure 5-16 shows the groove with the 7 added to the triad. The ♭7 defines the groove as a definite dominant chord (1, 3, 5, ♭7).

Figure 5-17 shows the groove with the mode added in its entirety (root, 2, 3, 4, 5, 6, ♭7). The mode fills out the harmonic content of the groove. You're now solidly entrenched in the Mixolydian mode, and you have a solid box. Notice that in a box your left hand doesn't have to shift.

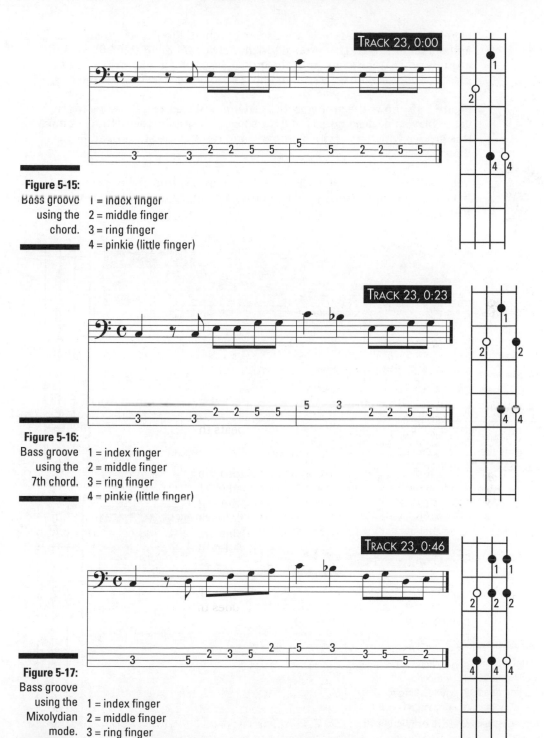

Figure 5-15:
Bass groove
using the
chord.

1 = index finger
2 = middle finger
3 = ring finger
4 = pinkie (little finger)

Figure 5-16:
Bass groove
using the
7th chord.

1 = index finger
2 = middle finger
3 = ring finger
4 = pinkie (little finger)

Figure 5-17:
Bass groove
using the
Mixolydian
mode.

1 = index finger
2 = middle finger
3 = ring finger
4 = pinkie (little finger)

Figure 5-18 shows the groove with some chromatic tones added both inside and outside the box. This groove is definitely developing some flavor and attitude now. At the same time, the groove is getting a bit more difficult to play. Your left hand has to shift to play a chromatic tone outside the box.

Figure 5-19 shows the groove with dead notes added as a finishing touch. You get to play some dead notes to fill the space and solidify the rhythm. Compare this groove with the previous grooves, and retrace the steps of adding each device.

You don't want to use all of these devices in every groove, but you do want to have them close at hand so that you can beef up a groove whenever you feel the urge to do so.

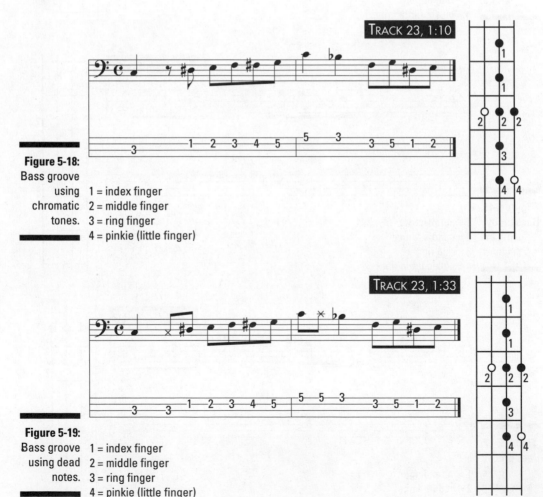

TRACK 23, 1:10

Figure 5-18:
Bass groove
using
chromatic
tones.

1 = index finger
2 = middle finger
3 = ring finger
4 = pinkie (little finger)

TRACK 23, 1:33

Figure 5-19:
Bass groove
using dead
notes.

1 = index finger
2 = middle finger
3 = ring finger
4 = pinkie (little finger)

Part III
Making the Moves, Creating the Grooves

The 5th Wave   By Rich Tennant

In this part . . .

Welcome to the elite society of bassists. This part helps you unlock the deep mysteries of bass playing. Chapter 6 tells you how to move comfortably to the higher notes of the bass, and Chapter 7 shows you how to create your own bass grooves. Chapter 8 lets you shine with some hip solo licks and fills.

Chapter 6

Expanding the Range: Going for the Second Octave

*T*he bass guitar is a near-perfect instrument. All the strings are tuned symmetrically. Aside from one small exception, you can reach all the notes of any one-octave scale without shifting your left hand. However, when you look at the bass, you may notice one thing — it's *long*. It may be easy to reach the notes without having to shift your left hand out of position when you're playing a scale in one octave. But it's another matter entirely when you want to expand your range of playing from one octave into the second octave (the same scale using higher or lower notes). This chapter helps you develop methods to easily reach the higher and lower notes in the second octave (the upper and lower registers).

When One Just Isn't Enough: Playing Two Octaves

When you play two octaves (see Chapter 5 for a complete explanation of octave), you need to shift your left hand to reach all the notes.

To shift your hand smoothly, be aware of what your hand needs to do next. In other words, you want to anticipate where your hand will be for the next *several* notes (not just for the *next* note) so that your musical phrase or scale can flow smoothly even though your hand is making a shift. You don't want your listener to hear an awkward hesitation in the music as you fumble around for the next note.

As I explain in the next few sections, practicing scales and chords over two octaves is the perfect way to develop a seamless shifting technique.

Two-octave major scales

Figure 6-1 shows you the structure of any two-octave major scale, except the E-major scale, which begins on the open (unfretted) E string. Figure 6-2 shows you the structure of the E-major scale, beginning on the open E string.

The following instructions explain how to play the two-octave major scale step by step. Be sure to refer to Figure 6-1 while you're playing. (If you happen to be a lefty, please read "right hand" to mean "left hand," and vice versa.)

1. **Press the index finger of your left hand down on any note on the E string, the thickest string.**

   Strike the string with your right hand to sound the note. This note is going to be your root (the first note in the scale).

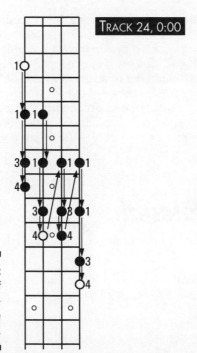

TRACK 24, 0:00

Figure 6-1:
Structure of the two-octave major scale.

2. **Shift your left hand by two frets along the E string toward the bridge, and press down with your index finger.**

   You are now two frets above the previous note. Strike the string with your right hand.

3. **Stay in position (don't shift) and press the ring finger of your left hand down on the E string.**

   Strike the string with your right hand.

4. **Stay in position and press the pinkie of your left hand down on the E string.**

   Strike the string with your right hand.

5. **Stay in position and move the index finger of your left hand from the E string across to the next string, the A string (the second-thickest string).**

   Strike the string with your right hand.

6. **Shift your left hand by two frets along the A string toward the bridge, and press your index finger down on the string.**

   This note is two frets above the previous note. Strike the string with your right hand.

7. **Stay in position and press the ring finger of your left hand down on the A string.**

   Strike the string with your right hand.

8. **Stay in position and press the pinkie of your left hand down on the A string.**

   Strike the string with your right hand. You are now exactly one octave above the original starting note from Step 1.

9. **Stay in position and move the index finger of your left hand from the A string across to the D string (the second-thinnest string).**

   Press down your index finger, and strike the string with your right hand.

10. **Stay in position and press the ring finger of your left hand down on the D string.**

    Strike the string with your right hand.

11. **Stay in position and press the pinkie of your left hand down on the D string.**

    Strike the string with your right hand.

12. **Stay in position and press the index finger of your left hand on the G string (the thinnest string).**

    Strike the string with your right hand.

13. **Shift your left hand by two frets along the G string toward the bridge, and press your index finger down on the string.**

    This note is two frets above the previous note. Strike the string with your right hand.

14. **Stay in position and press the ring finger of your left hand down on the G string.**

    Strike the string with your right hand.

15. **Stay in position and press the pinkie of your left hand down on the G string.**

    Strike the string with your right hand. Voilà! You're now exactly two octaves above the original starting note from Step 1.

As you're practicing two-octave scales, keep in mind that you can finger them several different ways. I prefer the patterns in Figures 6-1 through 6-4 because they're the most consistent no matter what note you start on. (If you discover a pattern you like better, by all means use it. You won't hurt my feelings . . . well, maybe a little.) Remember that whatever pattern you settle on, you want to stick to it so that your hands develop *muscle memory*. When your hand muscles get used to playing two-octave scales one particular way, they never forget. Before you know it, the scales will seem to play themselves.

The only position that has its own unique scale pattern is the E scale, which starts on the open E string. This position can be found at the low end of the neck near the nut. (If you have trouble identifying the nut, see Chapter 1 for details about the anatomy of the bass guitar. Hint: It doesn't have a shell.)

You begin playing the scale in E by merely striking the open (nonfretted) E string. You don't have to press the string down to play the root (E, the first note of the scale in E) — just strike it. Figure 6-2 shows you the structure of the E-major scale.

To play the second note, press your index finger onto the E string at the second fret (eliminating the shift of Step 1 described in the previous list and shown in Figure 6-1). You then follow Steps 2 through 15 in the previous list to play the rest of the E-major scale.

To descend the scales, reverse the order and shift toward the nut.

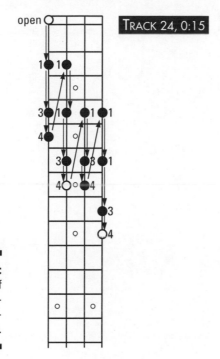

TRACK 24, 0:15

Figure 6-2:
Structure of
the two-
octave E-
major scale.

Two-octave minor scales

As with the major scale from the previous section, you can play the two-octave minor scale more than one way. Figure 6-3 shows the structure of the two-octave minor scale. Every minor scale (except the E-minor scale) follows the same pattern.

The following instructions explain how to play the minor scale step by step. Be sure to refer to Figure 6-3 as you're playing this.

1. **Press the index finger of your left hand down on the E string, the thickest string.**

   Strike the string with your right hand to sound the note. This note is your root.

2. **Stay in position (don't shift) and press the ring finger of your left hand down on the E string.**

   Strike the string with your right hand.

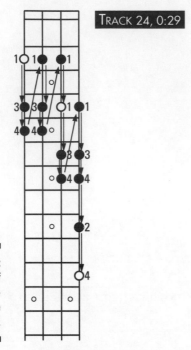

TRACK 24, 0:29

Figure 6-3:
Structure of
the two-
octave
minor scale.

3. **Stay in position and press the pinkie of your left hand down on the E string.**

   Strike the string with your right hand.

4. **Stay in position and move your index finger across from the E string to the next string, the A string (the second-thickest string).**

   Press down your index finger, and strike the string with your right hand.

5. **Stay in position and press the ring finger of your left hand down on the A string.**

   Strike the string with your right hand.

6. **Stay in position and press the pinkie of your left hand down on the A string.**

   Strike the string with your right hand.

7. **Stay in position and move the index finger of your left hand from the A string across to the D string (the second-thinnest string).**

   Press down your index finger, and strike the string with your right hand.

8. **Shift your left hand by two frets along the D string toward the bridge, and press your index finger down on the string.**

   Your index finger is two frets above the previous note. Strike the string with your right hand. You're now exactly one octave above the original starting note from Step 1.

9. **Stay in position and press the ring finger of your left hand down on the D string.**

   Strike the string with your right hand.

10. **Stay in position and press the pinkie of your left hand down on the D string.**

    Strike the string with your right hand.

11. **Stay in position and move the index finger of your left hand across from the D string to the G string (the thinnest string).**

    Press down with your index finger, and strike the string with your right hand.

12. **Stay in position and press the ring finger of your left hand down on the G string.**

    Strike the string with your right hand.

13. **Stay in position and press the pinkie of your left hand down on the G string.**

    Strike the string with your right hand.

Keep your eyes on the fret that you just played with your pinkie. The next note, which is played with your middle finger, is two frets above the last note, so your hand has to move a distance of four frets in order to place your middle finger on the proper fret (as described in the next step).

14. **Shift your left hand by four frets along the G string and place your middle finger two frets above the previous note (which was played by your pinkie).**

    Press down with your middle finger, and strike the string with your right hand.

15. **Stay in position and press the pinkie of your left hand down on the G string.**

    Strike the string with your right hand. You're now exactly two octaves above the original starting note from Step 1.

The E-minor scale is the odd scale out (again) because it requires a different pattern from all the other scales. Figure 6-4 shows you the structure of the two-octave E-minor scale.

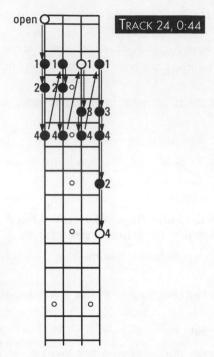

TRACK 24, 0:44

Figure 6-4:
Structure of
the two-
octave E-
minor scale.

To play the E-minor scale, follow these steps (and refer to Figure 6-4):

1. **Strike the open (unfretted) E string with your right hand.**

2. **Press the index finger of your left hand down on the second fret of the E string.**

   Strike the string with your right hand.

3. **Stay in position and press the middle finger of your left hand down on the E string.**

   Strike the string with your right hand.

4. **Stay in position and press the pinkie of your left hand down on the E string.**

   Strike the string with your right hand.

5. **Stay in position and move the index finger of your left hand across to the next string, the A string.**

   Press down with your index finger, and strike the string with your right hand.

6. **Stay in position and press the middle finger of your left hand down on the A string.**

   Strike the string with your right hand.

7. **Stay in position and press the pinkie of your left hand down on the A string.**

   Strike the string with your right hand.

8. **Stay in position and move the index finger of your left hand across to the next string, the D string.**

   Press down with your index finger, and strike the string with your right hand. You're now one octave above the original starting note (E) in Step 1. At this point, you can follow Steps 9 through 15 from the previous list to complete the second octave.

To descend the minor scale, simply reverse the order of the previous numbered lists and shift toward the nut instead of the bridge.

Two-octave major arpeggios

You're playing what's called an *arpeggio* when you play chord tones in sequence (root, 3, 5, octave), and onto the next 3 and 5 in the second octave (for more on chord tones, see Chapter 5). *Arpeggios* are notes in a chord played one after the other in ascending or descending order. When playing an arpeggio, you can reach several of the notes without shifting your left hand. Even though the arpeggio has a lot fewer notes than the scale, playing it is more difficult (but not impossible). Because the notes of arpeggios are spread further apart, arpeggios are perfect tools for practicing shifts.

When you shift your left hand to play an arpeggio, you always shift it by two frets. To make this task easy, keep your eyes glued to the index finger of your left hand. By watching this finger, you can measure your shift (always two frets) without having to divert your eyes to the note you're actually playing. To play an ascending arpeggio, set your index finger, play the note, and then shift your index finger (and thus the whole hand) two frets toward the bridge. Now instead of pressing your index finger down, press your ring finger down (it's in position already) and play *that* note. Your eyes have moved only two frets, but you're playing a note *four* frets above the previous note.

Figure 6-5 shows the pattern for all the two-octave major arpeggios except E major.

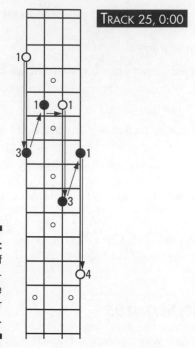

TRACK 25, 0:00

Figure 6-5:
Structure of
the two-
octave
major
arpeggio.

The following steps explain how to play the two-octave major arpeggio that applies to all keys except E. Be sure to refer to Figure 6-5 while you're playing.

1. **Press the index finger of your left hand down on the E string.**

    Strike the string with your right hand. This note is your root.

2. **Shift your left hand by two frets along the E string toward the bridge (aim with your index finger, but don't press your index finger down on the fret!). Press your ring finger (now four frets from the previous note) down on the E string.**

    Strike the string with your right hand.

3. **Stay in position and move the index finger of your left hand across to the A string.**

    Press down with your index finger, and strike the string with your right hand.

4. **Stay in position and move your index finger across to the D string.**

    Press down with your index finger, and strike the string with your right hand. You're now one octave above the original starting note from Step 1.

5. **Shift your left hand by two frets along the D string toward the bridge (aim with your index finger), and press your ring finger down on the D string.**

   Strike the string with your right hand.

6. **Stay in position and move your index finger across to the G string.**

   Press down with your index finger, and strike the string with your right hand.

7. **Shift your left hand by two frets along the G string toward the bridge (aim with your index finger), and press your pinkie down on the G string.**

Strike the string with your right hand. You're now exactly two octaves above the original starting note from Step 1. To descend this arpeggio, simply reverse the order and shift toward the nut of the bass.

In the case of the two-octave arpeggio in E major (see Figure 6-6 for the structure), your first step is to strike the open E string (the root). You then set the index finger of your left hand on the second fret of the E string. (Don't play it; your index finger helps you position your left hand.) This shift puts your ring finger in position on the fourth fret of the E string. Press your ring finger down on the E string, strike the string with your right hand, and then follow Steps 3 through 7 in the previous list to complete the two-octave E-major arpeggio.

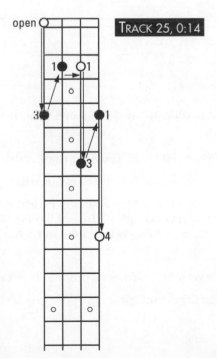

Figure 6-6:
Structure of the two-octave arpeggio in E major.

Two-octave minor arpeggios

The two-octave minor arpeggio is very much like the two-octave major arpeggio, except it's a minor chord. Figure 6-7 shows the pattern for every key except E minor.

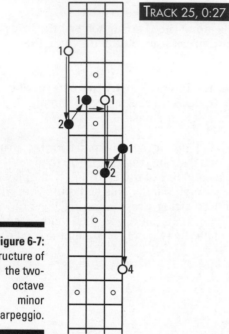

TRACK 25, 0:27

Figure 6-7:
Structure of
the two-
octave
minor
arpeggio.

To play the two-octave minor arpeggio, follow these steps (and refer to Figure 6-7):

1. **Press the index finger of your left hand down on the E string.**

   Strike the string with your right hand. This note is your root.

2. **Shift your left hand by two frets along the E string toward the bridge (aim with your index finger, but don't play it!), and press your middle finger (now three frets from the previous note) down on the E string.**

   Strike the string with your right hand.

3. **Stay in position and move your index finger across to the A string.**

   Press down with your index finger, and strike the string with your right hand.

4. **Stay in position and move your index finger across to the D string.**

   Press down with your index finger, and strike the string with your right hand. You're now one octave above the original starting note from Step 1.

5. **Shift your left hand by two frets along the D string (aim with your index finger), and press your middle finger down on the D string.**

   Strike the string with your right hand.

6. **Stay in position and move your index finger across to the G string.**

   Press down with your index finger, and strike the string with your right hand.

7. **Shift your left hand by two frets along the G string (aim with your index finger), and press your pinkie down on the G string.**

   Strike the string with your right hand. You're now exactly two octaves above the original starting note from Step 1.

To play the two-octave arpeggio in E minor (see Figure 6-8 for its structure), you first strike the open E string (the root). You then set the index finger of your left hand on the second fret of the E string. (Don't play it; your index finger helps you position your left hand.) This shift puts your middle finger into position on the third fret of the E string. Now press your middle finger down on the E string, strike the string with your right hand, and follow Steps 3 through 7 in the previous list to complete the two-octave arpeggio in E minor.

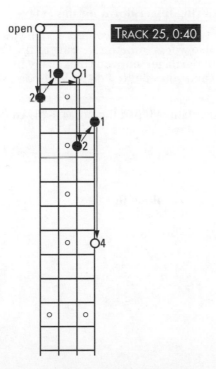

open

TRACK 25, 0:40

Figure 6-8:
Structure of
the two-
octave
arpeggio in
E minor.

To descend these arpeggios, simply reverse the order and shift toward the nut of the bass.

Finding Any Note in Any Octave

Playing notes in a two-octave range can be challenging. All the notes occur in at least two places on the neck of the bass. Knowing where the alternative notes are located allows you to play two-octave scales and two-octave arpeggios easily and efficiently anywhere on the fingerboard. Look in Chapter 3 to find where the notes are on the neck. The following list explains three methods to help you remember how to find the notes you want on any part of the neck.

- ✔ **The *octave method*, also called the *two-strings/two-frets* method.** This is the most common method for finding the same note in a different place. Here's how to do it:

    1. **Start by placing your left-hand index finger on a note on the E string.**

        You can find the same note an octave higher by letting your ring finger cross two strings and land on the D string. The ring finger naturally positions itself on the octave of the original note, two frets above the index finger.

    2. **Press your left-hand ring finger down for the octave.**

        Your octave note is two strings and two frets above your original note. This method also works from the A string to the G string, and you can use your middle finger and your pinkie. If you have a note on the G or D string and you want to find its lower octave, just reverse the process.

        Figure 6-9 shows the relationship of the notes using the two-strings/two-frets (or octave) method.

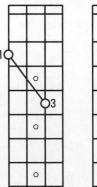
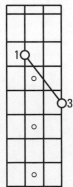

Figure 6-9:
Two-strings/
two-frets
method.

✔ The *handspan-plus-two-frets method.* Whereas the previous octave method helps you locate a note two strings away, this method helps you locate a note on the adjacent string.

1. **Start by pressing down a note on the A string with your left-hand index finger, and strike it with your right hand.**

2. **Now shift your left hand two frets toward the bridge and move your pinkie from the A string to the E string.**

3. **Press your pinkie down on the E string in that position and play that note.**

You now have the same note in the same octave as your original note on the A string. You can also use this method when going from the D string to the A string, and from the G string to the D string. This process also works in reverse.

Figure 6-10 shows the relationship of the notes in the handspan-plus-two-frets method.

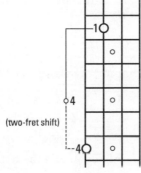

Figure 6-10:
Handspan-
plus-   (two-fret shift)
two-frets
method.

✔ **The marker method.** If you need to locate a note on the same string, use the markers (dots) imbedded on the side and face of your bass neck. If you look at the neck, you can see one section — on the 12th fret — that has two dots in the space of one fret. This fret is your octave marker for your open strings. You can play the octaves for all the open strings (E, A, D, and G) at this fret.

For example, the octave of open E is right at the double dot on the same string. If you want to play the octave of low F on the E string (the note on the first fret of the E string), you can find its octave one fret above the double dot (on the 13th fret). If you want to play the octave of low G on the E string (the note at the first dot of the E string), you can find its octave at the first dot past the double dot (15th fret) of the E string. This marker method applies to all the other strings, as well. See Chapter 3 for more on note position.

You can practice finding notes by choosing a note at random (C, for example) and then locating all the instances of that note on your bass neck. When you're finished, move on to another note (A♭, for example). Repeat this exercise until you cover all 12 notes: C, C♯/D♭, D, D♯/E♭, E, F, F♯/G♭, G, G♯/A♭, A, A♯/B♭, and B. (A ♯ raises a note by one half step, and a ♭ lowers it by one half step.)

Doing the Old Switcheroo: Using Inversions

Sometimes you may find that it sounds good to begin playing a chord, such as a triad (1, 3, 5), not on the root but on the 3rd or 5th (see Chapter 5 for more about chords and triads). To do this, you need to be able to *invert* (switch the order of the notes around) your basic major and minor chords.

For example, take the C triad (C-E-G). Instead of playing C-E-G, you can play the E first, the G second, and the root (the C) last, making it E-G-C. Or you can play the G first, the root C second, and the E last, making it G-C-E. These switches are called *inversions*. You can play any of the inversions in this section in one position without shifting your left hand.

Never, ever, ever lose track of your root (see Chapter 5 for information about the root). Everything you do as a bassist is based on the root. If you know where your root is, you can locate all the other notes related to it.

Major chord inversions

Try playing the inversions for the C major chord. If you add the octave to the C-major triad, you get root, 3, 5, and octave (or C-E-G-C).

Figure 6-11 shows you the major chord, with C as the root. In this chord, C is also in the *bass*. Here, the term *bass* refers to the note that sounds the lowest in any chord. Start with the C on the 8th fret of the E string to play the C-major chord. Be sure to keep your hand in position by starting the inversion with your middle finger on the root.

Now find the 3rd of the root C (it's the E on the 7th fret of the A string). Take a look at Figure 6-12, and play the C-major chord with the 3rd in the bass by following the grid. The chord is now E-G-C-E. E is now in the bass, but C is still the root.

Next, find the 5th of C, which is G. You find the G on the 10th fret of the A string. Follow the grid in Figure 6-13 and keep your hand in position. The chord is now G-C-E-G. G is now in the bass, but C is still the root.

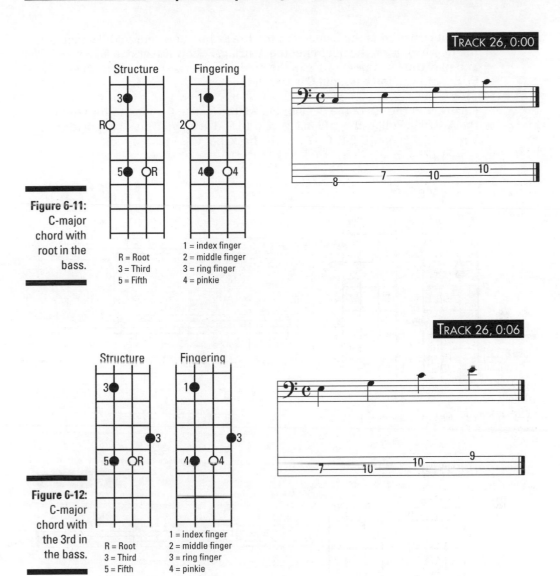

Figure 6-11:
C-major
chord with
root in the
bass.

Figure 6-12:
C-major
chord with
the 3rd in
the bass.

Minor chord inversions

Figure 6-14 shows you the C-minor chord with the root, C, in the bass. This chord is C-E♭-G-C. Begin with the C on the 8th fret of the E string and be sure to keep your hand in position. (No matter where you are or what chord you play, don't lose sight of your root.)

Now find the 3rd of the C-minor chord, the E♭. Position your middle finger on the E♭, which is on the 6th fret of the A string. Follow the grid in Figure 6-15 and play the C-minor chord with the 3rd in the bass. The chord is now E♭–G–C–E♭. E♭ is now in the bass, but C is still the root.

Finally, find the 5th of the C-minor chord, the G. The G is on the 10th fret of the A string. Follow the grid in Figure 6-16 and keep your hand in position. Your chord is now G–C–E♭–G. G is in the bass, but C is still the root.

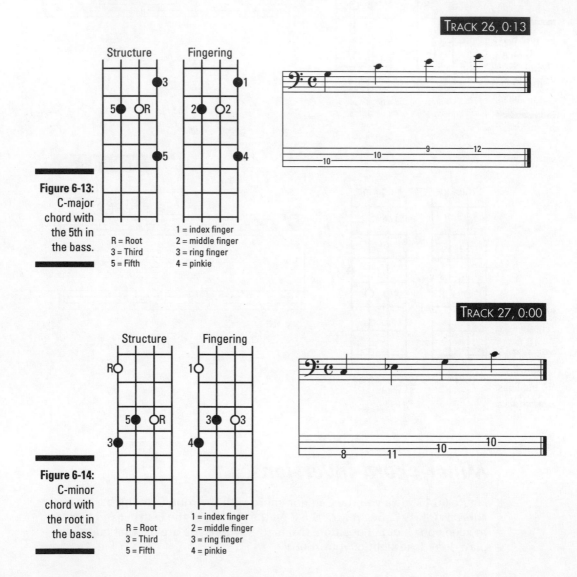

TRACK 26, 0:13

Structure   Fingering

●3   ●1
5● OR   2● O2
●5   ●4

Figure 6-13:
C-major
chord with
the 5th in
the bass.

R = Root   1 = index finger
3 = Third   2 = middle finger
5 = Fifth   3 = ring finger
                4 = pinkie

TRACK 27, 0:00

Structure   Fingering

RO   1O
5● OR   3● O3
3●   4●

Figure 6-14:
C-minor
chord with
the root in
the bass.

R = Root   1 = index finger
3 = Third   2 = middle finger
5 = Fifth   3 = ring finger
                4 = pinkie

You can use the same patterns to invert any major or minor chord.

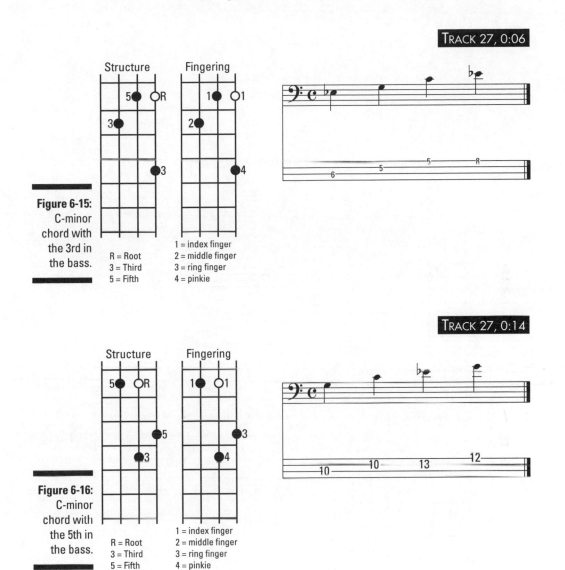

Structure Fingering

Figure 6-15:
C-minor
chord with
the 3rd in
the bass.

R = Root
3 = Third
5 = Fifth

1 = index finger
2 = middle finger
3 = ring finger
4 = pinkie

Structure Fingering

Figure 6-16:
C-minor
chord with
the 5th in
the bass.

R = Root
3 = Third
5 = Fifth

1 = index finger
2 = middle finger
3 = ring finger
4 = pinkie

Chapter 7

Creating the Groove

*W*hat do rock, funk, blues, reggae, and all the other musical styles have in common? They each have their own distinctive groove. A *groove* is a short musical phrase (a group of notes) that a bassist plays repeatedly throughout a tune. Grooves establish the rhythm and harmony (chords and scales) for the band and the listener. Knowing how to create grooves in different styles is absolutely essential for a bass player — not to mention a lot of fun.

This chapter introduces you to the wonderful world of grooves. To get the most out of the chapter, you need to have a handle on two vital concepts. Hmmm, if the groove establishes rhythm and harmony, could those two vital concepts be . . . rhythm . . . and harmony? Yes! Rhythm gets the audience snapping their fingers, and harmony sends them home singing. (You can find out more about rhythm in Chapter 3 and more about harmony in Chapter 5.)

Are you ready? Then get into the groove!

Anatomy of a Groove: Putting Together the Necessary Elements

A good groove can make you tap your feet, bob your head, and snap your fingers. You can move the same groove from chord to chord in a tune without changing the basic phrase. Sounds wimpy? Actually, grooves are anything but wimpy. One of my teachers (a long, long time ago) told me something I'll never forget: With the right groove, a good bassist alone can move a whole roomful of people. A groove is constructed of several elements, and you can use the different elements to create your own earth-shaking grooves. Check out the guidelines in the next section to help you get started.

Rattling the groove skeleton

The human skeleton consists of about 206 bones, while the groove skeleton consists of just two bones . . . uh . . . notes. The first two notes of any groove are what I refer to as the *groove skeleton*. A groove can contain other notes besides the groove skeleton, but these first two notes are the most important because they establish the root of the chord, the tempo for the tune, and the feel of the rhythm. The following list takes a closer look at each one of these elements.

- **The root of the chord:** You usually play the root as the first note of your groove. The root of any chord (or scale) is the most important note in that chord — it's the note your ear gravitates toward (the most satisfying note). The second note, or the other half of the groove skeleton, is usually a chord tone (root, 3, 5, or 7) that further defines the chord. With these two notes, you give the listener a good idea of the harmony in a tune. You can find the chord tones for each *tonality* (sound) in Chapter 5.

- **The pulse (tempo) of the tune:** Music has a certain pulse. The *pulse* is the speed at which you count 1-2-3-4, or the speed at which you tap your feet in time with a tune. The pulse can be fast, slow, or something in between. The time that elapses between the first note and the second note of the groove skeleton establishes the pulse for the groove and for the song, and lets the listener know how fast the music is.

- **The feel of the rhythm:** You can divide a beat only so many ways: into quarters, eighths, sixteenths, or triplets (no, not babies . . . *triplets* divide a beat into three equal parts. See Chapter 3 for more on rhythm). When you choose the division of the beat for your groove skeleton, you signal the feel of the groove and the song to the listener. The feel has nothing to do with tempo (see previous bullet). Different feels can be applied to the same tempo. A *feel* can give the listener a sense of urgency or a sense of laziness in a tune, all without changing the overall tempo of the music.

Figure 7-1 shows how the groove skeleton creates different feels.

When you listen to the grooves from Figure 7-1, tap your feet in tempo. (You can hear the count-off, which establishes the tempo, at the beginning of the track.) Notice how the tempo for all six of these grooves remains the same. Also notice that all six grooves use exactly the same notes. Even so, as you listen to these grooves, pay special attention to how very different they are from each other. Each one has its own unique characteristics, created simply by slight changes in the rhythm of the two notes in the groove skeleton. This shows the power of the groove skeleton: If you change the groove skeleton and leave everything else exactly as is, you still end up with a completely new groove. In this track, the groove skeleton is the only thing that changes from groove to groove.

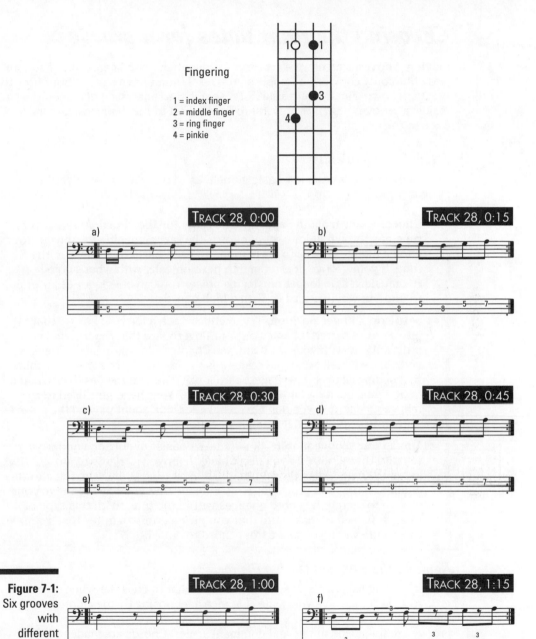

Figure 7-1:
Six grooves
with
different
groove
skeletons.

Choosing the right notes for a groove

Playing grooves is an elusive art form. I remember when I came out of school and could only copy other people's grooves. I didn't have a clue about how to create my own. Finally, after years of research and analysis, I discovered what makes a groove . . . *groove*. Yes, there's a method to the madness, and a science to the art.

A few basic guidelines

The following list gives a few basic guidelines to remember when you're creating any groove:

- ✓ **Choose notes from the appropriate scale for the chord.** Almost every tune has its own unique set of chords that accompanies the music. Your choice of notes needs to correspond to each particular chord in the tune. If your groove doesn't match harmonically with what's going on in the music, it's no longer music; it's noise. You can check out Chapter 5 to find out which scales go with which chords.

- ✓ **Settle on a finger position.** Try to choose notes for your groove that fit into a *box* (a pattern of notes on your fingerboard that requires no, or very little, shifting with your left hand; see Chapter 5 for more info). The less you shift your left hand, the easier it is to play the groove. You may think that sliding all over your fingerboard looks cool, but the best bassists tend to hold one position for as long as possible. Your hand gets used to a certain sequence, and you don't even have to think about playing the groove (after you've practiced it enough, of course).

- ✓ **Make your groove mobile.** Some tunes consist of only one underlying tonality throughout, so you don't have to move your groove around (just listen to some James Brown tunes). In most tunes, however, the chords change as the tune proceeds, which means that you have to move your groove to match the chord changes within the tune. With this type of tune, you need to make sure that you pick a group of notes that's simple to execute when you move from chord to chord.

Ranking the best and leaving the rest

The preceding list gives you a general idea of what to consider when creating a groove. Now let me give you some guidance in choosing the best notes to incorporate into your groove. The three most commonly used scales in a groove are the major, minor, and dominant scales. Chords are made up of the root, the 3, the 5, and sometimes the 7 of the scale they're related to. Check out Figure 7-2 for the structure of the major (Ionian), minor (Dorian), and dominant (Mixolydian) scales. Take a look at Chapter 5 for more on these scales.

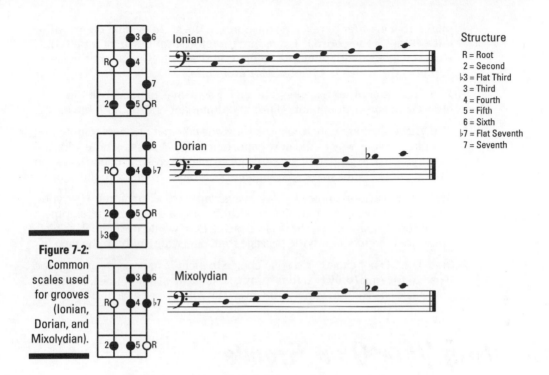

Structure

R = Root
2 = Second
♭3 = Flat Third
3 = Third
4 = Fourth
5 = Fifth
6 = Sixth
♭7 = Flat Seventh
7 = Seventh

Figure 7-2:
Common scales used for grooves (Ionian, Dorian, and Mixolydian).

Not all notes are created equal. Certain notes in a scale sound better in a groove than others. The following notes are the prime choices for your grooves (listed in order of importance):

1. **Root:** No question about it: You have to know the root of each chord in the tune. The root identifies the sound of the chord for your band and for the listener. For example, a D-minor chord has D as the root; an E-dominant chord has E as the root. The root is the most important note in a chord. Your band counts on you to define the sound of each chord for them. That's why bassists play the root as the first note every time the chord changes, so play that root with authority.

2. **5th:** The 5 reinforces the root, and it's fairly neutral (it fits over any major, minor, or dominant chord). The interval (distance) between the root and the 5 is the same for major, minor, and dominant chords. If you have a lot of chord changes between major, minor, and dominant in a tune, the root and 5 combination is the perfect choice for your groove notes.

3. **3rd:** The 3 identifies the chord as either major or minor. Choosing the 3 also forces you to settle on a hand position. If the chord is major and therefore requires a major 3, start your groove with your middle finger

on the root in order to reach all the notes in the scale for that chord without shifting. If the chord is minor and therefore requires a minor 3 (♭3), start the groove with your index finger on the root. (Check out the fingering of the scales in Chapter 5 for more info.)

4. **7th:** The 7 is another excellent choice for a groove, especially if the chord is minor or dominant. Minor and dominant chords both have a ♭7.

5. **4th:** The 4 is a great note to play as a *passing note* (an unstressed note that you play on your way to the next important note). A passing note adds a little spice to the groove (it gives the groove an interesting sound). Just be careful not to emphasize a passing note, as it tends to obscure the chord.

6. **6th:** The 6 is a good choice to play as a *neutral note.* (No matter what your chord is, the 6 will generally fit.) As with the 4, you don't want to emphasize it too strongly. Using the 6 as a passing note would be ideal. Passing notes are used to smooth the passage from one strong note to the next.

7. **2nd:** The 2 is not exactly a terrific choice to include in your groove. It's too close to the root (only two frets away), so it clashes, and it doesn't give your bass line enough variety. However, the 2 can work as a passing note.

Creating Your Own Groove

With a little help from your friend (that's me!), you can create your own groove. The process that goes on in your head each time you have to decide on any groove for a tune is the same, no matter what kind of chord you're playing (major, minor, or dominant).

If you haven't already, you may want to take a look at the section "Choosing the right notes for a groove," earlier in this chapter, to familiarize yourself with the important decisions you need to make *before* creating a groove.

Covering the "basses": Creating dominant, minor, and major grooves

The process in preparing to play any groove is the same, but you need to make a few adjustments to accommodate your groove to each kind of chord: dominant, minor, and major (see Chapter 5). Read on for some help creating unforgettable grooves.

The dominant groove

Imagine that you're getting together with a bunch of other musicians to play some music. The guy in charge says, "Let's jam in D7." (He's talking about playing in D dominant.) Don't panic. The following list gives you some guide-lines for determining what notes to play during a D7 jam. Figure 7-3 shows you the process.

1. **Determine the root of the chord.**

   In this case, the chord is D7, so the root of the chord is D (see Figure 7-3a).

2. **Decide what kind of groove skeleton you want to play.**

   Figure 7-3b shows your basic choices. The example uses two eighth notes, but feel free to experiment with the other possibilities. In fact, let your ear decide which rhythm sounds best for the given situation. (For more on the groove skeleton, see "Rattling the groove skeleton," earlier in this chapter.)

3. **Choose the appropriate scale for the chord.**

   For the D7 chord in this example, the proper scale is D Mixolydian (see Figure 7-3c). See Chapter 5 to find out which scale goes with which chord.

   To play the D-Mixolydian scale, start the scale on the 5th fret of the A string and end on the 7th fret of the G string. Choose the notes for your groove from this scale. You can pick the choice notes (see "Ranking the best and leaving the rest," earlier in this chapter, for details) from the intervals marked in Figure 7-3c. I chose the root, 5, and ♭7 for the simple groove, and the root, 3, 4, 5, and ♭7 for the complex groove (see Figure 7-4).

4. **Position your left hand.**

   You want to play the groove with the least amount of effort, so you need to avoid any unnecessary shifting with your left hand.

   Start the D-Mixolydian scale with the middle finger of your left hand on the root D (5th fret of the A string). You can reach all the notes of the scale from this position without moving your left hand. Refer to Figure 7-3d for the fingering for this scale.

5. **Determine how mobile your groove needs to be.**

   If the tune has different chords (the roots change), your groove has to be *mobile,* or moveable from chord to chord. In this case, you need to make your groove simple. Choose only a few notes and make them easy to play.

   If you stay on one chord for awhile (which is the likely scenario if some-one wants to jam in D7), you can make your groove a bit more complex to keep it interesting. Refer to Figure 7-4 for both a simple and a complex version of the same groove.

6. **Enjoy playing your groove.**

   You read correctly. Have fun! Whatever groove you come up with, make it meaningful. Jamming isn't work — it's play!

Figure 7-3:
Creating
a groove
for D7 (D
dominant).

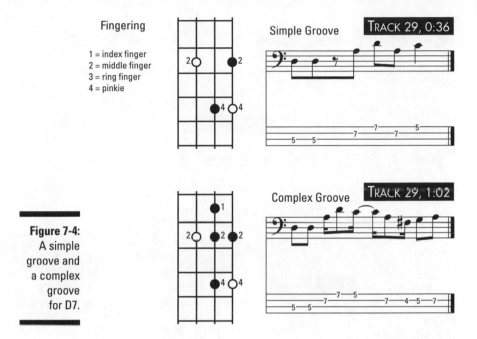

Fingering

1 = index finger
2 = middle finger
3 = ring finger
4 = pinkie

Simple Groove — TRACK 29, 0:36

Complex Groove — TRACK 29, 1:02

Figure 7-4:
A simple
groove and
a complex
groove
for D7.

The minor groove

You're playing with the band, jamming on a dominant groove . . . but wait . . .
what if the guy in charge yells, very enthusiastically, "Let's jam in D *minor*!"?
Uh, oh . . . a minor adjustment is in order. Relax. Figure 7-5 shows you the
process.

1. **Determine the root of the chord.**

   In this case, the chord is D minor (Dm or Dm7), so the root of the chord
   is D (see Figure 7-5a).

2. **Decide what kind of groove skeleton you want to play.**

   I show you the basic choices in Figure 7-5b. I chose the dotted eighth
   note and the sixteenth note as the groove skeleton, but you can experiment with the other possibilities.

3. **Choose the appropriate scale for the chord.**

   For the D-minor chord in this example, the proper scale is D Dorian (see
   Figure 7-5c). For more info about the D-Dorian scale, see Chapter 5.

   To play the D-Dorian scale, start the scale on the 5th fret of the A string
   and end it on the 7th fret of the G string. Choose the notes for your
   groove from this scale. You can pick the choice notes from the intervals
   marked in Figure 7-5c. I chose the root, 5, and ♭7 for the simple groove,
   and the root, ♭3, 4, 5, and ♭7 for the complex groove (see Figure 7-6).

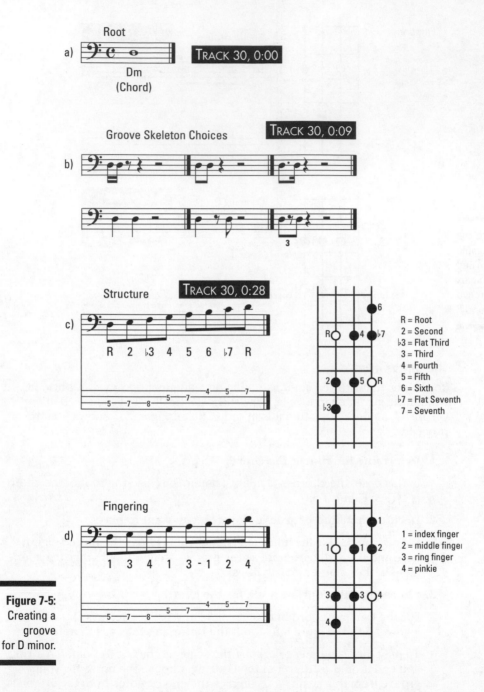

Figure 7-5:
Creating a
groove
for D minor.

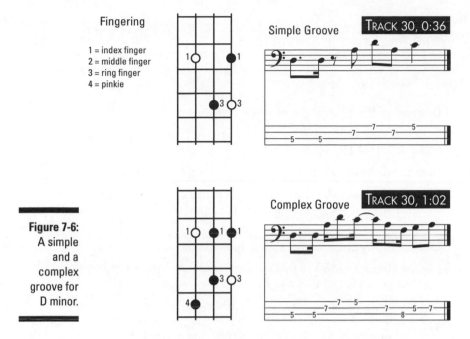

Fingering

1 = index finger
2 = middle finger
3 = ring finger
4 = pinkie

Simple Groove   TRACK 30, 0:36

Complex Groove   TRACK 30, 1:02

Figure 7-6:
A simple
and a
complex
groove for
D minor.

4. **Position your left hand.**

   You want to avoid any unnecessary shifts in your left hand. The D-Dorian scale requires one (itty, bitty) shift, however.

   Begin the D-Dorian scale with the index finger of your left hand on the root D (5th fret of the A string). From this position, you can reach all the notes of the scale from this position until you get to the G string. At that point, you need to shift your hand toward the nut by one fret to reach the remaining three notes. Check out Figure 7-5d on how to finger this scale.

5. **Determine how mobile your groove needs to be.**

   Your groove has to be mobile if the tune has different chords. In this case, be sure to create a groove that's simple. Choose only a few notes that are easy to play. Even though the D-Dorian scale requires you to shift your hand, you don't have to play every single note in that scale. You may well decide to choose only the notes of the scale that you can reach from one position (without shifting).

   If you stay on one chord for awhile (which is the likely scenario if someone wants to jam in D minor), you can make your groove a bit more complex to keep it interesting. Figure 7-6 shows both a simple and a complex version of the same groove. Notice that neither of the two grooves requires any shifting with the left hand.

The major groove

You're jamming away with the band on a minor groove, but what if the guy in charge yells (with uninhibited enthusiasm, "Let's jam in D major!"? Hmmm, does he really mean *major?* Here's the way to respond to that enthusiasm. Figure 7-7 shows you the process.

1. **Determine the root of the chord.**

   In this case, the chord is D major (D Maj, or D Maj7), so the root of the chord is D (see Figure 7-7a).

2. **Decide what kind of groove skeleton you want to play.**

   Figure 7-7b shows the basic choices. I chose the two sixteenth notes as the groove skeleton, but you can experiment with the other possibilities as well.

3. **Choose the appropriate scale for the chord.**

   For the D-major chord in this example, the proper scale is D Ionian (see Figure 7-7c). You can find more info on the Ionian scale in Chapter 5.

   To play the D-Ionian scale, you start the scale on the 5th fret of the A string and end it on the 7th fret of the G string. Choose the notes for your groove from this scale. You can pick the choice notes from the intervals marked in Figure 7-7c. I chose the root, 5, and 6 for the simple groove, and the root, 3, 4, 5, and 6 for the complex groove (see Figure 7-8).

4. **Position your left hand.**

   You want to avoid any unnecessary shifting with your left hand.

   Start the D-Ionian scale with the middle finger of your left hand on the D (5th fret of the A string), which is the root. You can reach all the notes of the scale from this position without moving your left hand. You can refer to Figure 7-7d for the fingering for this scale.

5. **Decide how mobile your groove needs to be.**

   If the tune has different chords — if the roots change — your groove has to be mobile (moveable from chord to chord), so the groove you create needs to be a simple one. Use only a few notes and make them easy to play.

   If you stay on one chord for awhile, you can make your groove a bit more complex to keep it interesting. You can see both a simple and a complex version of the same groove in Figure 7-8. In the case of the major chord, you have to consider one more thing when choosing the notes for the groove: The 7 of the Ionian scale doesn't sound all that great in a groove format, so avoid it if you can. Choose the 6 instead; the 6 is usually a great choice, but let your own ears decide what's right.

Root

a) 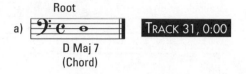 TRACK 31, 0:00

D Maj 7
(Chord)

Groove Skeleton Choices   TRACK 31, 0:08

b)

3

Structure   TRACK 31, 0:28

c)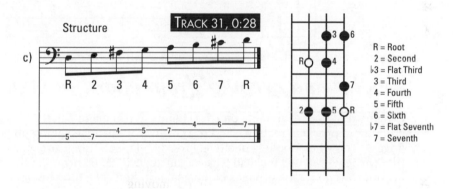

R 2 3 4 5 6 7 R

R = Root
2 = Second
♭3 = Flat Third
3 = Third
4 = Fourth
5 = Fifth
6 = Sixth
♭7 = Flat Seventh
7 = Seventh

Fingering

d)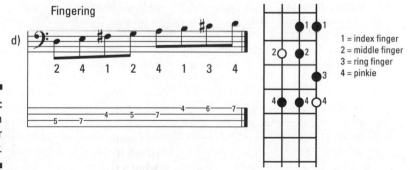

2 4 1 2 4 1 3 4

1 = index finger
2 = middle finger
3 = ring finger
4 = pinkie

Figure 7-7:
Creating a
groove for
D major.

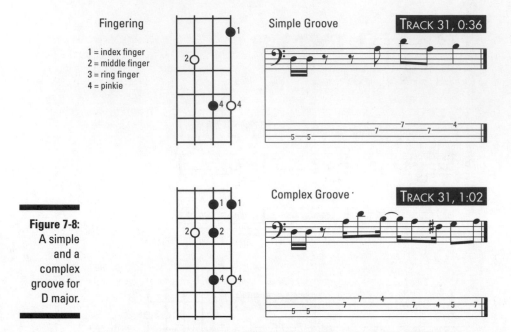

Figure 7-8:
A simple
and a
complex
groove for
D major.

Movin' and groovin' from chord to chord

Imagine that you're jamming on D7, D minor, and D major (all three are covered in the previous section), and the grooves are just cascading off your fingers. The whole room is positively rocking. In fact, things are going so well, that the leader of this musical extravaganza decides to surprise you by handing out the *chord charts* (pages of musical notation) of a tune he or she wrote the previous week.

The chords of the tune move all over the place and change between major, minor, and dominant more frequently than your lead-footed cousin Jimmy changes lanes on a four-lane highway. Should you tremble? Absolutely not. Just take a look at the chord chart in Figure 7-9 and find out where the roots are located. Using the concepts from the previous sections, come up with a simple groove that you can move easily from chord to chord.

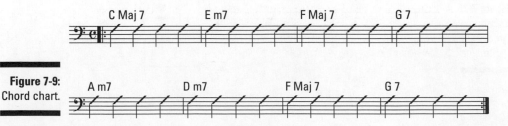

Figure 7-9:
Chord chart.

Using constant structure

Using constant structure is one way to move a groove easily between chords with different tonalities (major, minor, and dominant). *Constant structure* refers to a group of notes in a groove that can be moved from chord to chord regardless of whether the chords are major, minor, or dominant tonalities. The root and 5 of a scale are one of the most common constant structures for grooves and can be easily moved between chords. Grooves using the root and 5 are simple but powerful. In fact, most songs incorporate root-5 grooves. As you read the next list, see Figure 7-10 for tips on how to create a mobile groove.

1. **Create a groove.** To create a groove, take a look at the section earlier in this chapter "Covering the 'basses': Creating dominant, minor, and major grooves." Keep the groove simple, because you need to move it to several different chords. I chose a groove that doesn't require you to shift your hand to reach all the notes (see Figure 7-10a).

   To play this groove, you need access to two strings above your root, so choose the root on either the E string or the A string. You won't have enough strings to play this groove if you start on either the D or G string.

2. **Find the roots of the chords.** Look at your chord chart (simulated in Figure 7-9) and find the roots of the chords on the fingerboard of your bass. Remember that all your roots have to be on the E or the A string to play this groove. Figure 7-10b shows you where the roots for the chords on the chord chart are located on your bass.

3. **Practice moving the groove smoothly from one chord to the next.** You have to make these moves without any hesitation. Figure 7-10c shows the movement of the chords on your fingerboard.

Using chord tones

Another way to move a groove between chords with different tonalities is to use chord tones. *Chord tones* are the notes in any chord (root, 3, 5, and 7) that identify the chord type.

When you play a song that includes several tonalities, such as major, minor, and dominant, you need to make slight adjustments in your groove to play the chord tones. Your fingering changes as you move from one kind of chord to another. Keep the groove simple, because you have your hands full (pun intended) just changing the groove from chord to chord.

As you're reading the list, check out Figure 7-11 for an example of a mobile groove that uses chord tones.

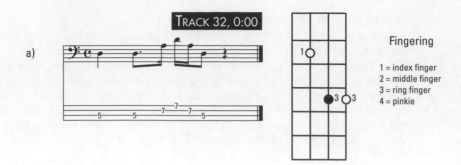

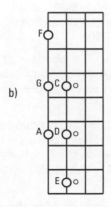

Figure 7-10:
Mobile
groove
using
constant
structure.

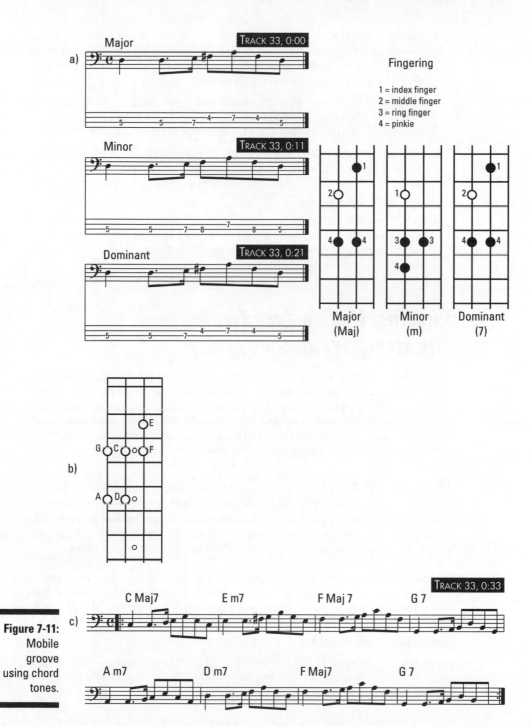

Figure 7-11: Mobile groove using chord tones.

1. **Create a groove.** Make your groove simple enough to handle. I chose a groove that includes the root, 3, and 5 of a chord. You can see the different patterns for major, minor, and dominant in Figure 7-11a. (For the sake of comparison, all the patterns start on D.)

   Practice this groove, starting on the same note to get comfortable with it. This groove covers two strings: the string you play the root on, and the one above it. You can start this groove on the E, A, or D string.

2. **Find the roots of the chords.** Using the chord chart (refer to Figure 7-9), find the roots of the chords on your fingerboard. Your roots can start on the E, A, or D string. Figure 7-11b shows you the locations of the roots for this particular chord chart.

3. **Practice moving the groove smoothly from one chord to the next.** You have to change your fingering from chord to chord. Perform these fingering changes without hesitation. Figure 7-11c shows the configuration of the groove for different chords.

Finding the perfect fit: The designer groove

Every now and then you hear a bass groove that simply knocks your socks off — a groove that seems to fit the song like a glove. I call these grooves *designer grooves;* you literally design them to fit perfectly with everything that is going on harmonically and rhythmically in a particular tune. In addition to the groove skeleton (see "Rattling the groove skeleton," earlier in the chapter, for details), designer grooves also have a *groove apex.*

The groove apex

An apex refers to the highlight of something, and in this case, the *groove apex* is the note that is the highlight of a groove. Every groove has an apex. The *groove apex* is usually either the highest or the lowest note of the groove. Either way, it's often the note furthest from the root of your groove.

Which note is the groove apex is open to interpretation. If you hear one note in a bass groove that really sticks out for you, that note is the groove apex. Accenting the groove apex makes your groove fit better with the music.

The upper groove apex

An *upper groove apex* is the highest note of a groove. Figure 7-12 shows a groove with a clear upper groove apex. Notice how the groove skeleton sets up the groove.

To practice how to play an upper groove apex, check out the exercise in Figure 7-13. This exercise focuses on the upper groove apex only and will greatly improve your ability to execute it on any note.

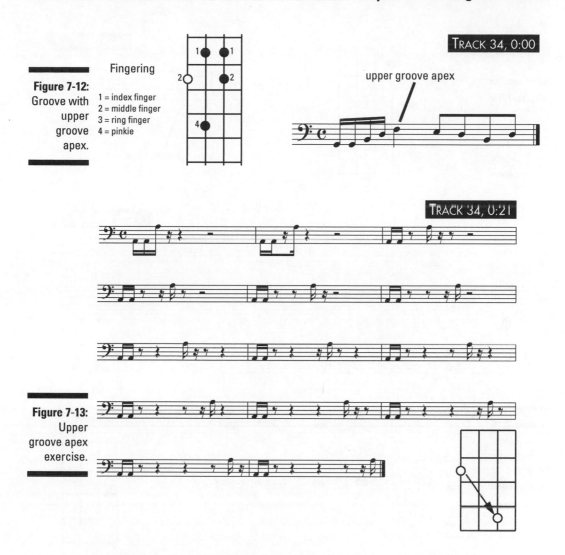

Figure 7-12: Groove with upper groove apex.

Fingering

1 = index finger
2 = middle finger
3 = ring finger
4 = pinkie

TRACK 34, 0:00

upper groove apex

TRACK 34, 0:21

Figure 7-13: Upper groove apex exercise.

The lower groove apex

The *lower groove apex* is the lowest note of a groove. Figure 7-14 shows a groove with a lower groove apex. Notice how the groove skeleton establishes the groove.

To get comfortable playing the lower groove apex, check out the exercise in Figure 7-15. This exercise shows you how to play the lower groove apex on any note.

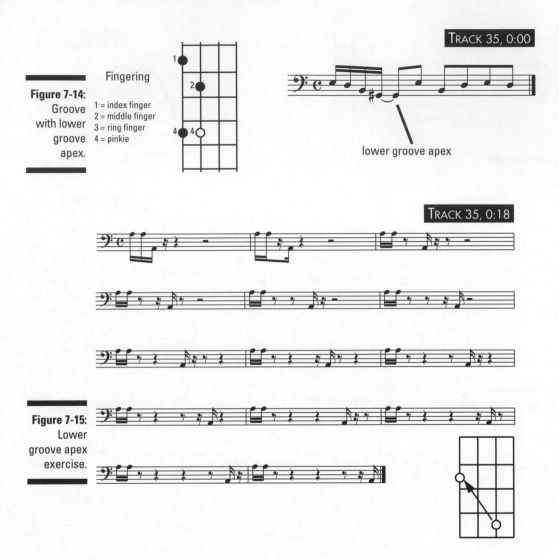

Figure 7-14: Groove with lower groove apex.

Fingering

1 = index finger
2 = middle finger
3 = ring finger
4 = pinkie

TRACK 35, 0:00

lower groove apex

TRACK 35, 0:18

Figure 7-15: Lower groove apex exercise.

In both the upper groove apex exercise (wow, that's a mouthful) and the lower groove apex exercise, the groove apex follows right behind the groove skeleton (the first two notes). These exercises are a great way to get comfortable playing not only grooves but rhythms as well.

When you're comfortable playing along with the CD, try playing these exercises without the CD, and with your metronome set at varying speeds (see Chapter 3 for more on the metronome).

Grooving with a Drummer

No instrument is more important to your well-being as a bass player than the drums. (By the way, the bass is just as important to the well-being of a drummer.) Bassists and drummers work hand in hand to create grooves. If you want to build great grooves (and great relationships) with drummers, you need to know what all the different drums on a drum set sound like and what they're generally used for. This section gives you a quick overview of the different types of drums. If you want to read more, you can always check out *Drums For Dummies,* by Jeff Strong (Wiley Publishing).

The bass drum

The bass drum is the lowest-sounding drum on the drum set. This drum is very closely aligned with your part as a bass player. Generally speaking, drummers play the bass drum on the first beat of a measure to start the groove and then play it at least once more within that measure. If you play notes that match the rhythm of the bass drum, you'll fit right in.

Figure 7-16 shows you how to match the rhythm of the bass drum. You can listen to Track 36 on the CD for a demonstration of how the bass drum sounds.

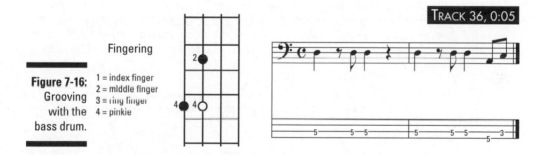

Figure 7-16: Grooving with the bass drum.

Fingering

1 = index finger
2 = middle finger
3 = ring finger
4 = pinkie

TRACK 36, 0:05

The snare drum

The snare drum is the loudest drum on the drum set. This drum is usually played on the *backbeat* (beats 2 and 4) of each measure. You can match up one of your notes with the snare drum, or you can create some *sonic space* (which simply means that you don't play at that moment) for the snare drum as it sounds out alone. (Hmmm, now there's an interesting concept: Instead of looking confused when you're lost, just give the band leader your most serious look and say that you're experimenting with sonic space.)

Listen to Track 36 on the CD for the sound of the snare drum, and take a look at Figure 7-17 to find out how to play with the snare and bass drums.

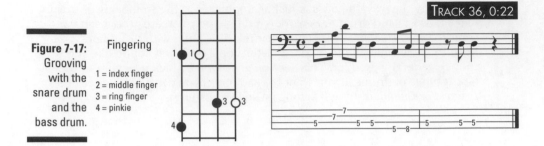

Figure 7-17:
Grooving
with the
snare drum
and the
bass drum.

The hi-hat

No, the hi-hat isn't something you wear on your head. The *hi-hat* (the two interconnected circular brass plates that snap together when played) is your real-life metronome. The drummer uses the hi-hat to mark the subdivisions of the beat (usually eighth notes or sixteenth notes) and keeps the hi-hat snapping right through a groove.

Sometimes, instead of using the hi-hat, the drummer uses one of the *cymbals* (the big, circular brass plates on the drum set) to keep the rhythm. You may have trouble hearing the hi-hat at first, but after you get used to listening for its constant sound, you'll be able to play your notes easily, because the rhythm of most of the notes you play on the bass are also played (rhythmically) on the hi-hat.

Listen to Track 36 on the CD for the sound of the hi-hat, and check out Figure 7-18 for a groove you can play with the hi-hat, the snare drum, and the bass drum.

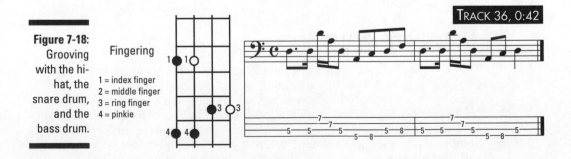

Figure 7-18:
Grooving
with the hi-
hat, the
snare drum,
and the
bass drum.

Chapter 8

Going Solo: Playing Solos and Fills

● ●

In This Chapter

▶ Choosing solo scales

▶ Playing fills in a groove

● ●

*I*magine that you're playing with a great bunch of musicians and you're hold-ing down a monster groove (see Chapter 7 for more on creating a groove) so solidly that the music takes on a life of its own. In fact, things are sounding so good that the other musicians decide to reward you with a solo — a chance to show off your bass *chops* (bass-speak for skills). Looks like you need to prepare for your moment in the sun, because when the time comes for your solo, you have to *burn* (bass-speak for showing off your chops).

This chapter presents three surefire scales that you can use to create a solo or a fill (a mini-solo) that will make you and everyone else *smoke* (bass-speak for dazzle).

Soloing: Your Moment to Shine

A *solo* is the music (musical and rhythmic line) you create when you're the featured player in a band. Solos are usually reserved for the traditional melody instruments, such as the guitar, saxophone, and trumpet, but bassists are also asked to perform a solo on occasion. Making a solo sound good is a bit more challenging for the bassist, because the sound of the instrument is very deep and you don't have a groove backing you. (You can't play a groove and a solo at the same time.) Despite these challenges, bass solos can be very effective in the hands of a good player. The next few sections explain how to play solos.

Playing with the blues scale: A favorite solo spice

The six-note blues scale is one of the most commonly used scales in soloing — and with good reason: It's comfortable to play, it's easy to move around, and it sounds great. The blues scale is a one-size-fits-all scale, no matter what the chord tonality. However, as with those one-size-fits-all pieces of clothing, the blues scale doesn't always give you a perfect fit. The notes may not relate perfectly with all the notes in the chord.

When you create a solo with the blues scale, it's going to sound bluesy. Let your ears be the judge of which notes you can linger on in the blues scale and which notes you should use as passing tones (unaccented notes that connect two strong notes). Just like salt for the soup: When you add the right amount, it's delicious; when you use too much, you spoil it.

You need three strings to complete the blues scale, so start on either the E or A string — on whichever string is the root of the chord you're playing (see Chapter 5 for more about chords). The following steps explain how to play a blues scale, and Figure 8-1 shows the structure of the blues scale.

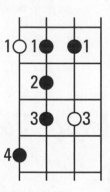

TRACK 37, 0:00

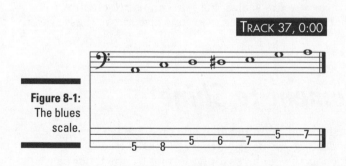

Figure 8-1:
The blues
scale.

1. **Press the index finger of your left hand down on the root of the chord (on the E or A string) and play the note.**

2. **Press your pinkie down on the same string and play the note.**

   This note is ♭3 (flat 3); it's one of the *blue* (slightly dissonant) notes.

3. **Press your index finger down on the next higher (thinner) string and play the note.**

   This note is a 4; it sounds fairly neutral.

4. **Press your middle finger down on the same string and play the note.**

   This note is a ♯4 (sharp 4); it's another blue note.

5. **Press your ring finger down on the same string and play the note.**

   This note is a 5; it's present in almost all chords.

6. **Press your index finger down on the next higher (thinner) string and play the note.**

   This note is a ♭7 (flat 7); it's usually a cool choice.

7. **Press your ring finger down on the same string and play the note.**

   This note is your octave; you've arrived at the root again.

Three strings. No shifts. The blues scale couldn't be easier.

You can use the notes of the blues scale in any order — not just straight up and down. You can also use the blues scale over any chord: major, minor, or dominant. Use the blues scale tastefully and sparingly; don't overdo it.

Figure 8-2 shows you some useful blues-scale licks. A lick, in this case, doesn't refer to how your dog welcomes you home. A *lick* is a short melodic phrase you play in a solo — a solo is a succession of licks. You can collect a repertoire of licks from your favorite musicians, and you can also create some of your own.

Playing with the minor pentatonic scale: No wrong notes

The structure of the minor pentatonic scale is very similar to the blues scale (which I cover in the section "Playing with the blues scale: A favorite solo spice"). However, the *minor pentatonic scale* has five different notes: one fewer note than the six-note blues scale.

You use the minor pentatonic scale when the tonality of the chord is minor. (For more on chord tonality, see Chapter 5.) You need to make sure that you have three strings available to complete the scale, so find your root on the E or A string. The following steps explain how to play the minor pentatonic scale, and Figure 8-3 shows the pattern of the minor pentatonic scale.

Figure 8-2: Blues-scale licks.

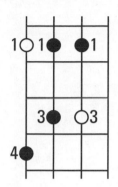

TRACK 38, 0:00

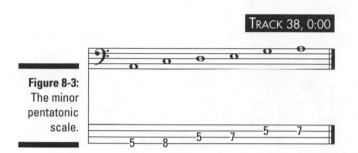

Figure 8-3:
The minor
pentatonic
scale.

1. **Press the index finger of your left hand down on the root of the chord (on the E or A string) and play the note.**

2. **Press your pinkie down on the same string and play the note.**

   This note is a ♭3 (flat 3); it's one of the main ingredients of the minor chord.

3. **Press your index finger down on the next higher (thinner) string and play the note.**

   This note is a 4; it's part of the minor scale. (See Chapter 5 for major, minor, and dominant scales.)

4. **Press your ring finger down on the same string and play the note.**

   This note is a 5; it's another main ingredient of the minor chord.

5. **Press your index finger down on the next higher (thinner) string and play the note.**

   This note is a ♭7 (flat 7); it's yet another main ingredient of the minor chord.

6. **Press your ring finger down on the same string and play the note.**

   This note is your octave; you've arrived at the root again.

Voilà! Three strings. No shifts. No problem.

As with the blues scale, you can use the notes of the minor pentatonic scale in any order when playing your solo — not just straight up and down. Use this scale over any minor chord. All the notes sound good when you play them over a minor chord, so you can land on any of them. If you find that your solo needs spice, use the blues scale.

Figure 8-4 shows some very useful licks that you can play using the minor pentatonic scale. This scale comes in handy in every solo, so add it to your repertoire.

Figure 8-4:
Minor
pentatonic
scale licks.

Using the major pentatonic scale: Smooth as can be

You can use the *major pentatonic scale* for two different chord tonalities: the major chord and the dominant chord. Think of this scale as a two-for-one deal. (For more on major and dominant chords, see Chapter 5.)

You need three strings to complete the major pentatonic scale, so start it on the E or A string. The following steps explain how to play the major pentatonic scale, and Figure 8-5 shows the structure of the major pentatonic scale.

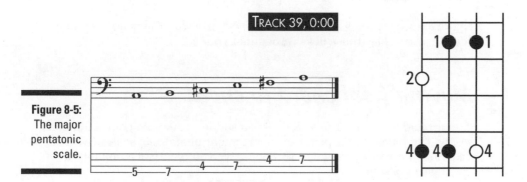

Figure 8-5: The major pentatonic scale.

TRACK 39, 0:00

1. **Press the middle finger of your left hand down on the root of the chord (on the E or A string) and play the note.**

2. **Press your pinkie down on the same string and play the note.**

   This note is a 2; it's a fairly neutral note that's part of the scales of both the major and dominant chords.

3. **Press your index finger down on the next higher (thinner) string and play the note.**

   This note is a 3; it's one of the main ingredients of both the major and dominant chords.

4. **Press your pinkie down on the same string and play the note.**

   This note is a 5; it's another main ingredient of the major and dominant chords.

5. **Press your index finger down on the next higher (thinner) string and play the note.**

   This note is a 6; it's another neutral note that's part of the scales used for major and dominant chords.

6. **Press your pinkie down on the same string and play the note.**

This note is your octave; you've arrived at the root again.

Three strings. No shifts. Okay, you're ready for the limelight.

You can use the notes of the major pentatonic scale in any order — not just straight up and down. Play this scale for any major or dominant chord. All the notes of the major pentatonic scale sound good with a major or dominant chord, so you're perfectly safe landing on any of them. If you find that things start to sound bland, you can add some spice in the form of the blues scale. (See "Playing with the blues scale: A favorite solo spice," earlier in the chapter, for more information).

Figure 8-6 shows some specific licks you can use with the major pentatonic scale. You can play these licks throughout your solo.

Moving from chord to chord

If your band is playing a tune and all of a sudden your solo comes up, don't worry. The blues, minor pentatonic, and major pentatonic scales (which I describe in the three previous sections) give you plenty of ammunition for playing a cool solo.

When performing a solo, you use the minor pentatonic scale for a minor chord, the major pentatonic scale for a major or dominant chord, and the blues scale for any chord.

The following steps give you some guidelines to follow when soloing for a tune that has all three of the common chords (minor, major, and dominant). The steps tell you how to approach each individual chord.

1. **Find the root of the chord.**

You need to make sure that you have enough strings to cover the entire scale, so stick with the E and A strings.

2. **Determine whether the chord is minor, major, or dominant.**

   a. **If the chord is minor, place your index finger on the root of the chord.**

   You're now in position to execute the minor pentatonic scale for this chord.

   b. **If the chord is either major or dominant, place your middle finger on the root of the chord.**

   You're now in position to execute the major pentatonic scale for this chord.

Track 39, 0:07

a)

Track 39, 0:25

b)

Track 39, 0:39

c)

Figure 8-6:
Major
pentatonic
scale licks.

3. **Add some spice to your solo by occasionally placing your index finger on the root of any chord and playing a blues-scale lick.**

Figure 8-7 shows you a chord chart for a tune. Listen to Track 40 on the CD for samples of soloing over these chords, and then try coming up with your own solo.

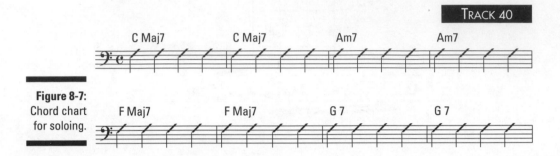

TRACK 40

Figure 8-7:
Chord chart
for soloing.

Creating Fills without Any Help from Your Dentist

Fills are mini-solos that give grooves a little flash every now and then. (Check out Chapter 7 if you're not sure what a groove is.) The purpose of the fill is to

- Lead you back to the beginning of the groove
- Give your *line* (the bass part you're playing) some variety
- Fill a little space when the rest of the band is quiet

A fill works the same way as a solo: You use the minor pentatonic scale as a fill when playing a minor chord, the major pentatonic scale as a fill when playing a major or dominant chord, and the blues scale as a fill when playing any chord. See "Soloing: Your Moment to Shine," earlier in this chapter, for more details on how to use these scales as solos.

A fill is usually short (only about two beats long), so you need to fit the notes of the fill within the two beats and blend them smoothly with the other notes.

A match made in heaven: Connecting your fill to the groove

You can take more liberties in terms of rhythm with a regular solo than you can with a fill. Because fills are a part of the groove, the rhythm for the fill has to relate closely to the rhythm of the groove.

When you put a fill into a groove, you need to be acutely aware of the number of beats you have to fill before returning to the beginning of the groove. You can't miss the beginning of a groove — not even for the greatest of fills.

Timing a fill

A fill within a groove lasts for about two beats — the *last* two beats of a measure. In other words, you play beats one and two (the first two beats of the measure) as a regular groove, and then you replace beats three and four (the last part of your groove) with a fill. Don't play a fill every time you play a groove, though, because it will obscure the groove, which is the sound the band depends on to guide them in rhythm and harmony. A fill is usually only played every fourth measure or every eighth measure.

Figure 8-8 shows examples of fills for major, minor, and dominant chords using eighth notes, triplets, and sixteenth notes. The following list guides you step by step through the process of creating a fill.

1. **Establish a groove.**

   (See Chapter 7 to find out how to establish a groove.)

2. **Determine where the third beat starts in your groove.**

   Play the groove up to the third beat, because that's where you'll be substituting the fill for beats three and four.

3. **Determine how many notes you can hit in two beats (beats three and four).**

   The two beats for the fill have a total of four eighth notes, six triplets, or eight sixteenth notes. (See Chapter 3 for more about rhythms.) A lot depends on the tempo of the groove and on how accurately you can fit the notes into the two beats of the fill before the first note of the next groove. You can fit more notes into a fill at slower tempos.

Figure 8-8 (a):
Two-beat
fills.

Figure 8-8 (b):
Two-beat
fills.

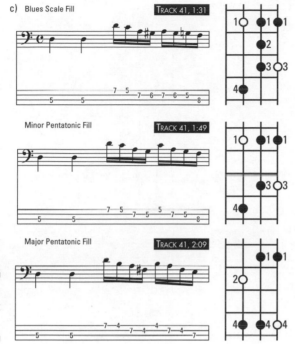

Figure 8-8 (c) : Two-beat fills.

4. **Work out a fill using the number of notes you can play (either four, six, or eight) using the appropriate pentatonic or blues scale for the chord of the groove.**

   For details on how the different scales relate to the different chords, see "Soloing: Your Moment to Shine," earlier in this chapter.

5. **Practice going back and forth between the groove and the fill until your transitions are seamless.**

   In order to create a successful fill, your groove must flow without hesitation.

6. **Play your fill no more than every four or eight bars so that each fill sounds special.**

   If you play your fill more than every four or eight bars, it will just sound like another groove.

When you feel comfortable playing the fills from Figure 8-8, incorporate them into some of your more complex grooves. (The grooves in Figure 8-8 are simply two quarter notes played on the first two beats, so you can concentrate on getting the fills right.) You can come up with a collection of your own favorite fills and incorporate them into your playing.

Part IV
Using the Correct Accompaniment for Each Style

The 5th Wave   By Rich Tennant

"First you play a G7 demolished chord followed by a fragmented 9th chord, then a perverted 32nd chord ending with a mangled 11th chord with a recovering 3rd."

In this part . . .

Whether you're into rock, pop, jazz, funk, blues, country, reggae, or world music, this part helps you maneuver your bass lines through any style of music that you may encounter. Versatility is a key asset for any bass player, and Part IV will help you build a repertoire of licks to draw from.

Chapter 9

Rock On! Getting Down with the Rock Styles

The term *Rock* encompasses a number of different styles — ranging from country rock to hard rock — all of which have certain traits in common. All rock styles use rhythms dominated by driving eighth notes. (For more on rhythm, see Chapter 3.) The bassist locks in tightly with the drums and plays grooves that stress the *root*, the first note of a scale. (You can find out about grooves in Chapter 7.) The main difference between each rock style, however, lies in the rhythmic and melodic feel of the bass lines.

Rock 'n' Roll: The Good Old Standby

Rock 'n' roll refers to the style of rock that originated in the 1950s and '60s (think Elvis Presley or Buddy Holly). The bassist maintains a quarter-note or eighth-note rhythm and a distinctive melodic bass line that spells out the harmony for the band and the listener. Check out Figure 9-1 for the first example of a rock 'n' roll accompaniment. The example uses one note — the root — with an eighth-note rhythm. (The open circle on the grid represents the root.)

Notice how the rhythm of the notes in Figure 9-1 is evenly divided, as well as how the bass locks in with the drums.

TRACK 42, 0:00

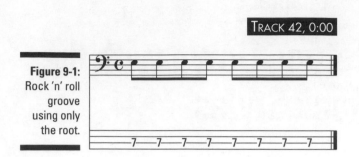

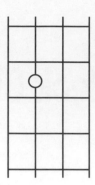

Figure 9-1:
Rock 'n' roll
groove
using only
the root.

You can start the groove in Figure 9-1 with any finger, because only one note is used — the root. You don't have to worry about the chord tonality. (Chapter 5 discusses tonality.)

You can play any of the grooves featured in this chapter in any key (starting with any root) by using the grids in the figures. You just have to make sure that you have enough frets and strings at your disposal — usually four or five frets and three strings.

In Figure 9-2, you add the 3 and 5 (the third and fifth note of the major scale) to the groove to form the chord. (Check out Chapter 5 for a definition of chords.) In the grid, the root is the open circle, and the solid black dots are the other chord tones (the notes in the chord). Figure 9-2 has to be played with your middle finger on the root to avoid shifting during the groove.

TRACK 42, 0:12

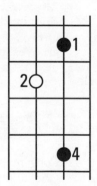

Figure 9-2:
Rock 'n' roll
groove
using notes
from the
chord.

Notice how the eighth notes are driving the rhythm in Figure 9-2. The bass and drums are tightly locked in with each other. The choice of the bass notes indicates to the band members the tonality of the chords: major, minor, or dominant.

You can alter the examples in this chapter to fit any tonality. Simply lower the regular 3 to a ♭3 to change the tonality from major to minor, or raise the ♭3 to a regular 3 to change it from minor to major. This change is not a major problem, just a minor adjustment.

The groove in Figure 9-3 is the same as the groove shown in Figure 9-2 with one exception: The groove in Figure 9-3 has a minor 3 (♭3) instead of a major 3 (or 3). The lowering of the major 3 to the ♭3 changes the entire chord into a minor chord. Start this groove with your index finger on the root to avoid any unnecessary shifting of your left hand.

TRACK 42, 0:23

Figure 9-3:
Rock 'n' roll groove in minor using notes from the chord.

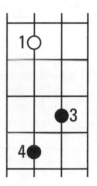

Figure 9-4 shows an example of a more elaborate rock 'n' roll groove using notes that come not only from the major chord but also from the Mixolydian mode. (See Chapter 5 for a discussion of modes.) Start this groove with your middle finger on the root.

TRACK 42, 0:35

Figure 9-4:
Rock 'n' roll groove using notes from the chord and mode.

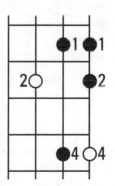

The groove in Figure 9-4 fits nicely over a dominant chord, which is a common chord in rock 'n' roll. The dominant chord consists of the root, 3, 5, and ♭7 of the Mixolydian mode or scale. Figure 9-5 shows you the thought process behind the creation of this groove.

Mode   Chord   7th Chord   Groove

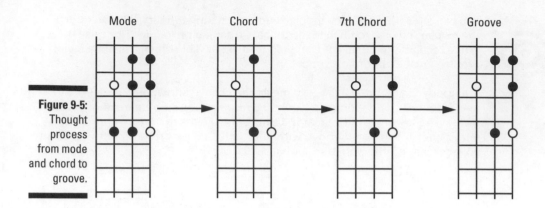

Figure 9-5:
Thought
process
from mode
and chord to
groove.

For a denser rock 'n' roll groove, check out Figure 9-6, which includes not only notes from the chord and its related mode (Mixolydian in this case) but also *chromatic tones* (notes outside the regular mode; see Chapter 5 for more on chromatic tones) that lead to the notes in the chord.

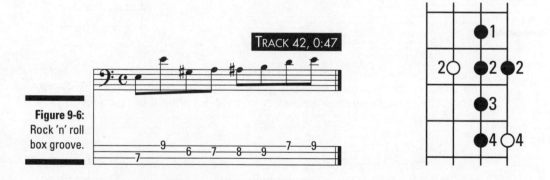

TRACK 42, 0:47

Figure 9-6:
Rock 'n' roll
box groove.

You can play all the notes of this groove in the same position as long as you start it with your middle finger. I call this a *box groove* because the positioning of the notes forms a *box;* your left hand is positioned so that your fingers can reach all the notes without shifting.

You can alter the groove from Figure 9-6 to play over a minor tonality by lowering the 3 to ♭3, which converts the dominant chord tonality into a minor tonality. (Check out Figure 9-7 to see what this groove looks like in a minor tonality.) To play the groove in Figure 9-7, start with your index finger on the root so that you don't have to shift your left hand.

You can also convert this groove into a major 7th tonality (see Figure 9-8). To do so, raise the ♭7 of the original groove (refer to Figure 9-6) and then play the groove using a major 7th chord (root, 3, 5, and 7). Play this groove with your middle finger on the root. (Check out Chapter 5 for info on major, minor, and dominant chords.) The major 7th tonality is not common in rock 'n' roll, but it's still useful to know how to play it for those rare cases.

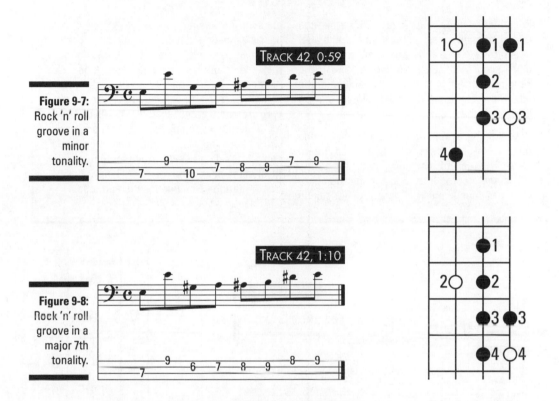

Figure 9-7:
Rock 'n' roll groove in a minor tonality.

TRACK 42, 0:59

Figure 9-8:
Rock 'n' roll groove in a major 7th tonality.

TRACK 42, 1:10

When accompanying a rock tune that has a major 7th tonality, you may want to substitute the 6 of the major mode for the 7 in your groove. The 6 softens the sound and makes it more palatable to the ear. Take a look at Figure 9-9 for an example of a 6 in a major 7th tonality.

With the 6 in place, you can use the groove in Figure 9-9 over a major 7th tonality as well as over a dominant tonality. The only difference between these two tonalities is the 7: The major 7th chord has a regular 7, while the dominant chord has a ♭7. A groove with a regular 7 clashes with a dominant chord; a groove with a ♭7 clashes with a major chord. In the groove shown in Figure 9-9, however, the 6 doesn't clash with either chord. (In fact, it sounds pretty good.) You can use this groove to give the other players of your band more leeway in their choice of notes. It doesn't lock them into having to choose between either a 7 or ♭7.

A history of rock styles from the bassist's perspective

Rock had its beginnings in the 1950s when the rhythm section (bass, guitar, drums, and piano) began to take on a more prominent role in popular music. With the invention in 1951 of the Fender Precision bass (the first popular electric bass), the electric bass guitar slowly started displacing the acoustic (upright) bass.

With the improvement of recording and sound technology, the bass could now be heard clearly instead of just being felt, and by the 1960s, the electric bass was the instrument of choice in popular music. The bass guitar gained an ever-increasing role in rock music, and bassists developed more melodic and complex lines to accompany the music. In the 1970s, hard rock and progressive rock emerged, along with faster and more complex bass lines — and steadily increasing volume. Bass lines of *driving sixteenth notes* (sixteenth notes played in a continuous even stream, often on one pitch) were becoming more common in accompaniment. Rock didn't simply abandon one style in favor of the next; it absorbed each new musical trend, sharing its unique feel and attitude.

TRACK 42, 1:22

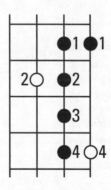

Figure 9-9:
Rock 'n' roll groove with a 6.

When you listen to the CD tracks corresponding to Figures 9-6 through 9-9, you can hear how one groove can be adapted to fit over different tonalities: the dominant (Figure 9-6), the minor (Figure 9-7), the major 7th (Figure 9-8), and a major tonality with a 6 instead of a 7 (Figure 9-9).

You can change the sound of a groove to a different tonality by changing the 3, the 7, or even the 5. Check out Chapter 5 for more on scale/chord compatibility.

Rock: Moving into Something a Bit More Edgy

Rock, which is a collective term for rock styles, also refers to a particular style of playing. *Rock* is often less melodic (for a bass player) and even more driven than rock 'n' roll. The eighth notes are *squared off* (equally divided over the beat), and the tempo is generally on the fast side. Check out the sounds of Adam Clayton of U2, or the late John Entwistle of The Who if you want to hear a great rock bassist.

Figure 9-10 shows a rock groove that uses only the root. (See Chapter 5 for more on roots.) The notes are the same as those in the rock 'n' roll groove from Figure 9-1.

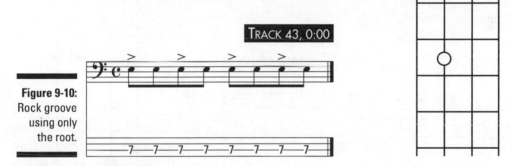

Figure 9-10: Rock groove using only the root.

Listen to the attitude of the groove in Figure 9-10. Notice how the *attack* (the way the notes are played) of the notes is more aggressive in rock than in rock 'n' roll. (See the previous section for more on rock 'n' roll.)

In Figure 9-11, you add the 3 and 5 to the root to form the chord — in this case, the minor chord with a ♭3. Remember, if you want to play this groove over a major tonality, you can simply change the tonality by raising the 3. Start this groove with your index finger to avoid shifting your left hand.

Figure 9-12 shows a more elaborate groove in a minor tonality that uses notes from the chord and the related minor mode. The minor modes are Aeolian, Dorian, and Phrygian. Most rock tunes use only Aeolian or Dorian. (Check out Chapter 5 for an explanation of the modes.) Try playing this groove using different roots. Make sure that you start the groove with your index finger (to keep your hand in one position).

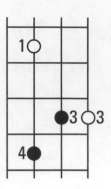

TRACK 43, 0:17

Figure 9-11:
Rock groove
using a
minor chord.

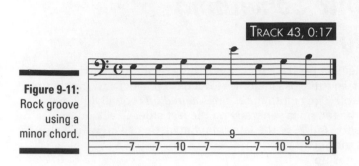

The box groove uses notes from the chord and mode along with the chromatic tones from outside the mode, which lead to the main chord tones. Figure 9-13 shows how to play a box groove in the rock style. Start this groove with your index finger on the root.

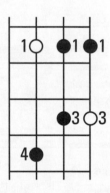

TRACK 43, 0:36

Figure 9-12:
Rock groove
using a
minor mode.

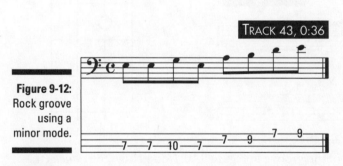

The rock groove in Figure 9-13 is very *dense*, meaning that it has a lot of different notes.

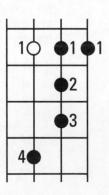

TRACK 43, 0:53

Figure 9-13:
Rock box
groove in
minor.

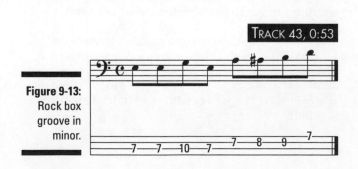

Hard Rock: Going at It Fast and Furious

Hard rock, which includes metal and its numerous offspring, is the fastest category of rock. The rhythm is hard and driving, and the tempo can be downright wicked (as in superfast). You may frequently encounter sixteenth notes (see Chapter 3) in this style. Hard-rock bass lines are often based on minor pentatonic sounds (check out Chapter 8 for pentatonic scales).

When you play unison *riffs* (licks with the same notes in the same rhythm, played together) with other band members in hard rock music, you want to get your sixteenth notes up to speed so that you can keep up with the guitar player. (For an example of a typical unison riff, check out Figure 9-17.) Listen to Tom Hamilton of Aerosmith or John Paul Jones of Led Zeppelin if you want to hear an excellent bassist who plays in this style.

Figure 9-14 shows a hard-rock bass groove played on the root only, using a combination of eighth and sixteenth notes.

Hard rock grooves often sound very aggressive (like the one in Figure 9-14).

The groove in Figure 9-15 adds the ♭3 and 5 to the root, giving it a minor tonality. Minor is the most common chord choice in hard rock, but you may occasionally encounter major tonalities as well. Start this groove with your index finger on the root.

Listen to the dark minor quality of the groove in Figure 9-15.

Figure 9-16 shows a bass groove that includes notes from both the minor chord and the minor modes. You can really feel your fingers move when you play this groove. Make sure that you start with your index finger on the root

TRACK 44, 0:00

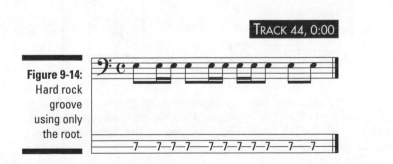

Figure 9-14:
Hard rock groove using only the root.

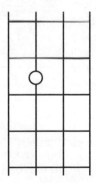

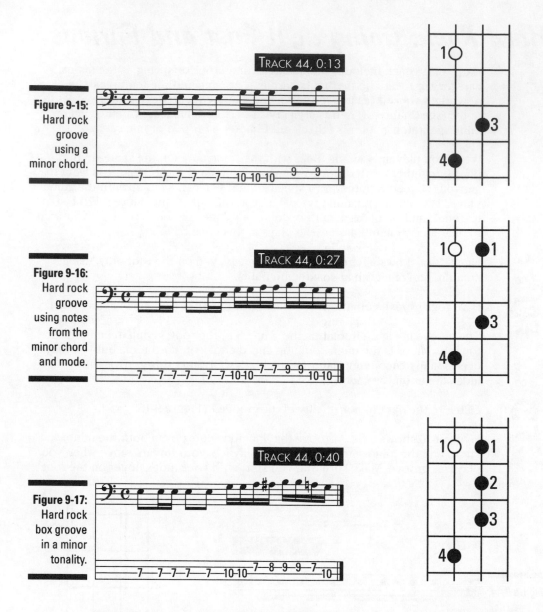

TRACK 44, 0:13

Figure 9-15:
Hard rock groove using a minor chord.

TRACK 44, 0:27

Figure 9-16:
Hard rock groove using notes from the minor chord and mode.

TRACK 44, 0:40

Figure 9-17:
Hard rock box groove in a minor tonality.

The hard rock groove in Figure 9-17 uses a chromatic tone (a note outside the regular minor mode) to embellish the bass line. This example shows a typical box groove (no shifts with the left hand) that's played on the bass and guitar in unison (not by the same person, of course).

Listen to the busy but melodic line of the groove in Figure 9-17.

Progressive Rock: Breaking Some (But Not All) of the Boundaries

Progressive rock refers to a style that goes beyond the traditional boundaries of rock but still uses the same basic chords, scales, and rhythms. Sixteenth notes are far more common in progressive rock than in the other rock styles (except for hard rock), and the harmonic structure of progressive rock grooves is more complex.

As with the other rock styles, the beats in progressive rock tunes are evenly divided. (See Chapter 3 for info on beat divisions.) However, the bass lines are more melodic than in some of the other rock styles. *Odd meter* — an odd number of beats in a measure — may also be used. (See Chapter 13 for a more detailed explanation of odd meter.) Progressive rock is a style of musical exploration. John Myung of Dream Theatre and Geddy Lee of Rush are two great progressive rock bassists.

Figure 9-18 shows a root-based progressive rock groove with rhythmic variation — the rhythm of the notes switches between eighth and sixteenth notes.

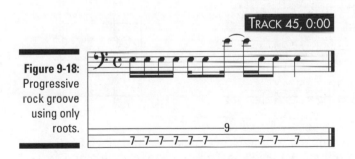

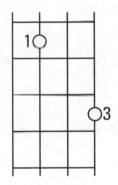

Figure 9-18:
Progressive rock groove using only roots.

The groove in Figure 9-19 uses the ♭3 and 5 to form a minor chord. The octave (which is a root, as well) is also used. Start this groove with your index finger on the root.

The tie in this groove creates *syncopation* (a tied note that anticipates a beat; for more on ties, check out Chapter 3). You create a syncopation by striking a note where it's not expected and then failing to restrike the note where it *is* expected. When playing this groove, you anticipate the beat by playing a note sooner than expected. This technique gives the music a kick, like a roller coaster that suddenly drops toward the ground when you don't expect it.

In Figure 9-20, you get to explore the notes of the minor scale beyond the root, ♭3, and 5 of the minor chord. Start with your index finger on the root to avoid any unnecessary shifts in your left hand.

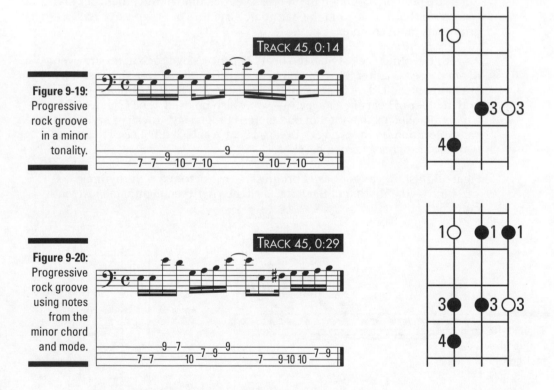

Figure 9-19:
Progressive rock groove in a minor tonality.

Figure 9-20:
Progressive rock groove using notes from the minor chord and mode.

Figure 9-21 shows an example of a progressive rock bass line played in the box (which means no shifting of the left hand). Notice that some of the notes are outside the regular minor mode — these are chromatic tones. (See Chapter 5 for more info on chromatic tones.) You can see (and feel) how busy this style can be. With this groove, you strike 15 of the 16 possible sixteenth notes (one is tied). Make sure that your hands are warmed up (see Chapter 4 for some great exercises) before you dive in and start playing this groove.

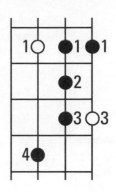

Figure 9-21:
Progressive
rock box
groove in
minor.

Pop Rock: Supporting the Vocals

The term *pop* is short for popular music (yes, I know that leaves it wide open), which refers to a style of rock that's popular with a wide range of the general population.

Ever heard of a band called The Beatles (with Paul McCartney on bass)? How about Elton John? (Several bassists play with Elton John, but the great Pino Palladino stands out.) In pop music, the song tells a story, so you don't want to overshadow the vocals with an outrageous bass line.

Figure 9-22 shows the quintessential singer/songwriter groove that you so often hear in pop. The beat is divided equally and often set up (approached) by an eighth note. The eighth note and the quarter note are the most frequent note choices for pop bass lines.

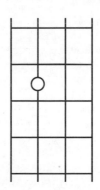

Figure 9-22:
Pop rock
groove
using only
the root.

Figure 9-23 shows a pop rock groove that uses a major tonality. When playing this groove, you add the 3 and 5 to fill out the chord (major). Make sure that you start this groove with your middle finger on the root.

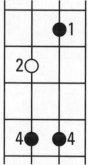

Figure 9-23:
Pop rock groove using a major tonality.

TRACK 46, 0:12

Notice how the bass hooks up with the drums for the groove in Figure 9-23.

Figure 9-24 shows a pop rock groove that uses notes in the dominant tonality. The first half of the measure sets up the feel for this groove. The last half of the measure is much busier; it sets up the calm first half of the next repetition of the groove. The groove builds up tension and then releases to a satisfying resolution. (You can read all about tension and release in Chapter 5.) You use notes from the major mode for this groove. Start with your middle finger on the root to keep your left hand in position.

Figure 9-24:
Pop rock groove using notes in the dominant tonality.

TRACK 46, 0:24

Figure 9-25 shows a box groove (no shifts) that uses the dominant chord, the mode (Mixolydian in this case), and a chromatic tone outside the mode. Remember to start the groove with your middle finger on the root.

TRACK 46, 0:37

Figure 9-25:
Pop rock
box groove
in dominant
tonality.

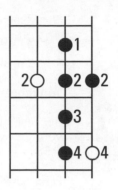

Listen to the solid establishment of the groove (in Figure 9-25) in the first half of the measure and the embellishment in the second half of the measure.

Blues Rock: A Bit More Organized

The bass lines in blues rock are very distinctive and repetitive. They form a little countermelody to accompany the real melody. When thinking of great blues rock bassists, the Allman Brothers' late bassist Berry Oakley comes to mind, as does Donald Duck Dunn of the Blues Brothers and Booker T. & the MGs.

In a blues style, the chords move in a specific sequence called the *blues progression*. The official term for the blues progression is the *I-IV-V progression* (1-4-5 progression). The chords are either all dominant or all minor tonalities, except for the two measures of V, which are almost always dominant. Figuring out a blues progression is pretty straightforward. Here's what you do:

1. **Determine the root of your tune's starting chord (C, for example).**

   This chord is your I chord (or 1 chord).

2. **Using the scale of the I chord (C in this case), find the 4 and 5 (F and G in this case — the 4 and 5 of the C-dominant or C-minor scale).**

   For a blues progression in C, F will be the root of the IV chord, and G will be the root for the V chord.

You now have the roots for your I-IV-V progression. The sequence used in the vast (and I mean *vast*) majority of blues tunes is

✔ 4 measures of I (C in the example from the previous list)

✔ 2 measures of IV (F)

  ✔ 2 measures of I (C)

  ✔ 2 measures of V (G)

  ✔ 2 measures of I (C)

You repeat this chord sequence throughout the song.

Because blues songs almost always move harmonically in a certain sequence, your groove needs to be easily moveable as well. Use notes that are easy to reach — within three strings and four frets.

Figure 9-26 shows a blues rock groove that uses only the root. Start the groove with either your middle finger or your ring finger on the root. The beat, as with all the rock styles, is evenly divided.

TRACK 47, 0:00

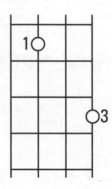

Figure 9-26:
Blues rock
groove
using only
the root.

The groove in Figure 9-26 uses the octave for variety.

Figure 9-27 shows a groove that adds the 3 and 5 to spell out the chord (a major chord). You start the groove with your middle finger on the root so that you don't have to make any shifts with your left hand. The groove in Figure 9-27 uses only two strings, making it easy to move from chord to chord.

The groove in Figure 9-28 adds notes from the mode (Mixolydian in this case) to the 3 and 5 to really flesh out the dominant tonality. (Check out Chapter 5 for an explanation of modes, chords, and tonalities.) Start this groove with your middle finger on the root.

The groove in Figure 9-29 adds some chromatic tones to the scale tones and chord tones. You can play this groove in one position (which makes it a box groove); just start it with your middle finger on the root, and make sure that you don't shift your left hand. In this particular case, you may also start with your index finger, because the groove uses only three frets.

The dense blues rock groove in Figure 9-29 has lots of tightly spaced notes (half steps apart).

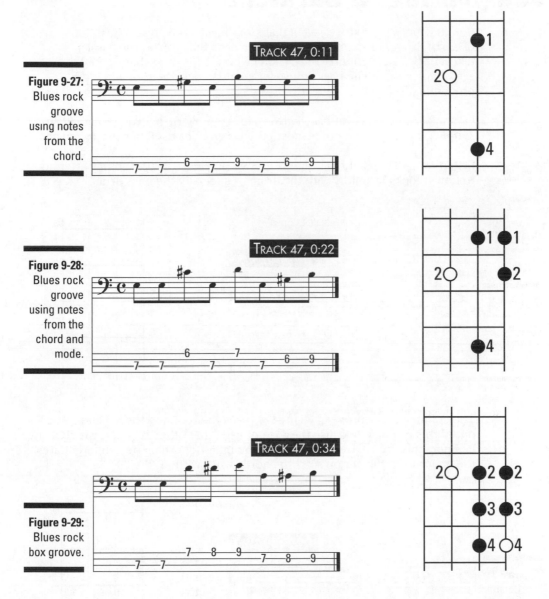

TRACK 47, 0:11

Figure 9-27: Blues rock groove using notes from the chord.

TRACK 47, 0:22

Figure 9-28: Blues rock groove using notes from the chord and mode.

TRACK 47, 0:34

Figure 9-29: Blues rock box groove.

Country Rock: Where Vocals Are King, and You Take a Backseat

Country tunes tell a story — and that story needs to be heard (just think of Garth Brooks or Kenny Rogers). That means that you, as the bassist, take a back seat in country rock. (Don't worry. You get to shine in funk; see Chapter 11). In the bass groove for country rock, the root and the 5 predominate.

Figure 9-30 shows a root-based groove for country rock. Even though it's a simple groove, it's one of the most popular grooves used in country music.

Listen to the simplicity of the bass groove (in Figure 9-30), and pay attention to how it locks in solidly with the drums, especially the bass drum.

TRACK 48, 0:00

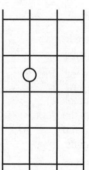

Figure 9-30:
Country rock groove using only the root.

The country rock groove in Figure 9-31 uses the root and the 5. I leave the 3 out of this example because the 3 is not used that often in country rock. You can play this groove over both major and minor chords. The 3 differentiates the major from the minor, so both chords work without the 3.

TRACK 48, 0:12

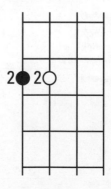

Figure 9-31:
Country rock groove using notes from the chord.

Notice that the 5 is played below the root in the groove shown in Figure 9-31. The 5 can also be played above the root.

Figure 9-32 shows a country rock bass groove that uses the mode (the root and 5, plus one other note from the mode). In most country rock songs, you have to keep the bass line simple. Start this groove with your pinkie on the root; your ring finger works, too.

Notice the simplicity of the groove in Figure 9-32, even with the added note.

The box groove in Figure 9-33 uses a chromatic tone outside the mode. This bass groove is simple and locked in with the drums. Grab your 10-gallon hat and play 'til the cows come home . . . and make sure that your left hand is in position by starting with your pinkie on the root; you can also use your ring finger.

Figure 9-32: Country rock groove using the mode.

Listen to the simplicity of the bass groove in Figure 9-33. Notice how it remains unobtrusive despite the added notes. You don't want anything to distract from the melody and words of the song.

Strap on your bass and rock the joint. You have enough material in this chapter to keep jammin' for quite a while.

Figure 9-33: Country rock box groove.

Chapter 10

Swing It! Playing Styles That Rely on the Triplet Feel

*T*ri-pe-let, *tri*-pe-let, *tri*-pe-let . . . snap your fingers while you say it out loud, accenting the italicized syllables. Now take a wild guess at what kind of feel (rhythm) this chapter is about. That's right, it's the *triplet feel,* and all the styles that I feature in this chapter are based on it. The triplet styles come in two flavors: swing and shuffle.

In music that has a triplet feel, each beat of a four-beat measure is broken into three equal parts. Instead of counting "1, 2, 3, 4," you count "1-trip-let, 2-trip-let, 3-trip-let, 4-trip-let." You hear four triplets in each measure, or 12 hits (occurrences) total.

Swing: Grooving Up-Tempo with Attitude

The *swing style* originated in the late 1920s and early 1930s. The music of Glenn Miller and Benny Goodman typifies the early swing era. Bands like The Brian Setzer Orchestra bring swing to today's music scene. In swing style, the first note is *slightly* longer than the second — long, short, long, short — and it gives the feeling of . . . swinging, of course.

The bass line in swing style is predictable but cool (it makes you want to snap your fingers). The vast majority of swing tunes are based on a major or a dominant tonality. (I cover tonality in Chapter 5.)

Figure 10-1 shows you a groove in a major tonality, using a major pentatonic scale. (See Chapter 8 for an explanation of pentatonic scales.) Start this groove with your middle finger to avoid any shifting of your left hand.

TRACK 49, 0:00

Figure 10-1:
Swing
groove
using a
major
pentatonic
scale.

Notice how the notes of the bass line in Figure 10-1 are played on the beat and how the drums subdivide each of those beats into — that's right — triplets.

Figure 10-2 shows an example of a swing groove using a mode — in this case, the common Mixolydian mode. (Check out Chapter 5 for information about modes.) Again, your bass line is concentrated on the beats, whereas the drums subdivide the beat into triplets.

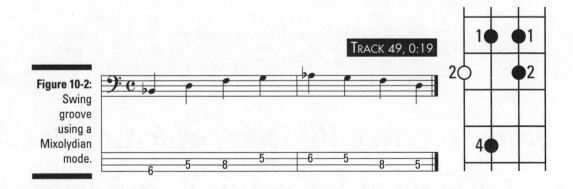

TRACK 49, 0:19

Figure 10-2:
Swing
groove
using a
Mixolydian
mode.

You can move all the grooves in this chapter from chord to chord (check out Chapter 7 for more on moving grooves from chord to chord); just practice taking a groove pattern from any grid and moving it to different roots. Consistent fingering is the key to success for moving these grooves smoothly.

Jazz: Going for a Walk

The walking bass line in jazz style is a more creative form of bass playing than the other swing styles because you choose new notes each time you play the same song. The walking bass line was developed by upright bassists, such as Ray Brown, Milt Hinton, Paul Chambers, and Ron Carter, but now it's also commonly played on the bass guitar.

Creating a walking bass line is one of the more elusive art forms in the bass world, but this section takes you through it step by step (pun intended) so that it doesn't seem so frightening. A *walking bass line* simply walks through the appropriate scale of each chord, one note per beat, hitting every beat of each measure.

The formula for a successful walking bass line is simple:

1. **Beat One: Determine the chord tonality (major, minor, dominant, or half-diminished; see Chapter 5 for more about chord tonalities), and play the root of that chord.**

2. **Beat Two: Play any chord tone of the chord, or any note in the scale related to that chord.**

   If you're not sure which scale belongs to which chord, check out Chapter 5.

3. **Beat Three: Play any chord tone or scale tone of the chord.**

   Yep — same as Step 2, but try to pick a different note.

4. **Beat Four: Play a leading tone to the next root.**

   A *leading tone* leads from one chord to the next. The sound of the leading tone is not related to the current chord; it's related to the chord you're approaching. In other words, the leading tone prepares the listener's ear for the sound of the new chord. The most important point to understand about a leading tone is that it aims for the *following* chord's root. For example, if you're going from a C chord to an F chord, your leading tone leads to *F* (never mind the C).

   Leading tones come in three types:

   - Chromatic (half-step)

   - Diatonic (scale)

   - Dominant (the 5 of the new chord)

   Figure 10-3 shows the location of each type of leading tone. The root of the new chord is represented by the open circle; the leading tones are represented by the solid dots. The arrows show which way the leading tone moves to resolve to the root of the new chord.

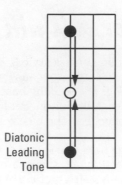
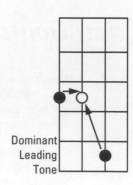

Figure 10-3:
The locations of the chromatic, diatonic, and dominant leading tones.

Chromatic Leading Tone

Diatonic Leading Tone

Dominant Leading Tone

> In a walking bass line, beat four of the measure is reserved for the leading tone.

You can walk through almost any jazz tune. To demonstrate the jazz walking style properly, I show you how to walk in a *jazz blues progression* (see Figure 10-4). In the figure, the chords are printed above each grid. The modes for each chord are clearly marked, and the leading tones are the last note in each sequence (follow the arrows). You can start this progression on any root. Figure 10-4 is written in B♭, but if someone asks for a jazz blues in C, just move the whole pattern up two frets (toward the bridge of the bass) and start your first note on C.

By the way, playing this pattern is easy (despite the complex sound) because you don't have to shift your left hand. Just make sure that you start the pattern with your middle finger.

You can use a walking bass line for any jazz tune. Take your time when starting to play a new tune; you need to figure out the scales for each chord before you play it. The more you play, the faster you get.

The Jazz Two Feel: Getting the Job Done with Two Notes

The *jazz two feel* is a very subtle way of playing the triplet feel. With this style, you concentrate on playing two notes per measure — one on the first beat of the measure, and one on the third beat. The other beats are rests. Occasionally, you can play an additional note just before either of the main notes to set them up; make sure that you play this additional note with the triplet feel.

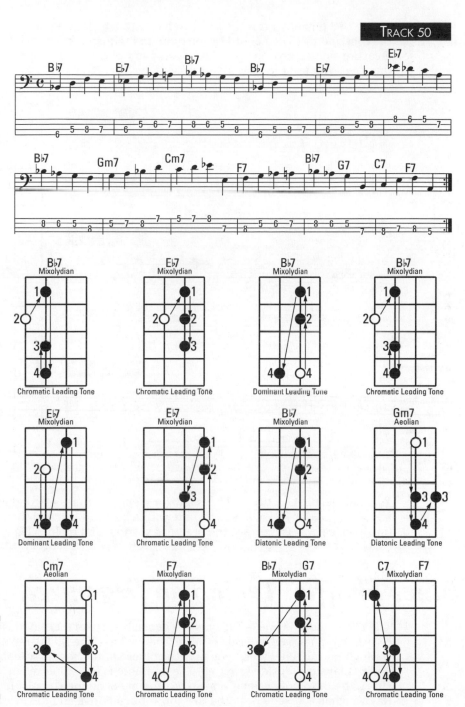

Figure 10-4: Jazz blues walking pattern.

Figure 10-5 demonstrates the jazz two feel with a bass line that uses only the root and the 5 of a chord (a common way to play the jazz two feel). The measure sounds broken up because you don't play on every beat. (That's the effect you want for this style.)

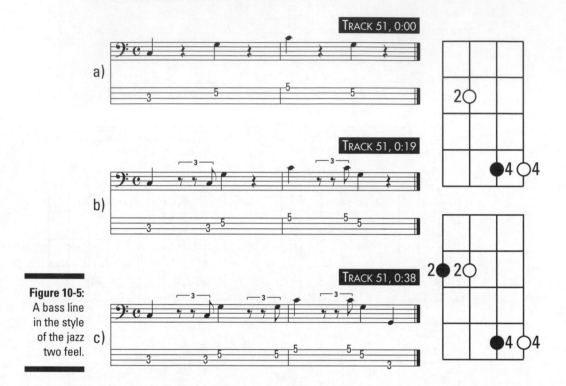

Figure 10-5: A bass line in the style of the jazz two feel.

You can use the jazz two feel bass line for most jazz tunes. A good way to take advantage of this feel is to start a tune with a jazz two feel and then break into a walking bass line (see the previous section, and refer to Figure 10-4).

Blues Shuffle: Taking an Organized Walk

The *blues shuffle* is one of the most recognizable triplet feels in music. The bass line is an organized walk — it's a walking bass line that is repeated throughout the tune. When you play the blues shuffle, you may feel like you're playing a lopsided rhythm. The first note is long, the second note is short, the third note is long, and so on. Tommy Shannon (bassist for Stevie Ray Vaughan), Roscoe Beck (bassist for Robben Ford), and the incomparable Donald Duck Dunn (of the Blues Brothers and Booker T. & the MGs) are three wonderful blues bassists who are very skilled at playing the blues shuffle.

Figure 10-6 demonstrates a blues shuffle groove that uses only one note — the root. You can use this groove for any chord.

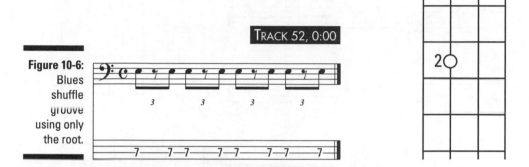

Figure 10-6:
Blues shuffle groove using only the root.

Figure 10-7 shows another example of a blues shuffle groove. The 3 and 5 are added to this groove to form a major chord. Start the groove with your middle finger.

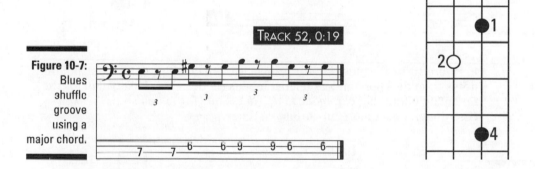

Figure 10-7:
Blues shuffle groove using a major chord.

In Figure 10-8, notes from the Mixolydian mode (see Chapter 5 for more about modes) are added to the root, 3, and 5, filling out the chord to form a dominant tonality. Start this groove with your middle finger on the root.

But what if the blues tune you're playing is on the sad side, in a minor tonality? (Actually, sad tunes are a strong possibility when you're playing the blues.) If you want to play the groove in Figure 10-8 over a minor tonality, you need to make a minor adjustment: Simply change the tonality by flattening the 3 (making it a ♭3). Figure 10-9 shows a blues shuffle that includes notes from the minor mode (Aeolian or Dorian mode).

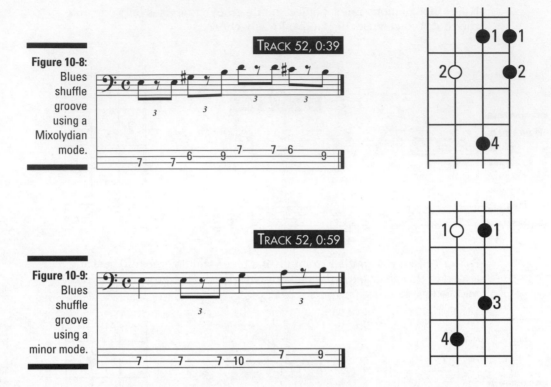

TRACK 52, 0:39

Figure 10-8:
Blues
shuffle
groove
using a
Mixolydian
mode.

TRACK 52, 0:59

Figure 10-9:
Blues
shuffle
groove
using a
minor mode.

In Figure 10-10, the blues shuffle groove is more complex. It includes not only notes from the chord and its related modes (in this case, Mixolydian for the dominant chord) but *chromatic tones* (notes moving in half steps) as well. (See Chapter 5 for more on chromatic tones.)

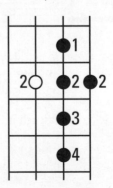

Figure 10-10:
Blues
shuffle
groove
using a
Mixolydian
mode with a
chromatic
tone.

TRACK 52, 1:19

And finally, Figure 10-11 shows a complex blues shuffle that you play over a minor tonality using a chromatic tone.

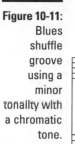

Figure 10-11:
Blues shuffle groove using a minor tonality with a chromatic tone.

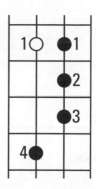

The grooves in Figures 10-10 and 10-11 use a strong *triplet figure* (three notes in a beat) on the last beat of the measure. This triplet figure helps establish the strong triplet feel for this style. Play around with these grooves and come up with some of your own. By the way, these grooves work great over a blues progression. (See Chapter 9 for the structure of the blues progression.)

Funk Shuffle: Combining Funk, Blues, and Jazz

Funk shuffle (also called *shuffle funk*) is a hybrid groove style, which means that it combines several elements of other styles — funk, blues, and jazz. When funk, which normally uses straight sixteenth notes, is combined with blues and jazz, which use triplets, the resulting combination is a lopsided sixteenth-note groove (a combination of long and short notes) — a very cool combination. This type of groove is pretty challenging, but some useful tricks of the trade can help make it a lot easier to play.

Check out Figure 10-12 for an example of a funk shuffle groove. This groove uses only the root (in two octaves) with an added *dead note* (a note that sounds like a thud; see Chapter 5 for a complete explanation). The drums are crucial in this style because they drive the rhythm along in tandem with the bass. You can start this groove with your index finger or middle finger on the low root (the starting note).

Figure 10-13 shows an example of a funk shuffle groove that uses notes common to both the Mixolydian (dominant) and Dorian (minor) modes. "Whoa! You mean the groove in Figure 10-13 fits over both dominant *and* minor?" Yep! This groove is not all that easy to learn, but after you get comfortable with it, you can get lots (and lots) of use out of playing it over any dominant or minor chord. In the funk shuffle style, almost all chords are dominant or minor.

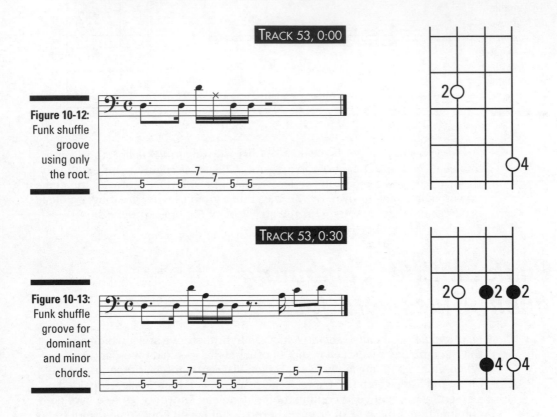

TRACK 53, 0:00

Figure 10-12:
Funk shuffle
groove
using only
the root.

TRACK 53, 0:30

Figure 10-13:
Funk shuffle
groove for
dominant
and minor
chords.

The funk shuffle in Figure 10-14 includes more notes from both the Mixolydian and Dorian modes; notice the cool syncopation — the way a note anticipates the beat it's expected on. (Chapter 9 covers syncopation.) The groove in Figure 10-14 can be used over most chords in shuffle funk tunes: Most of the chords are either dominant (Mixolydian) or minor (Dorian). Start the groove with your index finger or middle finger to keep it in the box (so that you don't have to shift your left hand).

TRACK 53, 0:59

Figure 10-14:
Funk shuffle
groove
using notes
from the
dominant or
minor
modes.

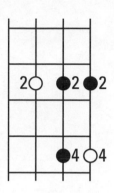

When you're grooving on a funk shuffle, you can keep going for hours and hours without getting the least bit bored; because of its complexity, a funk shuffle is going to keep you busy. Keep the shuffle funky, "'cause it don't mean a thing if it ain't got that swing."

Chapter 11

Making It Funky: Playing Hardcore Bass Grooves

"**G**imme the funk! You gotta gimme the funk!" When these words echo across the bandstand, they're directed at *you* (and your alter ego, the drummer). From Motown to hip-hop, the bass player takes a starring role in funk; your skill and dexterity are put to the test. These hardcore bass grooves are a real workout for any bass player. Funk is essentially party music, and your job is to keep every foot in the room moving to the beat.

The sixteenth note is the rhythm of choice in funk. You often play quite a few sixteenth notes in funk grooves. In this chapter, I give you a selection of prime funk grooves that you can use when the words "Gimme the funk!" echo across the bandstand.

R & B: Movin' to Some Rhythm and Blues

R & B (rhythm and blues) originated in the late 1940s. It is still one of today's most popular styles of music. R & B is dominated by *session players* — musicians who record with numerous artists. Generally, record producers hire the same rhythm section (session players) to accompany all of their artists. So you have the same bassist, drummer, guitarist, and keyboardist playing together for years and years on countless sessions with different artists. Tommy Cogbill (who played with such singers as Aretha Franklin and Wilson Pickett) and Chuck Rainey (who played with Aretha Franklin, Quincy Jones, and Steely Dan) are two great session players. Because of this tradition of using session players, you can hear excellent grooves behind some fabulous singers.

The bass groove in R & B consists of a fairly active bass line, locked in tight with the drums. Because R & B music often has such a busy bass line, the harmony includes both scale and chord tones — you need a lot of different notes to keep this bass line interesting. The use of *syncopation* (notes played between beats) makes the R & B groove funky. See Chapter 9 for a complete discussion of syncopation.

Figure 11-1 shows an R & B groove in a major tonality. (If you need help creating grooves for different tonalities — major, minor, and dominant — check out Chapter 7.) Start this groove with your middle finger to avoid shifting your left hand.

TRACK 54, 0:00

Figure 11-1:
R & B
groove
using a
major
(Ionian)
mode.

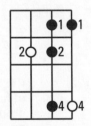

The groove in Figure 11-1 uses notes from the major chord and its related Ionian mode for a major tonality. (See Chapter 5 for information about mode and chord compatibility.) You can play this groove as a dominant tonality by playing the ♭7 instead of the 6.

Figure 11-2 shows an R & B groove in a dominant tonality using the Mixolydian mode. Start this groove with your middle finger to avoid shifting.

You have to listen carefully to hear the subtle difference between the grooves shown in Figures 11-1 and 11-2; only one note (the second to the last note) is different.

In Figure 11-3, you can see what the groove from Figure 11-1 looks like in a minor tonality. This groove is based on a Dorian or Aeolian mode (either one will do in this case), and it fits perfectly over a minor chord. Start the groove with your index finger.

Figure 11-2: R & B groove using a dominant (Mixolydian) mode.

Figure 11-3: R & B groove using a minor (Dorian or Aeolian) mode.

Dead notes and chromatic tones are frequently used in all funk styles, including R & B. (See Chapter 5 for an explanation of dead notes and chromatic tones.) Figure 11-4 shows you what the grooves in Figures 11-1, 11-2, and 11-3 look like with dead notes and chromatic tones added. The grooves in Figure 11-4 tend to sound fairly complex.

To keep your R & B grooves interesting, you may want to start with simple rhythm and note choices, and then add dead notes and chromatic tones as you get deeper into the tune.

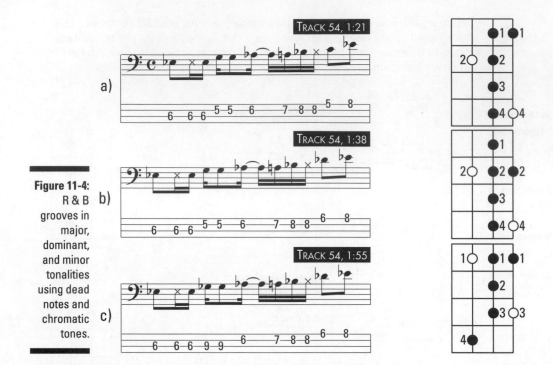

Figure 11-4:
R & B grooves in major, dominant, and minor tonalities using dead notes and chromatic tones.

The Motown Sound: Grooving with Variations

Motown is the name of a record label that got its start in Detroit in the late 1950s. The Motown style is actually part of the R & B family. Numerous singers recorded for Motown, and the vast majority were fortunate to be able to use the Motown house band — the famous Funk Brothers — for their recordings.

James Jamerson (also known as Funk Brother #1) not only defined the label's sound with his active, syncopated lines on hundreds of hits, he also forged the template for modern electric bass playing. Marvin Gaye, The Temptations, Stevie Wonder, and many other artists benefited from the outstanding groove-creating abilities of Jamerson and the Funk Brothers. Your bass skills can also benefit from the Jamerson/Motown-style grooves featured in this section.

Many of the Motown grooves use *constant structure*. Constant-structure grooves use notes that occur in more than one tonality. (The shared notes are called *common tones;* see Chapter 7 for more about constant-structure grooves.) You can play a groove using constant structure over any chord and still make it sound interesting.

Figure 11-5 shows a typical Motown groove that works over a major or dominant tonality. (This one even works for a minor tonality.) When you play the groove, start it with your pinkie.

Figure 11-5:
Motown groove using constant structure for major and dominant tonalities.

Notice how the groove in Figure 11-5 has a slight variation in the second measure. This variation is a Jamerson trademark.

Figure 11-6 shows a busy Motown groove using common tones for dominant and minor tonalities. This groove also sports chromatic tones in the second measure that lead back to the beginning of the groove. Start the groove with your pinkie.

Figure 11-6:
Motown groove using constant structure for dominant and minor tonalities.

The Motown bassists were the first generation of bass virtuosos. They influenced more modern bassists than you can shake a string at.

Fusion: Blending Two Styles into One

Fusion is the merging of two or more styles of music. Fusion generally refers to the combination of rock rhythms and jazz harmonies, but any combination of styles is possible. Fusion-style bass playing is intricate and complex and full of nervous energy and fast notes, yet it allows you to rock the joint with deep grooves. In this section, I show you bass grooves that use every trick in the book: scale tones, dead notes, chromatic tones, and plenty of sixteenth notes.

Figure 11-7 shows a busy fusion-style groove that you can play for either a major or dominant chord (Ionian or Mixolydian mode). Notice the use of dead notes and the chromatic tone that make the groove more interesting. Start the groove in Figure 11-7 with your middle finger; no shifts of the left hand are necessary (or desired). The groove is extremely busy, hitting all 16 of the sixteenth notes in the measure.

The groove in Figure 11-7 is challenging to play, so take your time with it. The extra effort will be well worth it when you feel comfortable enough to use it when playing with a band.

TRACK 56, 0:00

Figure 11-7:
Fusion groove for a major or dominant chord.

Figure 11-8 shows a fusion-style groove for a dominant chord (Mixolydian). Start this groove with your index finger.

TRACK 56, 0:33

Figure 11-8:
Fusion groove for a minor chord.

A brief history of fusion from the bass player's view

With the dawn of fusion in the 1970s, the role of the bassist was pushed to the forefront. Groups such as Return To Forever, with their astonishing bassist Stanley Clarke, and Weather Report, with the incredible bassist Jaco Pastorius, took bass playing to stratospheric heights. Suddenly bassists were expected to play blistering sixteenth-note grooves and perform solos like horn players. This era also saw the emergence of the *fretless bass* (a bass guitar without frets) — thanks to Jaco — as well as basses with more than four strings, such as the great session player Anthony Jackson's six-string contrabass guitar (with the addition of a low B string and a high C string) and the five-string (with a low B), which was a spinoff of Jackson's invention.

Many fusion-style tunes have an extended section of just one chord. With this type of tune, you don't have to move your groove from chord to chord. In other words, you can use a groove that covers all four strings of your bass. Figure 11-9 shows such a groove. This groove, which is based on a Mixolydian mode (for a dominant chord), requires no shifting if you start it with your middle finger. It may take a bit of effort to get it under your belt — I mean fingers — but the effort will be well worth it.

TRACK 56, 1:07

Figure 11-9:
Fusion groove over four strings on a dominant chord.

Funk: Sounding Heavy and Deep

Funk is not only a collective term for funk styles, it also refers to a particular style of playing. *Funk style* is normally percussive in sound. In fact, funk style is often played with a thumb (slap) technique (see Chapter 2). But fingerstyle is just as good at producing the percussive sound of funk. Flea (Red Hot Chili Peppers) and Victor Wooten (Béla Fleck and the Flecktones) are two excellent thumbers. Francis Rocco Prestia (Tower of Power) is a master of fingerstyle funk. Marcus Miller (a solo artist) is great at using both the fingerstyle and the thumb technique.

The note choices in funk style are often *neutral* (they work for more than one tonality); the emphasis is on rhythm. Figure 11-10 shows a funk groove that can be played over either a dominant or a minor chord. It has an aggressive attitude. Start the groove with your index finger or your middle finger.

TRACK 57, 0:00

Figure 11-10:
Funk groove
for a
dominant or
minor
tonality.

You can hear how this groove (shown in Figure 11-10) sounds when played with the fingerstyle technique. It can also be played with a thumb technique.

Figure 11-11 shows a funk groove that can be played over a major tonality. (It also works over a dominant tonality.) This groove represents a happy-sounding funk. This happy sound is not common, but sometimes the happy funk tunes have a way of sneaking up on you, so be ready.

TRACK 57, 0:28

Figure 11-11:
Funk groove
using a
major
tonality.

The groove in Figure 11-12 is a heavier funk groove in a minor tonality with a chromatic tone added. (The more notes in a funk groove, the lighter the groove; the fewer notes in the groove, the heavier the groove.) Start this groove with your pinkie or ring finger to keep the shifts to a minimum.

Figure 11-12: Heavy funk groove using a minor tonality.

Figure 11-13 shows a heavy funk groove in a major or dominant tonality. While the major tonality is not commonly found in funk, it's a good idea to be prepared in case you encounter one. Instead of making this groove a blatant major by adding a 3, you can avoid the 3 altogether by substituting the 6 (a neutral note). Start this groove with your pinkie to keep the shifts to a minimum.

Figure 11-13: Heavy funk groove for a major or dominant tonality.

In Figure 11-14, you have a funk groove that fits over both minor and dominant chords and is played in fingerstyle. Start this groove with your pinkie or ring finger.

Figure 11-15 shows you a finger-style funk in a major tonality (the counterpart of the groove from Figure 11-14). Start it with your pinkie.

No matter how you play the grooves in this section, make them funky. Practice them with a metronome (see Chapter 3) and make them precise — and above all, enjoy!

TRACK 57, 1:55

Figure 11-14: Fingerstyle funk for a minor or dominant tonality.

TRACK 57, 2:22

Figure 11-15: Fingerstyle funk using a major tonality.

Disco: Groovin' as the Ball Turns

Disco is dance music. With disco, you feel the repetitive groove setting the dance floor in motion. Disco had its heyday from the mid-1970s to the early 1980s. Bass player Bernard Edwards of the group Chic is well-known for his work during the disco era. The quintessential disco groove is played in octaves and fits over any chord.

Figure 11-16 shows a typical disco groove. You can start this groove with either your index or middle finger and move your hand with the notes as you play the octaves. Shifting is unavoidable when playing this particular groove, but at least your fingering doesn't change as you shift.

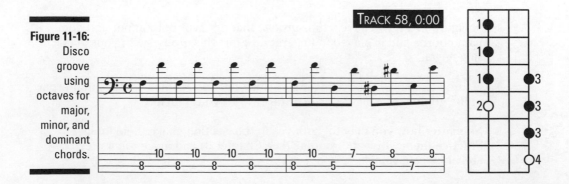

TRACK 58, 0:00

Figure 11-16: Disco groove using octaves for major, minor, and dominant chords.

A variation of this disco groove appears in Figure 11-17. With this groove, you double the notes on the high octave to give the bass line more rhythmic activity.

Figure 11-17:
Disco groove with doubled octaves for major, minor, and dominant chords.

TRACK 58, 0:19

The tempo of disco grooves is almost always on the fast side; you'll find them easy to dance to. (No surprise there.)

Figure 11-18 shows you a disco-style bass line that fits over a minor chord (a common tonality in disco). When you play it, make sure that you start with your index finger to avoid shifting.

Figure 11-18:
Disco groove for a minor tonality.

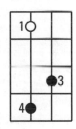

TRACK 58, 0:41

In Figure 11-19, you find the major and dominant version of the groove shown in Figure 11-18. The major tonality is not common in disco, but it's a good idea to be prepared for it in case you encounter one. Instead of making this groove a blatant major by adding a 3, avoid the 3 (and the ♭3) altogether and substitute the 4 (a neutral note). Start this groove with your index or middle finger to avoid shifting.

TRACK 58, 1:00

Figure 11-19: Disco groove for a major or dominant tonality.

Hip-Hop: Featuring Heavy Funk with Heavy Attitude

Hip-hop entered the music world in the 1990s. This style features a fat bass groove that sounds more laid-back than some of the other funk styles. Hip-hop is all about the message; the bass groove provides an important but unobtrusive accompaniment to the vocals. The bass line isn't very busy, but it's well-timed and repetitive. Raphael Saadiq is a well-known hip-hop bassist; he is best known for his work with D'Angelo and Tony Toni Tone.

Figure 11-20 shows a hip-hop-style bass groove. Start the groove with your ring finger.

TRACK 59, 0:00

Figure 11-20: Hip-hop groove.

The tonality in hip-hop is often minor, but it may occasionally be dominant. The groove doesn't move much from its starting chord. The feel and attitude are the most important features of the hip-hop groove.

Figure 11-21 shows another groove in hip-hop style, this time for a minor or dominant tonality. Start this groove with your middle finger.

TRACK 59, 0:27

Figure 11-21:
Hip-hop
groove for a
minor or
dominant
tonality.

Notice the long space between each note in this groove (Figure 11-21).

Figure 11-22 features a groove for a major or dominant tonality; it's for the happy hip-hoppers. Start this groove with your middle finger.

TRACK 59, 0:53

Figure 11-22:
Hip-hop
groove for a
major or
dominant
tonality.

A synthesizer is sometimes used to play the bass groove in hip-hop, but nothing grooves like the real thing.

Dance: If It Makes You Move, It's Good

Dance is a style that emphasizes on-the-beat playing, with syncopation (see Chapter 9) propelling the groove forward. Unlike the feel of disco style, which is light, dance style has a throbbing rhythm. (See "Disco: Groovin' as the Ball Turns," earlier in this chapter, for more details about disco.) The keyboardist, guitar player, and bassist often play the same *hits* (rhythm) in the groove.

Figure 11-23 shows a typical dance-style bass groove. This groove isn't too fancy, but it is effective. Because this groove uses only one note (the root), you can start it with any finger.

TRACK 60, 0:00

Figure 11-23:
Dance
groove
using only
the root.

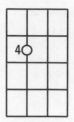

When you get the opportunity to be a little busier in a dance-style groove, use *common tones* (notes that fit over all the tonalities) so that you can keep the same groove going throughout the tune. Figure 11-24 shows you an example of a groove that uses only root, 2 (an octave up), and 5. This type of groove is popular in contemporary dance tunes. You need to make a small shift to play this groove, so start with your index finger.

TRACK 60, 0:20

Figure 11-24:
Contempo-
rary dance
groove
for major,
minor, and
dominant
chords.

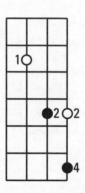

Sometimes you get the opportunity to dress up a dance groove and make it fancy. Figure 11-25 shows a dance-style groove with a few extra notes added as embellishments. The tonality is minor, so start this groove with your index finger.

TRACK 60, 0:39

Figure 11-25:
Dance-style
groove in
a minor
tonality with
embellish-
ments.

Figure 11-26 shows a dance-style groove for a major or dominant tonality. To avoid making it sound too happy, substitute the 3 with the 4 (which is still enough to keep everyone happy and dancing). You can start this one on your index or middle finger.

Figure 11-26:
Dance-style groove in a major or dominant tonality with embellishments.

TRACK 60, 1:00

Enjoy these grooves. If you have to leave a little sweat on your bass strings, remember that it's a small price to pay for the fun of funking it up.

Chapter 12

Sampling International Flavors: Bass Styles from Around the World

Ah, imagine it: Cool ocean breezes, white-sand beaches, palm trees, and, of course, the sound of great bass grooves with a native flavor. In this chapter, you discover how to play exotic bass grooves from South America and the Caribbean to South Africa. Rhythm is the all-important ingredient for bass grooves in these international styles. The harmony itself is often fairly simple.

Bossa Nova: Baskin' in a Brazilian Beat

If you've ever heard "Girl from Ipanema," you're familiar with bossa nova. Antonio Carlos Jobim, who wrote "Girl from Ipanema," is one of the best-known composers of bossa nova tunes. Bossa nova music (which is native to Brazil) has a light, swaying quality and a sensuous, easygoing groove. *Bossas* (short for bossa novas) are usually of medium tempo.

The bass line in bossa nova is almost always a root-5 combination (see Chapter 7), which fits over all major, minor, and dominant chords, and allows you to play a very repetitious bass groove.

The groove in Figure 12-1 shows a typical bossa nova groove for a major, dominant, or minor tonality. You can start it with either your index or middle finger, and you don't have to shift your left hand.

When bossa novas are played as jazz tunes, you occasionally encounter *half-diminished* chords where the 5 is flatted. In these cases, you satisfy the harmonic requirements for the half-diminished chord by simply playing a groove with a root and a ♭5.

Figure 12-2 shows a groove in a half-diminished tonality (Locrian mode; see Chapter 5 for more on modes). This groove is similar to the groove from Figure 12-1, but the 5 is changed to ♭5 to accommodate the ♭5 in the chord. To avoid shifting, start the groove with your index or middle finger.

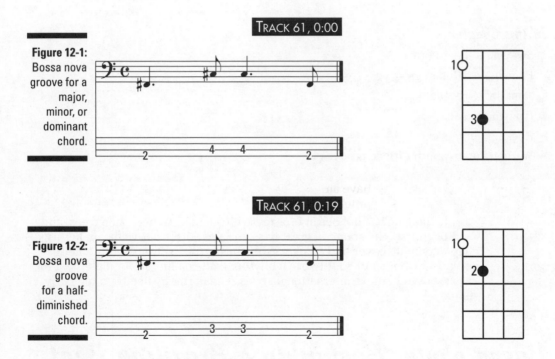

TRACK 61, 0:00

Figure 12-1: Bossa nova groove for a major, minor, or dominant chord.

TRACK 61, 0:19

Figure 12-2: Bossa nova groove for a half-diminished chord.

Afro-Cuban: Ordering Up Some Salsa (Hold the Chips, Please)

Afro-Cuban music is a mixture of Cuban and African rhythms, with musical elements from Puerto Rico, the Caribbean, Africa, Brazil, and other parts of South America thrown in for good measure. Lincoln Goines and Andy

Gonzales, two session players (see Chapter 11), are masters of this style. The Afro-Cuban style is often referred to as *Latin* or *salsa,* so don't be surprised when someone calls for salsa and expects to get the music instead of the sauce that goes with tortilla chips.

The bass groove in Afro-Cuban music often emphasizes the root and 5, but the *rhythmic syncopation* (notes played between the beats, on the offbeats) takes some getting used to. Afro-Cuban music has a fast-moving style, so buckle your seat belt. Figure 12-3 shows a bass groove that starts on the first beat of each measure. The groove includes syncopation, and it fits over major, minor, and dominant tonalities. Start this groove with your index or middle finger to avoid shifting.

TRACK 62, 0:00

Figure 12-3: Afro-Cuban groove for a major, minor, or dominant chord.

In Figure 12-4, you have an Afro-Cuban groove that's similar to the one in Figure 12-3 (syncopation and all), but this one is for a half-diminished chord. Start this groove with your index or middle finger.

TRACK 62, 0:12

Figure 12-4: Afro-Cuban groove for a half-diminished chord.

Figure 12-5 shows another version of the groove from Figure 12-3, but this time with a syncopation added at the beginning of the measure. Playing notes off the beat takes a little getting used to, but it provides a very cool feel after you get the hang of it. Start the groove in Figure 12-5 with your index or middle finger.

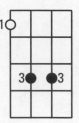

Figure 12-5: Afro-Cuban groove with syncopation for a major, minor, or dominant chord.

TRACK 62, 0:18

The groove in Figure 12-6 uses the same syncopated rhythm as the one in Figure 12-4, but this time a ♭5 is substituted for the 5 to accommodate a half-diminished chord. Start this groove with your index or middle finger.

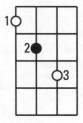

Figure 12-6: Afro-Cuban groove with syncopation for a half-diminished chord.

TRACK 62, 0:42

Reggae: Relaxing with Offbeat "Riddims"

Reggae music is most often associated with Jamaica and the Caribbean islands. The trademarks of reggae bass are a thuddy sound (short, dark notes) and offbeat rhythms (syncopation) — which is usually spelled and pronounced "riddims" by reggae musicians. Aston "Family Man" Barrett (who played with Bob Marley) and Robbie Shakespeare (who played with Peter Tosh) are two giants of reggae bass. Modern bassists, such as P-Nut of the group 311, also play this style to perfection.

With reggae, you often hear a lot of *space* (rests when the bassist is not playing). Figure 12-7 shows an example of a reggae groove with a lot of space. This groove fits over a minor chord, which is a common chord in reggae music. Start this groove with your index finger to avoid shifting, and keep the length of each note short.

If you want to play the groove in Figure 12-7 over a major or dominant chord, you need to change the ♭3 in the chord to a 3. Figure 12-8 shows a version of this groove adapted for a major or dominant chord. Start the groove with your index finger.

Figure 12-7: Reggae groove for a minor chord.

TRACK 63, 0:00

TRACK 63, 0:31

Figure 12-8: Reggae groove for a major or dominant chord.

You may sometimes hear a reggae bass groove that has a flurry of notes. Figure 12-9 shows you such a groove, which is structured in a tonality that fits over major, minor, and dominant chords. You can start this groove with either your index or middle finger.

TRACK 63, 1:02

Figure 12-9: Reggae groove for a major, minor, or dominant chord.

The *drop-one* technique, where the bassist doesn't play on the first beat of the measure, is a typical reggae device. Figure 12-10 shows you a drop-one reggae-style bass groove for a major or dominant chord. Start this groove with your middle finger.

Figure 12-10:
Drop-one reggae groove for a major or dominant chord.

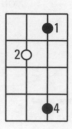

When listening to the groove shown in Figure 12-10, notice how the drummer hits on the *downbeat* (the first beat of the measure), and the bassist follows right after.

Figure 12-11 shows the minor version of this groove. You start this groove with your index finger.

Use the previous reggae grooves as a blueprint for creating your own grooves, and listen to a lot of reggae bands for inspiration. Better yet, take your bass with you on a vacation to Jamaica!

Figure 12-11:
Drop-one reggae groove for a minor chord.

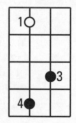

Soca: Blending American and Calypso Party Sounds

Soca is a combination of American Soul *(So-)* and Caribbean Calypso *(-Ca)*. This style is fast, driving, and a lot of fun. The feel often emphasizes the *weak beats* of a measure (the beats in the middle of the measure) rather than the downbeat.

The soca groove in Figure 12-12 uses notes that fit over a major or dominant chord. Notice the heavy use of *offbeats* (notes played between the beats) after the first measure. You may find this music difficult to play until you get used to hearing it. Start the groove with your middle finger.

TRACK 64, 0:00

Figure 12-12: Soca groove for a major or dominant chord.

The minor version of this groove is shown in Figure 12-13. The groove has the same structure, but this time you play the ♭3 instead of the 3 for the chord. Start this groove with your index finger.

TRACK 64, 0:19

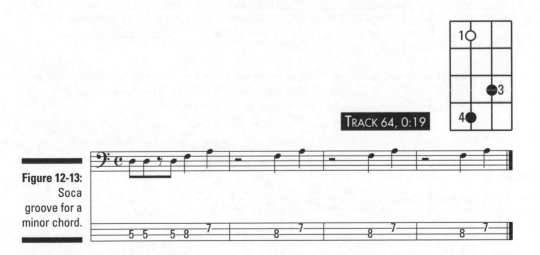

Figure 12-13: Soca groove for a minor chord.

In Figure 12-14, you have a soca groove that uses notes common to major, minor, and dominant chords. You can start this groove with either your index or middle finger.

Figure 12-14:
Soca
groove for a
major,
minor, or
dominant
chord.

TRACK 64, 0:30

Combining Reggae and Rock: The Distinct Sound of Ska

Ska is a motley combination of Caribbean and American styles. Think of it as mixing the offbeat rhythms of reggae with the driving force of rock. (See Chapter 9 for more on rock music.) Ska is very *up-tempo* (fast) and filled with high energy. Sting (most famous for his work with the Police) has been a prime force in ska music, playing some of the most memorable ska bass parts, which are often quite busy.

The ska groove in Figure 12-15 is an example of a busy bass line using notes that fit over major, minor, or dominant chords. No shifting is necessary. You can start this groove with your index or middle finger.

TRACK 65, 0:00

Figure 12-15:
Ska groove
for a major,
minor, or
dominant
chord.

Notice that the bass groove in Figure 12-15 does not start on the first beat of the measure, which is often the case in ska.

In Figure 12-16, you have a ska groove that uses the notes for a major or dominant chord; you get to play it on the downbeat of the measure. Start this groove with your middle finger.

TRACK 65, 0:16

Figure 12-16: Ska groove for a major or dominant chord.

The minor version of the groove in Figure 12-16 is shown in Figure 12-17. If you start this groove with your index finger, you don't have to shift your left hand.

TRACK 65, 0:37

Figure 12-17: Ska groove for a minor chord.

South African: Experimenting with Exotic Downbeat Grooves

South African music is an exotic blend of native rhythms with European and Caribbean influences. Bakithi Khumalo, whose bass playing is a wonderful example of South African style, recorded some excellent bass lines with Paul Simon.

The groove in Figure 12-18 shows an example of how a South African groove can say a lot with few notes. This groove fits perfectly over a major or dominant chord. Start with your middle finger to avoid shifting, and don't even try to sit still when playing.

TRACK 66, 0:00

Figure 12-18: South African groove for a major or dominant chord.

Listen to how the bass and drums interact to give the groove in Figure 12-18 its downbeat quality.

Figure 12-19 shows the minor version of this groove. The minor version simply replaces the 3 with a ♭3, which changes your fingering. You need to start this groove with your index finger.

TRACK 66, 0:21

Figure 12-19: South African groove for a minor chord.

In Figure 12-20, you have a South African groove that uses *neutral notes* — root, 5, and 2 an octave up — notes that fit over major, dominant, and minor chords. This groove does require a small shift with your left hand, but this shift is easy if you start with your index finger.

TRACK 66, 0:33

Figure 12-20:
South
African
groove
for a major,
dominant, or
minor chord.

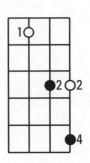

All the grooves in this chapter provide you with a whole new way to use rhythm. So the next time you feel like visiting an exotic location, grab your bass instead of your sunscreen and visit these exotic places musically.

Chapter 13

Playing in Odd Meters: Not Strange, Just Not the Norm

Generally, when you say that something is odd, you're implying that it's out of the ordinary or unusual. In music, playing in an *odd meter* means playing a tune that doesn't have the usual four beats per measure. The word *odd* also refers to uneven numbers. Each measure in an odd meter tends to have an odd number of beats. For example, a tune may have three, five, seven, or more beats per measure. So is playing in odd meter a daunting task? Not at all. You don't even have to count past three. In this chapter, I show you how to handle odd meters with ease and grace.

An Odd-Meter Oldie but Goodie: The Waltz

The waltz is the most common of all odd-meter styles. In fact, the waltz is so common, that it's not thought of as being in odd meter at all. A waltz has three quarter notes per measure (thus the 3/4 symbol in Figures 13-1 and 13-2 at the beginning of the staff), and your count is **1**-2-3, **1**-2-3, and so on. (*Note:* You accent the bold numbers.) You frequently encounter the waltz in musicals and jazz, so it's a good idea to be ready with grooves for the waltz.

The waltz is a technical breeze for the bass player; you usually play only one or two notes per measure, but remember to keep counting. Figure 13-1 shows a typical waltz accompaniment for the bass. Simply play the root or 5 on the first beat of the measure. This accompaniment fits over major, minor, and dominant chords.

TRACK 67, 0:00

Figure 13-1:
Waltz accompaniment for major, minor, and dominant chords.

If you want to spice up your waltz a little, add a note (such as the 5) on beat three — the last beat of each measure. Three-quarter time is so common and so easily recognizable that, by the time you hit the fifth measure or so of the waltz, you don't even have to think about the rhythm. Three-quarter time feels natural.

Figure 13-2 shows another waltz accompaniment that fits over major, minor, and dominant chords. It's a bit fancier than the example in Figure 13-1 because of the added note, but it's still simple.

TRACK 67, 0:16

Figure 13-2:
Waltz accompaniment using two notes for major, minor, and dominant chords.

The sound of the waltz evokes images of imperial ballrooms in the heart of Europe, filled with ladies dressed in floor-length ball gowns and gentlemen in tuxedos who are turning in circles to the music. Yeah, these guys were party animals, too . . . well . . . sort of.

Beyond the Waltz: Navigating Compound Beats in Odd Meter

The structure of any measure in an odd meter can be divided into groups of two beats and three beats. That's right, it's just a matter of twos and threes. For example, if you have to count to seven in a measure, break it up into groups of two beats and three beats. Instead of counting "one, two, three, four, five, six, seven," count in either of the following ways:

- ✔ "One, two, three, one, two, one, two"
- ✔ "One, two, one, two, one, two, three"

The number of beats is the same, but dividing the count into sets of two and three makes the phrasing manageable.

When choosing the notes you play for tunes in odd meters, select notes that fall naturally into groups of two and three, and connect the groups rhythmically or harmonically. (I explain how to do this in the following sections that discuss playing in odd meters of 5/4 and 7/4, the two most common odd meters besides the waltz.) Remember that this concept of grouping the notes works for any type of odd meter.

5/4 meter: Not an impossible mission

When you play a tune in 5/4 meter, you have five beats (five quarter notes) per measure instead of the usual four. If you've ever watched the TV show *Mission Impossible* and heard its distinctive musical theme, you've heard a tune in 5/4. You can think of 5/4 as either a group of two beats followed by a group of three beats, or as a group of three beats followed by a group of two beats. Take a look at Figure 13-3 to see how the beats are grouped.

You can translate these groupings into music by playing your notes as a group of two beats followed by a group of three beats, or vice versa. You can count the groove in Figure 13-4 as **1**-2-**3**-1-2 or as **1**-2-**1**-2-3 (accenting the bold numbers). The notes in the groove in Figure 13-4 fit over major, minor, and dominant chords.

The groove in Figure 13-5 shows a clear three-two grouping in 5/4 meter, but some of the quarter notes are divided into eighth notes, which doesn't change the meter at all. When you look at this figure, notice that

✔ The first group of notes (the group of three) consists of six eighth notes, which equal three quarter notes.

✔ The second group (the group of two) consists of two quarter notes.

✔ The combination equals five beats in all.

The notes fit over major, minor, and dominant chords.

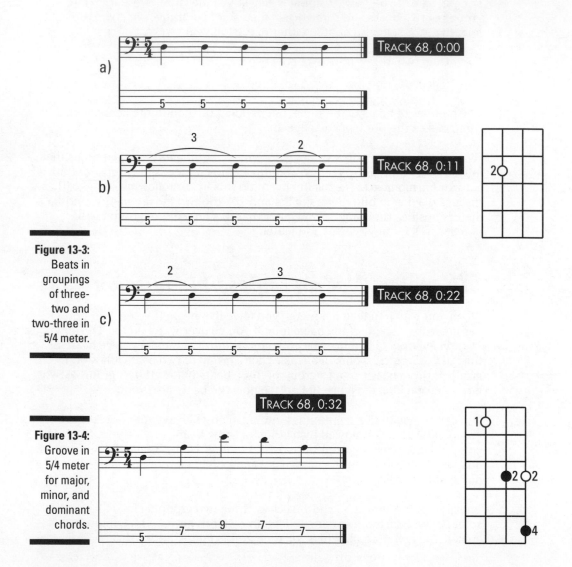

Figure 13-3: Beats in groupings of three-two and two-three in 5/4 meter.

Figure 13-4: Groove in 5/4 meter for major, minor, and dominant chords.

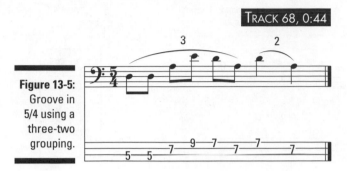

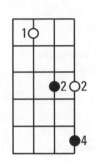

Figure 13-5:
Groove in
5/4 using a
three-two
grouping.

Notice the distinctive lopsided feel of the groove shown in Figure 13-5: It has a busy first part for three beats, followed by a less busy part for two beats.

Figure 13-6, on the other hand, shows you a clear two-three grouping in 5/4 meter. When you look at this figure, notice that

✔ The first group of notes (the group of two) consists of two quarter notes

✔ The second group of notes (the group of three) consists of six eighth notes

The notes fit over major, minor, and dominant chords.

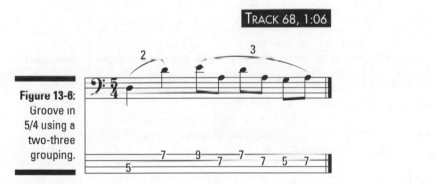

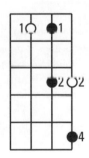

Figure 13-6:
Groove in
5/4 using a
two-three
grouping.

The feel of the groove in Figure 13-6 sounds different from the one in Figure 13-5, yet both are examples of 5/4 meter.

If you want to get really fancy with your 5/4 meter, you can subdivide your beats into sixteenth notes, which requires some funky finger work (see Chapter 3 for more information). Figure 13-7 shows a groove in a two-three grouping using sixteenth notes. The notes in this groove fit over major, minor, and dominant chords, so you don't have to worry about the tonality.

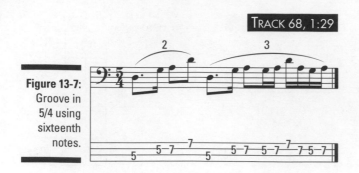

Figure 13-7: Groove in 5/4 using sixteenth notes.

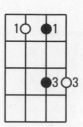

With the examples in this section, you can see that playing a solid groove in a 5/4 meter isn't such an impossible mission (should you choose to accept it).

7/4 meter: Adding two more beats

The 7/4 meter works the same way as the 5/4 meter, but it has two more beats per measure. Form groups of two and three notes, and you're all set to embark on the creation of a perfectly fine bass groove in 7/4. The song "Money," by the group Pink Floyd, is a very successful tune in a 7/4 meter.

The possible groupings of beats for a measure in 7/4 are: three beats, plus two beats, plus two beats — in any order. Take a look at Figure 13-8 to see the different groupings of beats in 7/4 meter.

You can translate these groupings into music by combining your notes into two groups of two beats and one group of three beats. Group the notes any way you like. You can count the groove shown in Figure 13-9 as **1**-2-3-**1**-2-**1**-2, **1**-2-**1**-2-3-**1**-2, or **1**-2-**1**-2-**1**-2-3. The notes in this groove fit over major, minor, and dominant chords.

The groove in Figure 13-10 is a clear three-two-two grouping in 7/4 meter. When you look at this figure, notice that

- ✔ The first group (the group of three beats) consists of a quarter note (the first beat) followed by two eighth notes (the second beat) and another quarter note (the third beat).

- ✔ The second group (a group of two beats) consists of four eighth notes.

- ✔ The third group (the other group of two beats) consists of four eighth notes, as well.

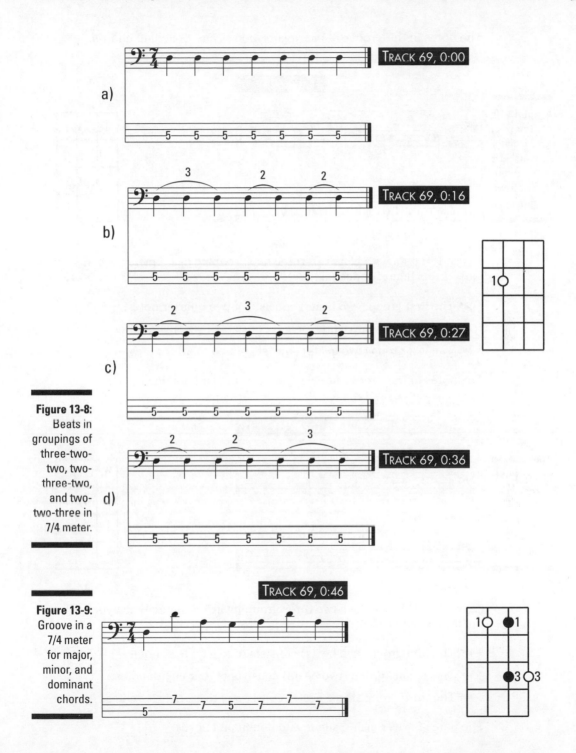

Figure 13-8:
Beats in groupings of three-two-two, two-three-two, and two-two-three in 7/4 meter.

Figure 13-9:
Groove in a 7/4 meter for major, minor, and dominant chords.

The notes in this groove fit over major, minor, and dominant chords.

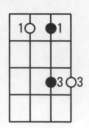

Figure 13-10: Groove in a 7/4 meter using a three-two-two grouping.

Figure 13-11 shows a clear two-three-two grouping in 7/4 meter. When you look at this figure, notice that

- ✔ The first group (two beats) consists of two quarter notes.
- ✔ The second group (three beats) consists of six eighth notes.
- ✔ The last group (two beats) consists of two quarter notes.

The notes in this groove fit over major, minor, and dominant chords.

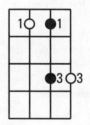

Figure 13-11: Groove in a 7/4 meter using a two-three-two grouping.

Figure 13-12 shows a two-two-three grouping in 7/4 meter. When you look at the figure, notice that

- ✔ The first group (two beats) consists of two quarter notes.
- ✔ The second group (two beats) consists of four eighth notes.
- ✔ The third group (three beats) consists of three quarter notes.

The notes fit over major, minor, and dominant chords.

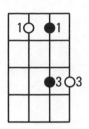

Figure 13-12:
Groove in
7/4 meter
using a two-
two-three
grouping.

And if you're brave, here's a 7/4 meter groove subdivided into sixteenth notes for some mind-boggling and finger-boggling playing. Figure 13-13 shows a groove in a two-three-two grouping using sixteenth notes. The notes in this groove fit over major, minor, and dominant chords.

Figure 13-13:
Groove in
7/4 using
sixteenth
notes.

The selection of odd-meter grooves in this chapter gives you plenty to choose from when you want to sound even-tempered playing odd-metered grooves.

Part V

Taking Care of the One You Love: TLC for Your Bass Guitar

The 5th Wave   By Rich Tennant

"Gee thanks, but I don't think a gingham neck cozy and peg board bonnet really goes with the rest of my bass guitar."

In this part . . .

Your bass may seem rugged and nearly indestructible, but it does have a soft side that cries out for your attention. This part gives you all the information you need to ensure that your bass will have a long and happy life. Chapter 14 shows how to change your strings, and Chapter 15 explains how to perform basic maintenance and set-ups to keep both you and your bass happy.

Chapter 14

Changing the Strings on Your Bass Guitar

In This Chapter

▶ Removing old or damaged strings

▶ Attaching new strings

▶ Keeping your new strings in good condition

"*W*hat kind of strings do you use?"

"I dunno. They came with the bass."

Some bassists think that you don't need to change strings on a bass until they unravel — and then only if you absolutely need that particular string. If this were true, you'd be waiting a long time to change your strings, and eventually the only sound you'd get out of your poor old strings would be a dull thud.

The fact is, bass strings need to be changed regularly. The dirt from your fingers and dust particles from the air wear them out. In addition, they get metal fatigue from being under constant tension. (Hey, come on! Don't *you* get fatigued when you're under constant tension?) Old strings lose their *brightness* (clarity of sound) and *sustain* (the length of time that a note rings out), get sticky, and become hard to tune.

In this chapter, I lead you step by step through the painless process of changing the strings on your bass.

Knowing When It's Time to Say Goodbye

How do you know when it's time to replace your strings? Here are some clues that signal a change is necessary:

- ✔ **The strings show wear and tear.** You can see dark spots along the strings, probably as a result of dirt stuck in the windings of the steel. You may also see corrosion (or rust spots) on the strings.

- ✔ **The strings sound dull and lifeless.** Your notes don't *sustain* (ring out for an extended length of time), and hearing an exact pitch is difficult. Playing a harmonic for tuning is also a challenge. (See Chapter 2 for more on tuning with harmonics.)

- ✔ **The strings feel sticky and stiff.** Unless you eat a cinnamon roll before playing your bass, this is a sure sign of trouble. (Like with swimming, you should always wait at least a half-hour to play bass after eating a cinnamon roll.)

- ✔ **Jimmy Carter was president when you last changed your strings, or you just can't remember *when* you changed them last.**

Off with the Old: Removing Bass Strings

Before you can put new strings on your bass, you need to remove the old ones.

Always replace all your strings at the same time. The strings wear at the same rate. So when you replace them all simultaneously, you ensure that they all sound the same; in other words, you ensure that one doesn't sound clearer than the others.

The quickest way to remove your old bass strings is to simply take wire cutters (sturdy ones; bass strings are pretty thick) and cut the string at the thin section between the *tuning post* (the round metal post connected to a tuning head that has one end of the string wound around it) and the *nut* (the little bar near the tuning posts that has a groove for each string; see Chapter 1).

If you're afraid that the string is going to whip across your face and leave a scar (imagine trying to explain that one), you can turn the tuning head to loosen the tension of the string before you cut it. Just remember which string is connected to which tuning post. After cutting the string, simply pull the coiled part of it off the tuning post, and then pull the other part through the bridge. Take a look at Figure 14-1 to see what this process looks like.

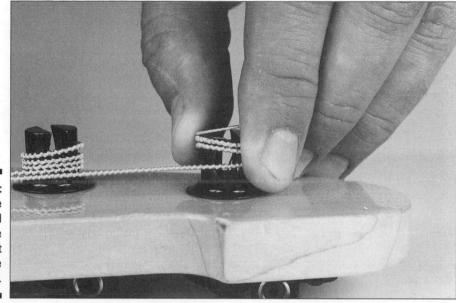

Figure 14-1:
Cut the
string and
pull the
coiled part
from the
tuning post.

If you want to save your strings as a spare set (in case one of the new strings breaks), don't cut the string. Just release the tension until you can grab the coiled end and pull it off the tuning post. Straighten the end of the string as best you can, and then pull the entire length through the bridge (see Figure 14-2).

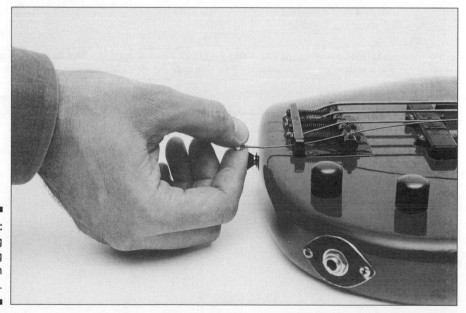

Figure 14-2:
Pulling
the string
through
the bridge.

One common myth says that you should change only one string at a time in order to maintain tension in the neck. I disagree. Take 'em off. . . . Take 'em all off. Your bass can handle it, and it gives you access to your fingerboard and pickups for some basic cleaning. (See Chapter 15 for info on how to clean your bass.)

On with the New: Restringing Your Bass

After you clip the old strings and clean any grime off the fingerboard, you renew the voice of your bass by adding brand-new strings. You need to be in a clean and comfortable environment for this, because there's not much point in putting on new strings if you're going to get sawdust all over them as soon as you're done. Be sure to lay your bass on a clean towel before you restring it.

Make sure that your wire cutters are nearby when you restring your bass. You'll need to cut the new strings down to size.

You attach strings to your bass at two points:

- ✔ At the bridge
- ✔ At the tuning posts

New strings are usually coiled in envelopes. The envelopes are numbered according to string size (the thickest string has the highest number). With most basses, the new string has to be pulled through a hole in the bridge, so that's the place to start. Here's a step-by-step guide to changing the strings of your bass guitar:

1. **Put a towel on the floor in front of you and lay the bass on the towel, with the neck pointing to the left (to the right if you're left-handed).**

2. **Remove the old strings.**

    (See the previous section for instructions on how to remove the old strings.)

3. **Take the thickest string out of its envelope (make sure that you leave the string coiled) and take a look at it.**

    Notice that it has a ring (called a *ball*) at one end; the other end is pointed, with its tip wrapped in silk. Figure 14-3 shows you what a coiled string looks like.

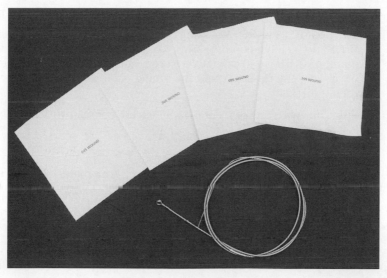

Figure 14-3:
Coiled
string with
envelope.

4. **Straighten the string and push the pointed end (the one without the brass ring) through the hole that's nearest you on the bridge.**

    Each string goes into a separate hole. Pull the string through the hole toward the nut. Make sure that the ball at the end of the string comes to rest against the bridge. Figure 14-4 shows how to perform this step.

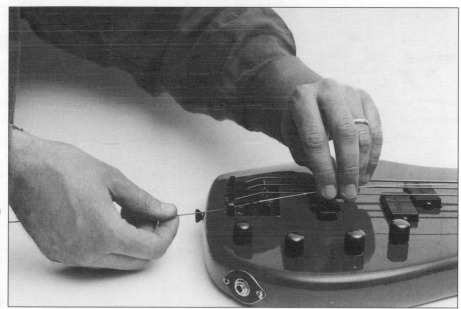

Figure 14-4:
Pulling
the string
through
the bridge.

5. **Pull the string until it's resting against its designated tuning post.**

(The post has a groove crossing the top and a hole in its center.) Make sure that you have enough string to extend 4 to 5 inches beyond the tuning post. This extra length ensures that your string is long enough to wind several times around the tuning post (so the string doesn't slip when tightened).

6. **With your wire cutters, cut off any excess string 4 to 5 inches past the post (see Figure 14-5).**

Cut only from the part of the string that's wrapped with silk.

WARNING!

Never cut the thick part of the string itself (the metal). If you cut this part of the string, it will simply unravel.

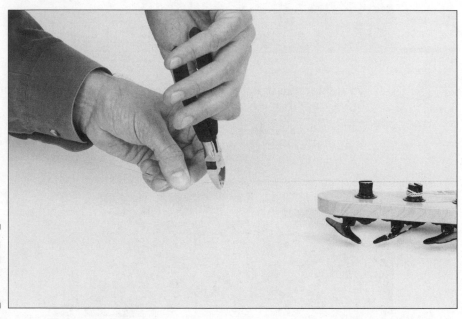

Figure 14-5:
Cutting
the string
to size.

7. **Take the tip of the string (now freshly cut) and stick it straight down into the hole in the center of the tuning post. Then bend the string to the side so that it rests in the groove at the top of the tuning post, and hold it there with one hand.**

Figure 14-6 shows you how to perform this step.

8. **Turn the tuning head with your left hand to increase the tension of the string.**

Make sure that the string winds *down* the post (you can guide it with the fingers of your right hand). This downward winding increases the slight bend (breaking angle) of the string against the nut and ensures that the string sits firmly in its groove on the nut, giving the notes better sustain.

At the same time, make sure that the other end of the string runs over the proper *saddle* (a small moveable part that has a groove for the string to fit into) at the bridge. Figure 14-7 shows a properly wound string, and Figure 14-8 shows how the string lies over the saddle.

Figure 14-6: Inserting the string into the tuning post.

 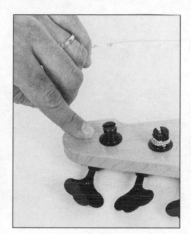

Figure 14-7: Windings of a string at the tuning post.

Figure 14-8:
The string at
the saddle.

9. **Repeat the entire process for all the other strings, moving from thick to thin.** Some basses have *string retainers* that hold the two thinnest strings close to the *headstock* (the top part of the neck). Pass the two thinnest strings under the string retainers before tightening them. Now tune them up. You need to go through the tuning process (described in Chapter 2) several times, because the strings stretch out and the neck bends forward under the increased tension. When your strings are in tune, you're ready to play.

Turn the tuning heads to wind the strings up. Don't wrap the strings around the tuning posts by hand; if you do, the strings will twist and lose their ability to sustain notes.

You can get many happy playing weeks (even months) out of your new strings. Just keep them reasonably clean so that you don't have to change them too often. New bass strings come at a price ($15 to $40 for a four-string set).

Ensuring a Long Life for Your Strings

After you get those new strings onto your bass, you want to do all you can to keep them in good, working condition, right? Well, increasing the life of your strings is easier than you think. All you have to do is follow two basic rules:

- ✓ Wash your hands before you touch your strings.
- ✓ Don't let any other people touch your strings unless they wash their hands first.

The natural oils and sweat in *clean* hands are hard enough on your bass strings. If you indulge in a greasy roast chicken or change the oil in your car before your next rehearsal, all that grease, grime, and dirt will end up on your strings. This kind of debris shortens string life drastically. So wash those paws before you play.

Chapter 15

Keeping Your Bass in Shape: Maintenance and Light Repair

*B*ass guitars are like their owners — tough, hard, and rugged — but only on the surface. Deep down, basses (like their owners) yearn for some tender, loving care and affection, and, of course, for some appreciation.

Despite the most careful handling and the best of care, however, your instrument is bound to collect battle scars. If you play your bass a lot, it needs to be cleaned regularly, and certain parts will need replacing from time to time — or at least tightening and adjusting. This chapter tells you what maintenance you can easily do yourself and what maintenance is best left to your friendly, neighborhood instrument repairperson.

Cleaning Your Bass Part by Part

Cleaning your bass is the most basic of maintenance jobs, and the first step is to wash your hands. No, really, I'm not kidding! The finish on the wood and hardware shows every fingerprint. So the least you should do is keep those fingerprints clean; don't enhance them with grime. The next few sections walk you through cleaning the various parts of your bass, one by one.

The body and neck

Cleaning the body of your bass is just like cleaning your favorite antique furniture: You need to do it very carefully. You can polish the finish with a cloth (such as an old sweat shirt), but use *guitar polish* (available in a spray bottle at any music store) instead of furniture polish. Guitar polish gets dust and dirt off your instrument and leaves your bass looking well cared for.

Apply a squirt or two (no, I don't mean your little brother) of the polish to the cloth and work it into the fabric. Then rub your bass down — work on the body (front and back) and the back of the neck. Your bass will love it. Keep the polish away from the strings and the fingerboard, though; I deal with them a little later on in this section.

The hardware

The *hardware* consists of all the brass and metal parts attached to the wood, with the exception of the frets and pickups. The tuning heads, bridge, and strap pins are all considered hardware. Rubbing the hardware down with a dust cloth helps keep it shiny. If too much dirt builds up on the hardware, you can use a mild brass polish from the supermarket to clean the metal. Make sure that the polish isn't abrasive and that it doesn't get onto the wood, because it will mar the wood.

The pickups

When it comes to cleaning your bass, the pickups are in a category all by themselves. A lot of dust accumulates where the wood meets the metal of the pickups (see Chapter 1 for a picture of the pickups on a bass guitar).

Whatever you do, don't use any liquids. Pickups are magnetic, and they can't deal with liquid. The liquid can cause them to short out, making it necessary to replace them.

Of course, getting new pickups every four weeks is one way to keep them clean. Otherwise, use cotton swabs to clean the area where your pickups meet the wood.

The fingerboard

The fingerboard consists of two major parts:

- The long wooden strip on the front of the neck
- The metal frets embedded in the long wooden strip

These two parts are made of very different materials, and each needs to be cleaned in its own special way. You can clean them only after removing your old strings and before restringing. (Check out Chapter 14 to find out how to restring your bass.)

The wood

Because the wood on your fingerboard is normally exposed, it's prone to drying out. To restore the wood to its original luster, use a dry cloth to get rid of the dirt, and then place a few drops (no more than five or so) of fingerboard oil (which you can get from your local music store) on a clean cotton cloth and work it into the wood. Let the oil dry thoroughly before rubbing down the fingerboard again to remove any excess oil. Apply oil to the wood every other time you change the strings. The wood absorbs fingerboard oil easily.

The frets

You can use a jewelry polishing cloth that has polish already soaked into it (available in any supermarket) to polish the frets. The cloth is inexpensive, and your frets will sparkle with joy (maybe not as bright as diamonds, but you never know).

When polishing the frets, don't use an abrasive jewelry polish that you have to pour out of a bottle. That stuff is rough on the wood of the fingerboard.

The strings

Yes, the strings need to be cleaned, as well. After all, they take the most abuse. You can simply wipe the strings with a dry cotton cloth after you're done playing. But using a couple drops of rubbing alcohol (available in any pharmacy) on a cotton cloth is even better.

Let the alcohol sink into the cloth for a few seconds. Then put a moist section of the cloth between your index finger and thumb and pinch one string at a time, rubbing the cloth up and down along the string's length.

Don't get any of the alcohol on the wood; it'll dry it out.

Check out Figure 15-1 for the proper method for cleaning bass strings.

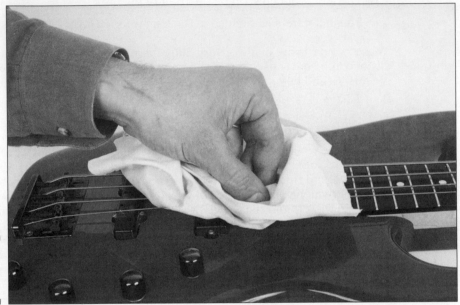

Figure 15-1:
Cleaning
the strings.

Making Minor Repairs to Your Bass

You can do minor repairs on your bass yourself in order to keep it in top-notch playing condition — tweaking a few screws, touching up a bit of finish, soldering a couple of electronic connectionszzzzzzzzzap! . . . well, maybe not the electronics.

The taming of the screw(s)

The parts of the bass guitar are held together in two ways: with glue and with screws. A *luthier* (a person who builds stringed instruments) uses specific glues for each type of wood on the bass. If anything that's supposed to be glued comes apart, take your instrument to a qualified repairperson.

If, on the other hand, a piece of hardware comes loose or starts rattling, you can simply screw it back where it belongs. Just remember one thing: Your bass has an array of different-sized screws. Most of the screws are of the

Phillips variety. Buy a set of screwdrivers at the hardware store and make sure that you have a perfect fit for each screw on your bass. Why do I say that? The reason is simple: If you force a screwdriver that doesn't fit into a screw, you'll end up stripping the head of the screw. If you don't feel comfortable putting the screws to your bass, don't mess around. Take your precious instrument to a qualified repairperson.

Taking care of the finish

The *finish* is the thin layer of lacquer that seals the wood of your bass.The finish is usually glossy; it looks beautiful when the instrument is new. The finish also serves a function: It protects the wood from severe changes in humidity. Low humidity makes the wood brittle and prone to cracking; high humidity causes the wood to swell and warp.

Collisions between your bass and other objects (such as the drummer's cymbals) may leave dings or cracks in the finish. If you want that perfect look back, you have to take your bass to a pro for refinishing, which can be costly. If you're not overly concerned with the look, or you think that battle scars are cool, seal the cracks with colorless nail polish. You can also try to match your bass's color with a small bottle of model paint from a toy store.

Be vigilant in protecting the back of your bass neck. If you scratch it, you'll be able to feel the scratch when you're playing. If the scratch is shallow, try to get it out by rubbing the entire neck up and down with 0000-grade (superfine) steel wool. Sand the entire length of the neck. The steel wool will give the back of the neck a very nice satin feel. If you still feel the scratch, have a repairperson refinish the neck of your bass.

Don't get too used to just sanding the scratches off the neck of your bass. Each time you sand the neck, even with the finest-grade steel wool, you take a layer of finish off. Eventually, none of the finish will be left, and you'll need to get the neck refinished. Of course, you'll be better off if you don't get your bass neck scratched in the first place.

Leaving the electronics to the experts

If you hear crackling when you turn the knobs, it may be a minor problem. Just turn the knobs vigorously back and forth to eliminate the crackling. If that doesn't do the trick — you guessed it — take it to a pro.

With the advent of high-tech basses that feature complex pre-amps and pick-ups, I simply don't touch the electronics. Take your bass to a pro to have any electronic problem fixed, unless you have a graduate degree in electrical engineering.

Adjusting the Bass Guitar

Your bass is a sturdy instrument, but every now and then it needs some slight adjusting. As the weather changes from season to season (provided you live in a location that has seasons), the wood in your bass also changes. The neck tends to bend or straighten slightly, causing the strings to either pull away from the frets or rest against them; this makes playing almost impossible.

You can counter the forces of nature by

- Tweaking the *truss rod* (a metal rod that runs inside the length of the bass neck)
- Adjusting the *saddles* (the little, moving metal parts of the bridge that have grooves for the strings to lie across)

Providing relief to the truss rod

The truss rod controls the curvature of your bass neck. Because the strings need space to vibrate freely over the entire length of the neck, your bass neck has to have a slight *relief* (curve) to give the strings room. Now notice that I said *slight* relief. If the relief is too great, the *action* (the space between the strings and frets) will be too large, and you'll need arms like Popeye's to press the strings down.

How much action is enough to keep the strings vibrating while still making them easy to press down? With your left hand, press the E string (the thickest string) down at the first fret. At the same time, press the E string down at the last fret with your right hand. The space between the E string and the neck (between the 7th and 12th frets) should be about the thickness of a credit card (finally, a good use for credit cards). You can have a little more space if you prefer, or slightly less space if you play very lightly.

To adjust the action, you need to turn a screw in the truss rod to change the curvature of the neck. The screw is located either on the headstock or at the other end of the neck.

On some basses, you have to remove the neck from the body in order to reach the screw of the truss rod. Don't attempt to loosen the screws at the back of the bass that hold the neck in place without first loosening the tension of the strings. Otherwise, the neck will snap off, stripping away the wood that holds the screws.

In most cases, you can adjust the truss rod with the small Allen wrench that comes with your bass. If you lose this wrench, you can get another one from your local music store or the bass manufacturer. On other basses, the screw of the truss rod requires a Phillips screwdriver, which doesn't come with the bass. (You can buy it at the hardware store.) If you have too much space between the E string and the neck, insert the Allen wrench or Phillips screwdriver into the screw and then tighten the truss rod by turning the wrench or screwdriver clockwise. If your strings buzz when you play on the first four frets (near the headstock), you need to loosen the truss rod by turning the wrench or screwdriver counterclockwise. Take a look at Figure 15-2 to see how to adjust a truss rod.

Figure 15-2:
Adjusting the truss rod.

Use only the specific wrench or screwdriver that fits into your truss rod. If you don't have the proper tool, get one from your local music store or the manufacturer of the bass. Don't try to force the truss rod with anything that doesn't quite fit. If you strip the truss rod, it'll cost you. Turn the truss rod only between one-quarter and one-half of a turn per day. You need to allow the wood to settle before you do any more adjustments.

Raising and lowering the bridge

You can also adjust the action of your bass by adjusting the saddles on the bridge. The saddles can be lowered or raised by turning the screws at the top with an Allen wrench. When you adjust the saddles, you lower and raise the string height (the action). Figure 15-3 shows how to adjust the saddles.

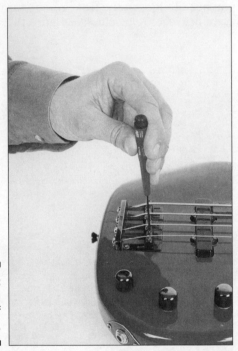

Figure 15-3:
Adjusting the height of the saddles.

Getting your bass set up by a repairperson initially is a good idea. After you get your bass back from the repairperson, take note of how high he or she set the saddles and how the strings feel. From then on, you can fine-tune your bass by comparing it to the original setup.

You can also use the saddles to adjust the intonation of your bass. If you hear your bass going out of tune when you play on the very high or very low frets, you need to adjust the intonation. To do this, find a screwdriver that fits into the screws at the back of the bridge. Turning these screws moves the saddles back and forth. You also need a tuner. Read the following steps and check out Figure 15-4 to find out how to adjust the saddles to correct the intonation:

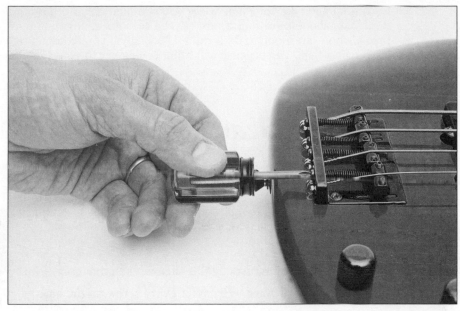

Figure 15-4:
Adjusting
the
intonation.

1. **Play the harmonic of one of the strings at the 12th fret, and tune the string to the tuner.**

   When the harmonic of the string is in perfect tune, play the same string by fretting it at the 12th fret and compare the pitch of the note with the pitch of the harmonic. (See Chapter 2 for how to play a harmonic.)

2. **If the fretted note is sharp compared to the harmonic, lengthen the string by tightening the screw.**

   This moves the saddle away from the neck. Now tune the string again using the harmonic. Compare the pitch of the harmonic with the fretted note, and keep adjusting the saddle until both the harmonic and the fretted note are in tune.

3. **If the fretted note is flat, shorten the string by loosening the screw to move the saddle toward the neck.**

   Tune the string using the harmonic, and keep adjusting the saddle until both the harmonic and fretted note are in tune.

4. **Repeat this process with all the strings.**

Be patient and take your time when you're adjusting your bass. It needs to be done only about four times a year (as the seasons change), but you have to take a whole afternoon to do it right, especially if you're adjusting your bass for the first time. The process will bring you closer to your instrument — you know, bass bonding.

Assembling a Cleaning and Repair Tool Bag

Before you attempt any of the adjustments or cleaning procedures I cover in this chapter, you need to make sure that you have all the required tools. Start assembling a tool set just for your bass. Here's a list of what needs to be in a bass tool bag (see Figure 15-5).

- Truss-rod wrench (usually the Allen wrench that comes with your bass)
- Screwdriver or Allen wrench for every screw on the bass

  A multi-screwdriver tool is okay, but you can get more leverage with separate screwdrivers. Make sure that you have a screwdriver or Allen wrench that fits the screws for the saddle.

- Rubbing alcohol (make sure it's in a bottle that won't leak)
- Cotton rags for cleaning (make sure to replace them once in a while)
- Super-fine steel wool
- Colorless nail polish (or a color that matches your bass)
- Electronic tuner (this needs to be part of your tool set if you adjust the intonation yourself)
- Wire cutters for changing your strings
- Jewelry polish cloth for polishing the frets

Be sure to keep your bass tools separate from your household tools so that they won't get lost or damaged. Besides, basses can get very jealous if they find out that *their* truss-rod wrench was used to tighten the bathroom faucet.

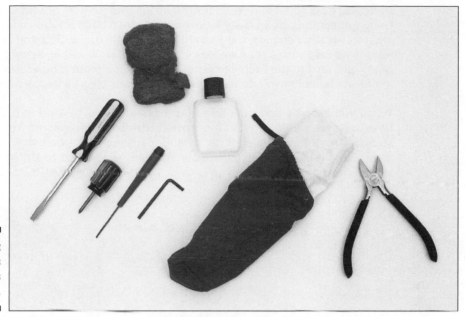

Figure 15-5:
Contents
of a bass
tool bag.

Storing Your Bass

Keeping your bass guitar happy is really quite simple. If you're comfortable, your bass will be comfortable. You want to keep it out of direct sunlight, and you want to keep it out of the snow — at least for any extended period of time. The safest place to keep your bass is in its case, but then it can be kind of a hassle to get to when inspiration strikes. If you want to keep your bass handy, place it on a sturdy bass guitar stand. Just make sure that you set it up in a safe corner of the room that doesn't get a lot of traffic. (In other words, don't place it in the path of the family dog, which just happens to be a clumsy Saint Bernard.)

If you have a *gig bag* (a soft, padded carrying pack), you can keep your bass in it when you're not playing. The gig bag gives your bass some protection (actually a good gig bag can give the bass a *lot* of protection) and allows you to get to it relatively easily.

Nearly all bass guitars are solid-body instruments (they're not hollow), making them quite sturdy. Solid-body bass guitars have a large tolerance for humidity and temperature change, but you still need to make sure that you keep your bass in an area with a reasonable temperature. For example, keeping your bass right next to the fireplace is not a good idea. Room temperature with moderate humidity will do the trick, making your bass as happy as a clam.

When you go away and can't take your bass with you, be kind to it. Put your bass in its case and keep it in a climate-controlled environment. You can stand it upright in a closet or lay it flat under your bed. Don't store your bass in a damp basement or an uninsulated garage. You want it to still love you when you come back, don't you?

Part VI
A Buyer's Guide: The Where and How of Buying a Bass

The 5th Wave   By Rich Tennant

"There's just something wrong about someone using a gold card to buy a bass guitar for a blues band."

In this part . . .

When you're ready to lay your hard-earned cash on the line, don't leave home without this part. Chapter 16 shows you how to choose the right bass, and Chapter 17 helps you pick out whatever else you may need to fulfill all your bass-ic needs.

Chapter 16

Love of a Lifetime or One-Night Stand?: Buying the Right Bass

....

....

*B*uying a bass guitar is an exciting experience, but it can also be a bit scary. You're about to commit a lot of hard-earned cash to the purchase of your bass. You're also about to commit yourself to becoming a bassist. Instead of borrowing a friend's instrument, you're now getting your very own personal bass guitar. Buying the right bass is a personal choice that only you can make; it's also a choice that you can only make every once in a while (unless you're independently wealthy), so choose wisely. This chapter helps you make the tough decisions when buying a new bass guitar. It also prepares you to step bravely into that music store as a bass player who knows exactly what to look for.

Assessing Your Needs Before You Buy

The single most important question to ask yourself before buying a bass is: "What do I want in a bass?"

Here's a really good piece of advice: Don't settle. If you find a bass that sounds great but doesn't feel good in your hands, don't buy it. If you find a bass that feels wonderful but sounds like a buzz saw, don't buy it. You *can* have the best of both worlds; you just have to look hard for it.

Also, keep in mind that bass guitars are flexible instruments. In other words, you can play your bass during the afternoon jazz cocktail hour at the local café before rushing off with it to play the rock 'n' roll set at the local pub in the evening. Then you can get up the next morning and use the same bass to record a country song at the studio. So set your buying priorities without worrying about what style of music you want to play.

The following are some other important points to consider when choosing your new instrument:

✔ **Feel.** The bass needs to feel good to you. Actually, it needs to feel good to your hands. You don't have to be an expert to determine whether a bass is right for you. Just pick it up and play a few notes. If the bass responds to your touch and doesn't feel awkward or stiff, it's a good candidate. Play lots of different basses when you shop for one so that you have some way of comparing the different models. Play a high-end (expensive) model for comparison, as well. (Those $2,500 basses usually feel *very* good.) And then see whether you can find a less expensive model that feels similar (or just buy the $2,500 one).

✔ **Sound.** The bass needs to sound good, not just to you but to the people you play with. (Of course, you can always find other people to play with.) It needs to have a clear, clean *bottom end* (low frequencies — what did you think that term meant?). If you want to alter the tone of the bass and dirty it up — fine. But make sure that you start out with a clean tone.

✔ **Looks**. Looks are a distant third behind feel and sound. I had a bass that played like a dream and sounded like Thor (the god of thunder) himself came down from the heavens . . . and it had the most obnoxious purple finish on the body, with grass-green silk windings on the strings to top it off. I was happy to buy it. (I used it mostly for recording, where nobody would see me.) Don't sacrifice tone or playability for looks. You can always have the bass refinished. However, if you can, pick a bass you also enjoy looking at (or rather, you enjoy being seen with).

Thinking long-term: The love of a lifetime

Some fledgling bassists feel that they have to *earn* that special bass; before buying the bass, they need to feel that they deserve it. Don't buy into that line of thinking. You only need to know if your level of commitment is strong enough, and nobody knows that better than you. If you're convinced that you're going to be playing bass for the rest of your life, or at least for the next few years or so, get the best bass you can afford (as long as it fulfills the criteria in the previous section). A great bass encourages you to play more, which makes you a better player.

In the long run, buying a good instrument right from the start is more cost-effective than constantly trading in mediocre instruments without ever buying the one you really want. Every time you trade in a used bass, you lose money. Make your bass yours for better or for worse, in sickness and in health.

Thinking short-term: Help me make it through the night

If you're not sure that you want to be a bassist, or you're just temporarily filling the bass chair for a band, go for a bass that feels good and has a good tone (and, yes, there is a difference between good and great), but don't break your bank account.

You can choose from a wide variety of bass guitars in the economy price range, and some of them are quite good. If you find that bass playing is growing on you, you can always get a better one later and keep the first one as a backup.

How many strings are too many?

Today's bassists face a variety of choices when choosing a bass. Not only do you have a huge selection of brand names to consider, you also have to decide whether to buy a traditional four-string bass or go for the extended range of a five-string bass, six-string bass, or beyond.

In the mid-1970s, Anthony Jackson — a top New York City session player best known for his work with Steely Dan, Chaka Khan, and Paul Simon — conceived of, and had luthier Carl Thompson build, a six-string contrabass guitar, with an extra high string and an extra low string. Soon after, other players saw his design and adapted the idea of adding a lower fifth string to compete with the extra low sounds of the keyboard bass on records. (After all, nobody plays better bass than a bassist.) The resulting five- and six-string configurations allow bassists to gain access to the low notes for groovy, synth-like (or synthesizer-like) bass lines, the high notes for clearer soloing and filling, and everything in between. Take a look at Figure 16-1 for some exotic six-string basses.

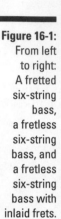

Figure 16-1:
From left to right: A fretted six-string bass, a fretless six-string bass, and a fretless six-string bass with inlaid frets.

Because the strings on five- and six-string basses are set up to have the same relation tonally to each other as the strings on the four-string bass, all the fingering grids in this book work for them as well. To determine which bass guitar is right for the style of music you want to play, figure out whether you need to venture into the extreme low or high register frequently.

If you play a lot of dance or hip-hop, a five-string bass with its extra low string may be right for you. If you want to get into fusion jazz, a six-string bass may be the answer for extensive soloing on the high string. However, a four-string bass can fulfill the bass function for any style just as well. So, like most of the other items on your shopping list, the number of strings becomes a question of personal preference.

To fret or not to fret

Fretless basses have a distinctive sound (sort of a growl). A fretless bass has no frets on the fingerboard. So when you play a fretless bass, you press the string directly onto the wood, just like with an upright bass (also called a *double bass*). In place of the frets, the neck has *markers* on either the top, where the frets would be, or the side of the fingerboard.

If you're just beginning to play and you're buying your first bass, I advise you not to get a fretless bass. A fretted bass is easier to play in tune; the frets cut off your string right at the correct note, whereas on a fretless bass your fingers are responsible for finding the correct intonation. You may well consider a fretless bass as your second bass when you reach the intermediate level or beyond. You may even want to use a fretless bass as your primary instrument after you become more familiar with the bass. (Listen to the recordings by Jaco Pastorius — see Chapter 18 — and Pino Palladino to hear masterful use of the fretless bass.)

Needs Are One Thing . . . Budget Is Quite Another

Now what about your budget? You need to decide how much money you can afford to spend on a bass and still have some left for an amp, a cable, and a few other essentials (which are discussed in Chapter 17). You can certainly play a bass without an amp — you just won't be able to hear it . . . and neither will anyone else.

If you feel that your commitment level is strong, buy a bass that can keep up with you throughout your playing career. An instrument like that will cost anywhere from about $700 to . . . the sky's the limit. If you're just starting out and you're not sure whether bass playing is for you (Are you serious? *Of course* it's for you!), you can get package deals that include a bass guitar and an amp for about $400. Beginner basses start at just under $200.

The lower your budget, the more important it is for you to try out several basses of the same brand before you settle on one. The quality is inconsistent, even within the same brand, in the lower price ranges. Some instruments may fall apart fairly quickly, while others may last for years and sound and feel great. Checking out magazines such as *Bass Player Magazine* and *Bassics Magazine* for articles that review and compare the quality of various basses is a good idea. And plan to play a lot of basses before deciding which bass to purchase. You may get lucky and find a diamond in the rough.

A Trip to the Bass-Mint: Where to Shop for Your Bass Guitar

Buying a bass is best done over the course of several days. This time frame allows you to take your time when comparing different basses and their prices, and also keeps you from falling prey to impulsive shopping. This decision may well change your life, so take your time.

Hitting the music stores

Visiting the biggest music store in your area, where you can look at (and listen to) the most basses in one place, is the best way to start your search. You may want to bring a friend who can listen objectively (and provide moral support for you). If this friend knows more about basses than you do, that's even better. Just remember, *you're* the one who's going to play it, so make sure that you choose what's best for you.

When you come face to face with a salesperson, be honest. Tell the salesperson that you're looking for a bass guitar and you'd like to try a few. Ask whether you can check out a Fender Precision and a Fender Jazz. The Fender Precision bass and the Fender Jazz bass are considered the standard for comparison. These basses sound great for any style of music, they look great, and they're real workhorses, too. If you can afford them, stick with the Fender basses made in America: Their quality is better than the quality of the imported models. Even if these basses are beyond your present budget, they give you a standard to compare the other basses to.

The salesperson is going to ask you what you're looking to spend, so come in knowing your budget. Also, prepare yourself to walk out of the store bassless. Before you plunk down all your savings from the past six months, you still have work to do. This first trip is your intelligence-gathering mission. You're trying to get an idea about which bass feels and sounds best to you.

When you sit down with a new bass, give it a once-over. Check to see whether the finish is even and all the seams are tight (especially where the neck joins the body), and whether the strings are evenly spaced on the fingerboard. The G string should be about the same distance from the edge of the finger-board as the E string, and all the strings should be about the same distance from each other. Take a look at Figure 16-2 to see evenly spaced strings on a fingerboard.

When you have the bass in your hands, check to see if the neck is securely attached to the body of the bass. The neck can be attached to the body in one of three different ways:

- **Bolt-on:** The neck is screwed onto the body with large screws.
- **Set-in (or glued in):** The neck is seamlessly glued into the body.
- **Neck-through:** The neck continues through the entire body of the bass, and the body wings are glued to the sides of the neck piece.

If the neck is bolted on, be sure that the neck doesn't shift when you move it from side to side. (Don't try to break it, just push and pull it lightly.) The neck and the body need to be solidly joined.

After you determine whether the bass is solid, ask the salesperson whether you can plug the bass into the best bass amp in the store to get the truest response on the instrument. Tune up the bass (see Chapter 2) and start playing. Play every fret on every string so you can make sure that the frets don't have high spots that make the strings buzz.

Next, play some music. If you've been practicing the grooves from Part IV of this book on a friend's bass, see what it feels like to play some of them on the new bass. If bass playing is new to you, just play a few notes and listen to the sound. Do you like it? Does it feel good? When you finish testing out the bass, move on to the next one. After you try all the basses in your price range (and maybe some that are beyond your price range), thank the salesperson and leave. Make sure that you know which models you like best and what they cost.

Try to resist the urge to buy a bass during your first trip to the store. You should take all of the information you gather and mull it over carefully before deciding which bass to buy.

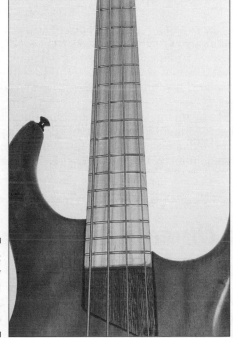

Figure 16-2:
Evenly
spaced
strings on a
fingerboard.

Hopping online

At this point, you can either go to the next music store on your list and repeat the process in the previous section, or you can see what you can find in the online music stores. I advise you not to buy a bass on the Internet without trying the model out in a store first.

When you have a pretty good idea which bass feels and sounds good in the store, you can concentrate on that model when you shop online. Get prices from the online stores and see whether your local music store can beat them. Sometimes getting a *service agreement* for your bass is worth paying a little extra money. With a service agreement, the store's technician will set up your bass for free every six months or so. (A set-up for your bass is the equivalent of a tune-up for your car.) If you feel comfortable buying your bass online and you can get a significantly better price, go for it. Make sure that you can return the bass if it's not as good as the one in the store.

Consulting newspaper ads

You can also check the classified ads in your local paper to see whether someone is selling the bass model you're looking for. As a general rule, newspaper ads state a price that leaves some wiggle room, so you may want to negotiate to get the price down. (Even if you can afford the stated price, negotiating gives you more cash for buying your amp.)

Be very careful to try out the bass and make sure that all the parts are working before kissing your hard-earned money goodbye. No guarantees are offered when buying a bass through a classified ad (unlike in the store). However, you may find an excellent instrument at a very reasonable price through a newspaper ad.

When Money Is No Object: Getting a Custom-Made Bass

If you have enough money at your disposal to go to a luthier, then that's a great route to take. A luthier can make an instrument especially for you. You need to tell the luthier what styles of music you like to play (even if the answer is "all of it"), how many strings you need, and whether you want to go fretless or fretted. (See "To fret or not to fret," earlier in the chapter, for more information.)

You can also pick the color of your bass. (Because the wood on custom-made instruments is usually so good, you may just want to go with the natural finish. After all, you don't spray paint a Rolls Royce.) The rest is best left to the luthier. He knows which wood types will sound best for the bass you desire.

You may have to wait awhile until your bass is ready, but let me tell you, the wait is well worth it. A custom-made instrument is one for a lifetime (and beyond). Meeting someone who's as passionate about building a bass guitar as you are about playing it is also nice.

Buying a bass comes down to this: What feels good to you? When you buy a bass, you build a relationship, so make it a good one.

Chapter 17

Getting the Right Gear for Your Bass Guitar

. . . .

In This Chapter

▶ Amplifying your bass

▶ Outfitting your bass

. . . .

*T*o share your bass grooves with the world — or even with the person right next to you — your bass guitar needs to be connected to an amplifier.

Most bass guitars have a solid body. Unlike instruments that have a hollow body, which acts as a *resonating chamber* (a cavity that resonates when notes are played, thus making the notes audible), solid-body instruments are simply inaudible without amplification. And because the notes that basses play are so low, they need a good amount of amplification. So, you need to take a trip to the music store to buy an amplifier — and while you're there, you might as well pick up a few other items for your permanent bass arsenal.

This chapter tells you exactly what you need to get to be a fully functional bassist who's ready for any playing situation. So take this book with you when you head out to the music store . . . and don't forget your wallet, too.

Making Yourself Heard: A Primer on Amplifiers and Speakers

The *amplifier* (or *amp* for short) is the unit that boosts the electronic signal of your bass and sends it to the *speaker,* which takes the signal and converts it into sound. The speaker is just as important as the amp. In fact, if you don't have a speaker attached to the amp, nobody will be able to hear you.

Guitarists can start out with a little 15-watt practice amp, but bassists don't have this option, because low notes require a lot more power than high notes. So you need to practice a little fiscal irresponsibility when purchasing your amp: You need to spring for a decent one.

Full-meal deal or à la carte: Combo or separate amp and speaker

You can amplify your bass in two basic ways:

- ✓ **With a separate amp and speaker.** The amp and speaker come as two separate units and are connected via a *speaker cable*. The advantage of buying separate units is that you can get an amplifier from a company known for making good-quality amps and a speaker from one that specializes in speakers. Additionally, the separate amp and speaker are more powerful, and they allow you to mix and match different amps and speakers.

- ✓ **With a combo amp.** A *combo amp* houses both the speaker and the amplifier in one unit, eliminating your need for a separate speaker. The combo amp is more portable than a separate amp and speaker. (You need to carry only one piece as opposed to two.)

Take a look at Figure 17-1 for an example of a combo amp and of a separate amp and speaker.

Figure 17-1:
A combo amp (left) and a separate amp and speaker (right).

I recommend that you start with a combo amp that has between 50 and 100 watts of power (it'll run you anywhere from $300 to $1,200). That's enough for practicing at home, rehearsing in the garage (get the car out first), and playing at the local pub. (Hint: Madison Square Garden is *not* a local pub, even if you live in New York City.) If you start playing at bigger venues — at parties and weddings — go for a performance amp and speaker with at least 300 watts. Yes, they're pricey (from $500 to $2,500 and beyond), but they're well worth it. You want to feel the rumble, don't you?

Opting for solid state or tubes

When buying an amplifier, you also have a choice between solid state and tube amplification.

- ✔ *Solid state amplification* refers to technology that uses transistors and/or microchips for amplification.
- ✔ *Tube amplification* refers to technology that uses vacuum tubes for amplification (like the red, glowing tubes in the back of old radios).

Selecting between solid state amplification and tube amplification is a personal choice, although some people swear by one or the other. Try several different amps (using *your* bass) at a music store to see which sound you prefer; you'll notice a subtle difference between the two.

If you don't have a strong preference for either solid state amps or tube amps, go for the solid state amp: It's usually less expensive for comparable power and quality, and it requires less maintenance. (A tube amp needs to have its tubes replaced every couple of years.)

Picking a speaker size

Amplifiers have a variety of different speaker sizes, whether you're buying a separate speaker or a combo amp.

The larger the speaker, the more boom you hear in the sound; the smaller the speaker, the clearer the tone (but with less of the bass sound).

Bass speakers that are 10 or 15 inches in diameter are best. (Some speaker cabinets have a combination of different speakers. For example, the cabinet may have a 15-inch and a 10-inch speaker in the same enclosure.)

Try different speakers with your bass to find out which one you prefer. You may want to start out with a 15-inch speaker and eventually graduate to a cabinet that has four 10-inch speakers. (Or you may want to go with the Grateful Dead's famous "wall of sound," which is several stories tall.) Just remember, you're the one who has to move all this equipment; you probably won't be able to count on your singer for help.

Setting the tone

Every amp has a control panel (see Figure 17-2) with a few knobs for adjusting the sound. These control panels are usually similar from amp to amp. Here's a quick rundown on what the knobs are used for:

- **Volume:** This knob raises or lowers the volume of your bass.
- **Bass:** This knob raises or lowers the low tones (frequencies) of your bass. If you don't have enough bass, the tone will sound tinny and weak; if you have too much bass, the tone will sound boomy and undefined.
- **Mid:** This knob adjusts the midrange tone. If you don't have enough midrange, the tone will sound undefined; if you have too much midrange, the tone will honk (not a pleasant sound). Sometimes amps have one knob for *high* mid and another for *low* mid.
- **Treble:** This knob adjusts the high tone. If you don't have enough high, the tone will sound dull; if you have too much high, the tone will sound piercing.

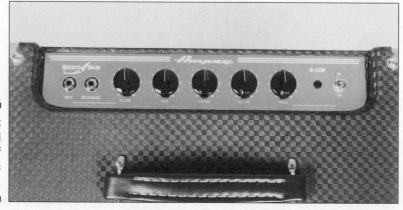

Figure 17-2:
The control panel of a bass amplifier.

Experiment with different settings, and remember that you have to readjust your settings to compensate for the unique acoustical qualities of the room where you're playing. Be sure to listen carefully to your sound during the sound check.

Needs, Wants, and Nonessentials: Rounding Out Your Equipment

Certain items are required for your career as a bass player; they simply come with the territory. Other items can make your life a lot easier if you have them. Finally, some items are just the icing on the cake; you won't miss a performance if you don't have them. This section covers these three types of equipment.

Must-haves

This section describes the items you absolutely must have in order to play comfortably (or at all).

Cases and gig bags

You need to be able to transport your bass safely from place to place, and you may have to do this during a blazing heat wave, a tropical monsoon, or a snowstorm. (For example, I recorded the CD for this book in New York City during one of the biggest blizzards of the year; the basses were safely in their cases while I was slogging through the storm on the way to the studio.) Two types of cases — hard-shell cases and (soft-sided) gig bags — give your bass ample protection.

Most basses come with a hard-shell case to protect it from the elements, as well as from anyone bumping into it. A hard case is great for traveling if other bags and suitcases may end up loaded on top of your precious bass.

If you live in a city and take public transportation, or you walk a lot, you may want to carry your bass in a gig bag. A *gig bag* is a soft case that protects your instrument from the elements but doesn't offer a lot of protection from people (or vehicles) bumping into it. However, hauling your bass in a gig bag is a lot easier than toting your bass around in a hard case: You carry a gig bag like a backpack, leaving your hands free to sign autographs for your adoring fans.

Other essentials

Whether you go for a hard case or a gig bag, you need to put several other items in the carrying case (along with your bass). The items you need to carry with you are

- ✔ **Cable:** You need a cable for connecting your bass to the amp. Without a cable, the best amp in the world won't be able to give you any sound.

- ✔ **Strap:** A strap helps you hold your bass while you're playing. The only other way to hold your bass in the proper position is to glue it to your belly. Ouch!

- ✔ **Electronic tuner:** An electronic tuner helps you tune your bass, especially in a noisy environment. You may also want to carry a tuning fork in case the batteries in your electronic tuner give out. (See Chapter 2 for more information about tuning.)

- ✔ **Extra set of strings:** Bass strings rarely break. But if they do break in the middle of a performance, you want to be ready. (See Chapter 14 for details about changing strings.)

- ✔ **Rubbing alcohol and cleaning cloth:** You want to keep your strings nice and bright, don't you? (See Chapter 15 for a discussion of cleaning.)

- ✔ **Wrenches and screwdrivers:** Anything to help you fix your bass when you're in a bind! If the problem is beyond the light repair discussed in Chapter 15, let a professional instrument repairperson handle it.

- ✔ **Metronome:** You may want to take your metronome in case you get a chance to practice when you're traveling. Even if you don't bring your metronome, make sure that you own one.

Figure 17-3 shows the contents that should be included in your case or gig bag.

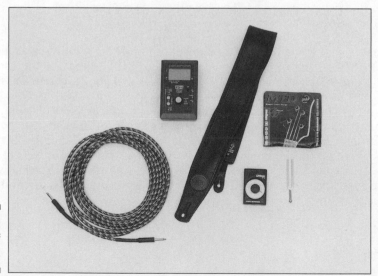

Figure 17-3:
Contents of
a bass bag.

Definite maybes

Some items make your life as a bass player easier, but you can function without them. Bassists generally prefer a clean sound, so they aren't as likely as guitar players to use all kinds of *effects* (gadgets that alter the sound). Two useful items, however, are

- ✔ **A chorus unit.** A *chorus unit* makes your bass sound like two basses being played together.

- ✔ **A volume pedal.** A *volume pedal* lets you adjust the volume with your foot, even in the middle of a tune.

Figure 17-4 shows a picture of a chorus unit and a volume pedal.

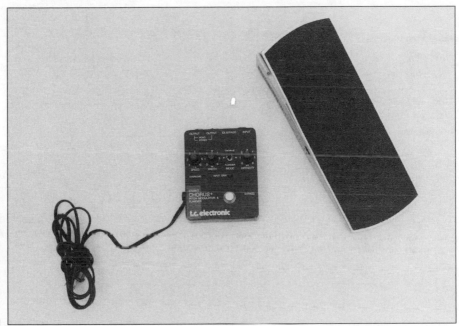

Figure 17-4:
A chorus unit and a volume pedal.

For those long hours of practicing, you may also find the following items useful:

- ✔ A stool for proper posture while playing
- ✔ A music stand to hold your charts (or this book)
- ✔ A stand for your bass

Figure 17-5 shows a picture of these items.

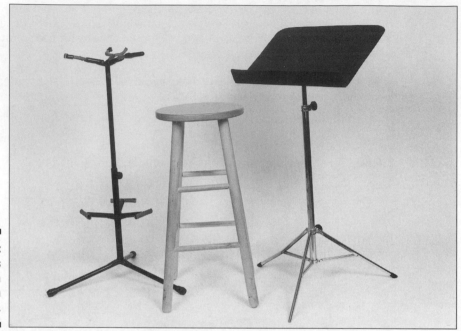

Figure 17-5:
A bass stand, a stool, and a music stand.

If you still have some cash to burn, get a good *headphone amp* (an amp that allows you to hear your bass over headphones). Figure 17-6 shows a head-phone amp. With one of these, you can play at all hours of the day or night without disturbing anyone. A wide variety of headphone amps are available, ranging in price from $30 to $300. The better the unit, the better your sound (and the more you'll want to practice).

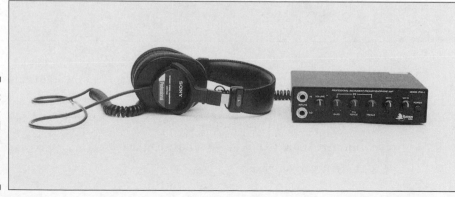

Figure 17-6:
A profes-sional headphone practice amp.

Chapter 17: Getting the Right Gear for Your Bass Guitar *275*

You can find most of the items in the previous list at any large music store. You may have to buy the stool from a furniture place (such as an "unfinished" furniture store) and the headphone amp via an online store, but the really large music stores usually have everything you need.

Extras

As a bass player, your job is to hold down the groove and keep the sound of the band tight, and that's best accomplished with a clean sound from the bass. But for a little special effect during a bass groove or solo, you may want to audition some other pedals besides the chorus unit and the volume pedal (both are described in the previous section). Here are some examples of other effects pedals you may want to use:

- **Flanger/phase shifter:** These devices create a whooshy, swirly sound, similar to the Hammond organ.

- **Digital delay:** This device creates an echo of the notes you play. You can also use the digital delay unit to record a short, rhythmic phrase that repeats as you play over it.

- **Distortion:** This device distorts your sound, making it rough and dirty. Distortion is mostly used for guitars, but basses can use it too. This device is great for hard-rock tunes.

- **Envelope filter:** This device makes your bass sound like a funky keyboard bass. It makes it sound as though a synthesizer is playing the bass part.

- **Octave pedal:** This device doubles your bass notes (either an octave above the note you're playing or an octave below).

- **Multi-effects unit:** A multi-effects unit is an all-in-one effects unit. It can be programmed to alter your bass sound in several ways at the touch of a foot pedal. Keep in mind, though, that a unit like this requires a lot of homework on your part. You have to find sounds you like, program them, and see how they work when you're playing in a band. You may find some cool sounds along the way. Just don't get carried away; you're the *bass* player, not the *guitar* player.

You can get these items at most large music stores, or you can order them online or through mail-order companies.

You can complete your arsenal at any time, but the essentials, along with the amp and speaker, are, well, essential. Fortunately, the essentials don't wear out very quickly, so you'll have them for years and years of joyful bass playing.

Part VII
The Part of Tens

"That's the third time tonight that's happened. They start out playing the blues, but by the end, everyone's playing a polka. I blame the new bass player from Milwaukee."

In this part . . .

A *For Dummies* book without a Part of Tens? No way!
Besides, *Bass Guitar For Dummies* has a special surprise for you: Chapter 18 lists ten excellent bassists you'll
want to know, and Chapter 19 runs down ten of the most
successful bass/drum combinations, with samples of their
styles that will have your fingers itching to play.

Chapter 18

Ten Innovative Bassists You Should Know

Certain bass players have a lasting mark on the entire bass world, regardless of which style of music they play. These innovators advance the instrument to new levels, influencing everyone who follows in their footsteps. Each of the bass players in this chapter has a unique style; it isn't easy to say how these giants influenced one another (it's sort of like saying "Which came first, the magnetic pickup or the steel string?"), so I simply put them in alphabetical order by first name.

Hey, so I'm a little different, but you sure can benefit from listening to these masters of the bass world. (If you'd like to see the Web sites of any of these bassists, I've included links to them on my own Web site, www.sourkrautmusic.com.)

Jack Bruce

Jack Bruce revolutionized the bass guitar in the '60s and '70s with his free-spirited, fiery approach to playing. His style is highly energetic and improvisational. As a result of Bruce's playing, the rock bassist's job expanded from a strictly supportive function to a much more prominent role. Jack is best known for his work with the rock group Cream. "Sunshine of Your Love" and "White Room" are signature Bruce tunes.

Jaco Pastorius

Hailed as the greatest electric bassist in the world, Jaco Pastorius restructured the function of the bass guitar in music. He was truly unprecedented, performing audacious technical feats. Jaco (he's typically referred to by his first name) played both fluid grooves and hornlike solos with equal virtuosity and incorporated harmonics into his playing as an additional musical tool (along with the regular notes).

He is best known for his work with the jazz-fusion group Weather Report and as a solo artist. Signature Jaco tunes include "Donna Lee" and "Teen Town."

James Jamerson

James Jamerson is the father of modern electric bass. He has played on more number-one hits than Elvis, The Beatles, The Beach Boys, and the Rolling Stones . . . *combined.* He was the main bassist for the Funk Brothers, the legendary rhythm section for the Motown label. Some of his signature tunes are "I Heard It Through The Grapevine" (check out the Gladys Knight version for some incredible bass playing) and "For Once In My Life."

John Entwistle

John Entwistle's nickname (among others) was "Thunderfingers." He is best remembered as the bassist for the rock group The Who. Entwistle developed a busy style of lead bass playing that included occasional explosive solos (and he was *loud*). He also performed as a solo artist. Signature Entwistle tunes include "My Generation" and "Who Are You."

Marcus Miller

A strong soloist and groove player, Marcus Miller is a multitalented musician and producer who just happens to play bass. He mixes soul, R & B, hip-hop, funk, and contemporary jazz and comes up with original works of stunning beauty and depth. He is best known for his work with jazzers Miles Davis and David Sanborn, as well as for his studio work and solo projects.

Paul McCartney

Perhaps the most famous bassist in history, Paul McCartney was one of the Beatles. He embarked on a solo career after the Fab Four's split in 1970. He pushed the bass to new levels in rock and pop music by playing with a melodic style that embellishes the vocals and melody of a tune. Signature McCartney tunes include "Something" and "Come Together" (among many, many others).

Stanley Clarke

Considered by many to be the liberator of the bass, Stanley Clarke pioneered the concept of "solo bass album" and brought the bass guitar (including his higher-pitched tenor and piccolo basses) from the back line to the front of the stage in a featured melodic role usually reserved for guitarists or horn players. Clarke is best known for his work with the jazz-fusion group Return To Forever and for his solo projects. Signature Clarke tunes include "School Days" and "Lopsy Lu."

Victor Wooten

Defying boundaries and categories, Victor Wooten is a modern bass virtuoso. Best known for his work with Béla Fleck and the Flecktones and as a solo artist, he's continually pushing the bass further and further into the limelight. Check out Wooten's bass playing on the CD *Live Art* with Béla Fleck and the Flecktones, and on his solo album *Show of Hands*. (And stay tuned — I think he has a lot more coming.)

Will Lee

Will Lee is living the dream of a bassist. As a top New York session player, Lee records and performs with stars in various musical styles that range from jazz (the Brecker Brothers) to rock and pop (Steely Dan, Barry Manilow) to soul (James Brown, D'Angelo) and everything in between. A musical chameleon whose superprecise bass lines enhance any contemporary style, he can be heard most nights on the popular *Late Show with David Letterman*.

X (Fill in Your Own)

This spot is yours to fill. Which bassist influenced you to pick up the bass (and this book) and made you want to play? X can be a world famous (and fabulous) rocker like Adam Clayton, Sting, or Flea; a jazz virtuoso like Alain Caron or John Patitucci; or a famous (to bassists) studio player like Lee Sklar or Anthony Jackson . . . or even your talented next-door neighbor or your teacher.

I have my favorite picked out, but this choice is yours.

Chapter 19

Ten Great Rhythm Sections (Bassists and Drummers)

The bass guitar, more than any other instrument, is at its best when tightly aligned with the drums. Together, the bassist and drummer drive the song with powerful grooves, constantly listening and reacting to each other. In this chapter, I introduce you to ten classic bass and drum combinations (sorted alphabetically by the last name of the bass player) that have enhanced a multitude of songs. If you listen to music at all (and I presume you do), you probably have heard most of these rhythm sections already. If you haven't, you should make a concerted effort to find recordings that feature these classic combinations — and then listen and enjoy!

On Track 70 of the CD that accompanies this book, you can hear brief examples in the styles of these masters. However, to get a sense of truly great bass grooves, you need to listen to the original recordings. Go directly to the source and get inspired by the same musicians who inspire me.

Bootsy Collins and Jab'o Starks

Bootsy Collins and Jab'o Starks are stellar as James Brown's rhythm section. Their work is one of the earliest examples of the complex interplay between bass and drums. Check out James Brown's recordings "Sex Machine" and "Super Bad" to hear their funky grooves. Figure 19-1 features a bass line in the style of their playing.

Figure 19-1:
Bass line
in the style
of Bootsy
Collins.

Donald Duck Dunn and Al Jackson, Jr.

Donald Duck Dunn and Al Jackson, Jr. recorded numerous hits for a number of artists as members of the house band for the Stax/Volts record label. Stax was one of the ultimate R & B record labels, featuring artists such as Sam and Dave, Otis Redding, Isaac Hayes, and many more. Listen to "(Sittin' On) The Dock of the Bay" and "In The Midnight Hour" to hear their soulful R & B grooves. Figure 19-2 shows you an example of a bass line in the style of Duck Dunn.

Figure 19-2:
Bass line
in the style
of Donald
Duck Dunn.

James Jamerson and Benny Benjamin

James Jamerson and Benny Benjamin combined to form the ultimate rhythm section for the Motown record label. Their playing can be heard on hits such as "I Was Made to Love Her" and "Going to a Go-Go." Check out Figure 19-3 for an example of Jamerson's style of playing.

Figure 19-3:
Bass line
in the style
of James
Jamerson.

John Paul Jones and John Bonham

John Paul Jones and John Bonham are best known for their work in the band Led Zeppelin. Songs such as "The Lemon Song" and "Ramble On" exemplify their work. Take a look at Figure 19-4 for an example of a bass line in the style of John Paul Jones.

Figure 19-4:
Bass line in
the style of
John Paul
Jones.

Joe Osborn and Hal Blaine

Joe Osborn and Hal Blaine were members of an elite assortment of session players who recorded a staggering number of hits during the "California Rock Explosion" of the '60s (when an unusually large number of hits were recorded by bands in California). Osborn and Blaine laid down solid grooves for the 5th Dimension, Simon and Garfunkel, the Mamas and the Papas, the Monkees, and many more. Figure 19-5 shows an example of a groove in the style of Joe Osborn.

Figure 19-5:
Bass line in
the style of
Joe Osborn.

Jaco Pastorius and Peter Erskine

Jaco Pastorius and Peter Erskine were both members of the pioneering jazz-rock-fusion group Weather Report during the high point of the band's popularity in the late '70s. Their complex interplay of bass and drums can be found in such tunes as "Birdland" and "Teen Town" (the *live* recordings, not the studio recordings). Check out Figure 19-6 for an example of a bass line in the style of Jaco Pastorius.

Figure 19-6:
Bass line
in the style
of Jaco
Pastorius.

TRACK 70, 1:23

Pastorius & Erskine

George Porter, Jr. and Zig Modeliste

The syncopated and rubbery style of George Porter, Jr. and John "Zigaboo" Modeliste represents New Orleans funk at its very finest. As members of the Meters from the late '60s to the late '70s, Porter and Modeliste laid down some of the most memorable grooves in history in such tunes as "Cissy Strut" and "Funky Miracle." Figure 19-7 features an example of a bass line in the style of George Porter, Jr.

Figure 19-7:
Bass line in
the style of
George
Porter, Jr.

TRACK 70, 1:43

Porter & Modeliste

Francis Rocco Prestia and David Garibaldi

The funk of the Oakland-based band Tower of Power was at its peak with the combination of Francis Rocco Prestia and David Garibaldi. Their solid sixteenth-note grooves can be heard on "Soul Vaccination" and "What Is Hip". Figure 19-8 features a bass line in the style of Francis Rocco Prestia.

Figure 19-8: Bass line in the style of Francis Rocco Prestia.

Chuck Rainey and Bernard Purdie

The power and nuances of Chuck Rainey's and Bernard Purdie's playing drove some of the best music recorded in New York in the mid '60s and '70s. They laid down the grooves for a diverse list of artists (from Aretha Franklin to Steely Dan). The Rainey-Purdie combination shines on tunes like "Until You Come Back To Me (That's What I'm Gonna Do)" and "Home At Last." Figure 19-9 shows a bass line in the style of Chuck Rainey.

Figure 19-9: Bass line in the style of Chuck Rainey.

Robbie Shakespeare and Sly Dunbar

Robbie Shakespeare and Sly Dunbar are widely considered the premier bass drum combination of reggae. Besides playing on dozens of records together, both were members of Peter Tosh's band in the late '70s. Shakespeare and Dunbar played some of the most memorable reggae grooves in history on such tunes as "Mama Africa" and "Whatcha Gonna Do." In Figure 19-10, you can see a bass line in the style of Robbie Shakespeare.

Figure 19-10: Bass line in the style of Robbie Shakespeare.

Part VIII
Appendixes

The 5th Wave   By Rich Tennant

"Okay- I'll front the band. But I want someone other than Dopey on bass guitar."

In this part . . .

This part of the book contains two appendixes bursting with useful information. First, Appendix A explains the organization of the CD. It provides a listing of each figure that corresponds to a CD track so you can see and hear the musical examples with ease. Second, Appendix B will have you itching to copy the pages of music and grid paper for your own bass grooves.

Appendix A

How to Use the CD

You can hear every example of music in *Bass Guitar For Dummies* on the CD found in the back of the book. The text explains the different techniques and styles, the figures show you examples in music notation, and the CD demonstrates how the examples sound when played correctly.

Having the CD ready to go in your CD player and then playing the appropriate examples as you read about them in the text is a great way to experience this book in all its glory. When you hear an example that you just have to try, grab your bass and play it. If the example is beyond your grasp, go to an earlier section and work on your technique.

Relating the Text to the CD

Every musical example in this book has a small black bar (the track bar) that tells you where that example is located on the CD. The track bar gives you the track number and the start time (in minutes and seconds) for the example. You can then cue up the CD to hear it.

Use the "track" or "track skip" button on your CD player to find the desired track. Then use the "cue/review," "fast forward," or "search" button to get to the start time of the example. For instance, if the track bar for a musical example reads "Track 18, 0:33," press the "track skip" button until you see 18 on your track display. Then press and hold the "cue" button until your "minute/second" display (next to the track number, which in this case is 18) reads 0:33 (or just a little less). Release the "cue" button and enjoy listening to the music.

If you want to play along with the CD, give yourself some extra time by cueing up a few seconds before the desired example starts (for example, in the case of "Track 33, 0:33," you may want to cue up to 0:28). When you give yourself a few extra seconds, you have time to toss the remote and get your bass into playing position before the music starts.

Count-offs

All the musical examples are preceded by a *count-off,* a rhythmic click that indicates the tempo of the music so that you know when to come in if you're playing along. Actually, the clicks are my friend Dave Meade (the drummer) banging away on a wood-block. Hey, did I tell you that this CD uses live musicians? You get to play the grooves with a real drummer and, on occasion, a real keyboard player (my friend Lou DiNatale).

If the music is in regular 4/4 meter, you hear four clicks before the music begins. If the music is in 3/4 meter, you get three clicks. If the music is in 5/4 meter, you get five counts before the music starts, and if it's in 7/4 meter, you get . . . that's right, seven clicks.

Stereo separation

Most of the examples (all the ones that feature bass and drums) are recorded in what's known as *stereo split,* where the bass is only recorded on one of the channels. (No, stereo split doesn't refer to some kind of yoga exercise.) In the examples, you can hear both the bass and the drums if the *balance control* on your stereo is in its normal position (straight up). If you want to hear more of the bass, just turn the balance control to the right. You can then listen to the bass part with a little bit of drums in the background. If you feel that you can hang with the drummer alone, just turn the balance control all the way to the left. You can then play to your heart's content with only the drums (and keys).

System Requirements

Note that this is an audio-only CD — just pop it into your CD player (or whatever you use to listen to music CDs).

If you're listening to the CD on your computer, make sure that your computer meets the minimum system requirements shown in the following list. If your computer doesn't match up to most of these requirements, you may have problems using the CD.

- ✔ A PC with a Pentium or faster processor; or a Mac OS computer with a 68040 or faster processor
- ✔ Microsoft Windows 95 or later; or Mac OS system software 7.6.1 or later
- ✔ At least 32MB of total RAM installed on your computer; for best performance, we recommend at least 64MB

✔ A CD-ROM drive

✔ A sound card for PCs; Mac OS computers have built-in sound support

✔ Media Player, such as Windows Media Player or Real Player

If you need more information on the basics, check out these books published by Wiley Publishing, Inc.: *PCs For Dummies,* by Dan Gookin; *Macs For Dummies,* by David Pogue; *iMacs For Dummies,* by David Pogue; *Windows 95 For Dummies, Windows 98 For Dummies, Windows 2000 Professional For Dummies,* and *Microsoft Windows Me Millennium Edition For Dummies,* all by Andy Rathbone.

Tracks on the CD

The following list shows the tracks on the CD, along with the track times and figure numbers that they match up with in the book. The list also provides a description of what you're listening to on each track.

Keep the CD with your book. The plastic sleeve protects it from scratches and stains, and when you grab your book for some playing, the CD will always be right where you expect it. Try to get into the habit of following along with the music notation as you're listening to the CD; this will get you used to seeing music as you hear it and familiarize you with sight reading.

Enjoy listening and playing along!

Track	Time	Figure	Description
1		n/a	Open strings
2	0:00	2-12, grid #1	Major scale
	0:18	2-12, grid #2	Minor scale
	0:34	2-13, grid #1	Open E major scale
	0:54	2-13 grid #2	Open A major scale
	1:14	2-13, grid #3	Open E minor scale
	1:32	2-13, grid #4	Open A minor scale
3	0:00	n/a	Tuning with harmonics
	0:09	n/a	Tuning via 5th fret
	0:20	n/a	Tuning via 7th fret
4		3-2	E minor rock groove

(continued)

Track	Time	Figure	Description
5		n/a	Playing with the metronome
6	0:00	3-6	Whole notes
	0:15	3-6	Half notes
	0:33	3-6	Quarter notes
	0:50	3-6	Eighth notes
	1:08	3-6	Sixteenth notes
	1:26	3-6	Triplets
7		3-9	Notes and rests
8	0:00	3-10 a	Beats as chunks of notes
	0:12	3-10 b	
	0:25	3-10 c	
	0:38	3-10 d	
	0:51	3-10 e	
	1:03	3-10 f	
	1:16	3-10 g	
	1:29	3-10 h	
	1:42	3-10 i	
	1:54	3-10 j	
	2:07	3-10 k	
9	0:00	n/a	Wrong finger slap
	0:10		Wrong finger pluck
	0:18		Correct strike
10		4-3	Right-hand accents
11		n/a	Right-hand string crossing
12		4-4	First line of left-hand permutations
13		4-6	Practice exercise for the right and left hands

Track	Time	Figure	Description
14	0:00	5-2	The structure of the major scale on a grid
	0:10	5-3	The structure of the natural minor scale
15	0:00	5-4	Structure and sequence of the major triad
	0:12	5-5 a	Accompaniments using the major triad
	0:36	5-5 b	
	1:01	5-5c	
16	0:00	5-6	Structure and sequence of the minor triad
	0:10	5-7 a	Accompaniments using the minor triad
	0:35	5-7 b	
	1:00	5-7 c	
17	0:00	5-8	Major chord and scale
	0:12		Minor chord and scale
	0:24		Dominant chord and scale
	0:35		Half-diminished chord and scale
18	0:00	5-9 a	Ionian mode (scale)
	0:09		Lydian mode
	0:16		Major 7th chord
	0:25		Mixolydian mode
	0:33		Dominant 7th chord
	0:41	5-9 b	Aeolian mode
	0:50		Dorian mode
	0:58		Phrygian mode
	1:06		Minor 7th chord

(continued)

Track	Time	Figure	Description
	1:13		Locrian mode
	1:21		Half-diminished chord
19	0:00	Sidebar figure	Melodic minor scale
	0:09		Harmonic minor scale
20	0:00	5-10	Using a chromatic tone in a major bass line
	0:25	5-11	Using a chromatic tone in a minor bass line
21	0:00	5-12	Using a chromatic tone outside the box in a major bass line
	0:23	5-13	Using a chromatic tone outside the box in a minor bass line
22		5-14	Using dead notes in a groove
23	0:00	5-15	Bass groove using the chord
	0:23	5-16	Bass groove using the 7th chord
	0:46	5-17	Bass groove using the Mixolydian mode
	1:10	5-18	Bass groove using chromatic tones
	1:33	5-19	Bass groove using dead notes
24	0:00	6-1	Structure of the two-octave major scale (F#)
	0:15	6-2	Structure of the two-octave E major scale
	0:29	6-3	Structure of the two-octave minor scale (F#)
	0:44	6-4	Structure of the two-octave E minor scale
25	0:00	6-5	Structure of the two-octave major arpeggio (F#)
	0:14	6-6	Structure of the two-octave arpeggio in E major

Track	Time	Figure	Description
	0:27	6-7	Structure of the two-octave minor arpeggio (F#)
	0:40	6-8	Structure of the two-octave arpeggio in E minor
26	0:00	6-11	C major chord with root in the bass
	0:06	6-12	C major chord with the 3rd in the bass
	0:13	6-13	C major chord with the 5th in the bass
27	0:00	6-14	C minor chord with the root in the bass
	0:06	6-15	C minor chord with the 3rd in the bass
	0:14	6-16	C minor chord with the 5th in the bass
28	0:00	7-1 a	Six grooves with different groove skeletons
	0:15	7-1 b	
	0:30	7-1 c	
	0:45	7-1 d	
	1:00	7-1 e	
	1:15	7-1 f	
29	0:00	7-3 a	Creating a groove for D7 (D dominant) — Root
	0:08	7-3 b	Groove skeleton choices
	0:29	7-3 c & d	Scale structure
	0:36	7-4	A simple groove for D7
	1:02		A complex groove for D7
30	0:00	7-5 a	Creating a groove for Dm (D minor) — Root
	0:09	7-5 b	Groove skeleton choices

(continued)

Track	Time	Figure	Description
	0:28	7-5 c & d	Scale structure
	0:36	7-6	A simple groove for Dm7
	1:02		A complex groove for Dm7
31	0:00	7-7 a	Creating a groove for D Maj7 (D major) — Root
	0:08	7-7 b	Groove skeleton choices
	0:28	7-7 c & d	Scale structure
	0:36	7-8	A simple groove for Dmaj7
	1:02		A complex groove for Dmaj7
32	0:00	7-10 a	Mobile groove using constant structure
	0:09	7-10 c	Progression
33	0:00	7-11 a	Mobile groove using chord tones — Major
	0:11	7-11 a	Mobile groove using chord tones — Minor
	0:21	7-11 a	Mobile groove using chord tones — Dominant
	0:33	7-11 c	Progression
34	0:00	7-12	Groove with upper groove apex
	0:21	7-13	Upper groove apex exercise
35	0:00	7-14	Groove with lower groove apex
	0:18	7-15	Lower groove apex exercise
36	0:00	n/a	The sound of the bass drum
	0:05	7-16	Grooving with the bass drum
	0:16	n/a	The sound of the snare drum
	0:22	7-17	Grooving with the snare drum
	0:34	n/a	The sound of the hi-hat
	0:42	7-18	Grooving with the hi-hat

Track	Time	Figure	Description
37	0:00	8-1	The blues scale
	0:07	8-2 a	Blues scale lick (played three times)
	0:25	8-2 b	Blues scale lick (played three times)
	0:40	8-2 c	Blues scale lick (played three times)
38	0:00	8-3	The minor pentatonic scale
	0:08	8-4 a	Minor pentatonic lick (played three times)
	0:26	8-4 b	Minor pentatonic lick (played three times)
	0:40	8-4 c	Minor pentatonic lick (played three times)
39	0:00	8-5	The major pentatonic scale
	0:07	8-6 a	Major pentatonic lick (played three times)
	0:25	8-6 b	Major pentatonic lick (played three times)
	0:39	8-6 c	Major pentatonic lick (played three times)
40		8-7	Progression for soloing
41	0:00	8-8 a	Two-beat fills using the blues scale in eighth notes
	0:14		Two-beat fills using the minor pentatonic scale in eighth notes
	0:30		Two-beat fills using the major pentatonic scale in eighth notes
	0:45	8-8 b	Two-beat fills using the blues scale in triplets
	1:01		Two-beat fills using the minor pentatonic scale in triplets
	1:16		Two-beat fills using the major pentatonic scale in triplets

(continued)

Track	Time	Figure	Description
	1:31	8-8 c	Two-beat fills using the blues scale in sixteenth notes
	1:49		Two-beat fills using the minor pentatonic scale in sixteenth notes
	2:09		Two-beat fills using the major pentatonic scale in sixteenth notes
42	0:00	9-1	Rock 'n' roll groove using only the root
	0:12	9-2	Rock 'n' roll groove using notes from the chord
	0:23	9-3	Rock 'n' roll groove in minor using notes from the chord
	0:35	9-4	Rock 'n' roll groove using notes from the chord and mode
	0:47	9-6	Thought process from mode and chord to groove
	0:59	9-7	Rock 'n' roll box groove
	1:10	9-8	Rock 'n' roll groove in a minor tonality
	1:22	9-9	Rock 'n' roll groove in a major 7th tonality
43	0:00	9-10	Rock groove using only the root
	0:17	9-11	Rock groove using a minor chord
	0:36	9-12	Rock groove using a minor mode
	0:53	9-13	Rock box groove in minor
44	0:00	9-14	Hard rock groove using only the root
	0:13	9-15	Hard rock groove using a minor chord

Track	Time	Figure	Description
	0:27	9-16	Hard rock groove with notes from the minor chord and mode
	0:40	9-17	Hard rock box groove in a minor tonality
45	0:00	9-18	Progressive rock groove using only roots
	0:14	9-19	Progressive rock groove in a minor tonality
	0:29	9-20	Progressive rock groove using the minor chord and mode
	0:46	9-21	Progressive rock box groove in minor
46	0:00	9-22	Pop rock groove using only the root
	0:12	9-23	Pop rock groove using a major tonality
	0:24	9-24	Pop rock groove using notes in the dominant tonality
	0:37	9-25	Pop rock box groove in dominant tonality
47	0:00	9-26	Blues rock groove using only the root
	0:11	9-27	Blues rock groove using notes from the chord
	0:22	9-28	Blues rock groove using notes from the chord and mode
	0:34	9-29	Blues rock box groove
48	0:00	9-30	Country rock groove using only the root
	0:12	9-31	Country rock groove using notes from the chord
	0:26	9-32	Country rock groove using the mode
	0:39	9-33	Country rock box groove

(continued)

Track	Time	Figure	Description
49	0:00	10-1	Swing groove using a major pentatonic scale
	0:19	10-2	Swing groove using a Mixolydian mode
50		10-4	Jazz blues walking pattern
51	0:00	10-5 a	Bass lines in the style of the jazz two feel
	0:19	10-5 b	
	0:38	10-5 c	
52	0:00	10-6	Blues shuffle groove using only the root
	0:19	10-7	Blues shuffle groove using a major chord
	0:39	10-8	Blues shuffle groove using a Mixolydian mode
	0:59	10-9	Blues shuffle groove using a minor mode
	1:19	10-10	Blues shuffle groove using a mode and a chromatic tone
	1:39	10-11	Blues shuffle groove in a minor tonality with a chromatic tone
53	0:00	10-12	Funk shuffle groove using only the root
	0:30	10-13	Funk shuffle groove for dominant and minor chords
	0:59	10-14	Funk shuffle groove using notes from the dominant or minor modes
54	0:00	11-1	R & B groove using a major (Ionian) mode
	0:28	11-2	R & B groove using a dominant (Mixolydian) mode
	0:54	11-3	R & B groove using a minor (Dorian or Aeolian) mode

Track	Time	Figure	Description
	1:21	11-4 a	R & B grooves in major with dead notes and chromatic tones
	1:38	11-4 b	R & B grooves in dominant with dead notes and chromatic tones
	1:55	11-4 c	R & B grooves in minor with dead notes and chromatic tones
55	0:00	11-5	Motown groove using common tones for major and dominant
	0:23	11-6	Motown groove in a dominant or minor tonality
56	0:00	11-7	Fusion groove for a major or dominant chord
	0:33	11-8	Fusion groove for a minor chord
	1:07	11-9	Fusion groove over four strings on a dominant chord
57	0:00	11-10	Funk groove for a dominant or minor tonality
	0:28	11-11	Funk groove using a major tonality
	0:57	11-12	Heavy funk groove using a minor tonality
	1:26	11-13	Heavy funk groove for a major or dominant tonality
	1:55	11-14	Fingerstyle funk for a minor or dominant tonality
	2:22	11-15	Fingerstyle funk using a major tonality
58	0:00	11-16	Disco groove using octaves
	0:19	11-17	Disco groove with doubled octaves
	0:41	11-18	Disco groove for a minor tonality

(continued)

Track	Time	Figure	Description
	1:00	11-19	Disco groove for a major or dominant tonality
59	0:00	11-20	Hip-hop groove
	0:27	11-21	Hip-hop groove for a minor or dominant tonality
	0:53	11-22	Hip-hop groove for a major or dominant tonality
60	0:00	11-23	Dance groove using only the root
	0:20	11-24	Contemporary dance groove
	0:39	11-25	Dance-style groove in a minor tonality with embellishments
	1:00	11-26	Dance-style groove in a major or dominant tonality with embellishments
61	0:00	12-1	Bossa nova groove for a major, minor, or dominant chord
	0:19	12-2	Bossa nova groove for a half-diminished chord
62	0:00	12-3	Afro-Cuban groove for a major, minor, or dominant chord
	0:12	12-4	Afro-Cuban groove for a half-diminished chord
	0:18	12-5	Afro-Cuban groove with syncopation for a major, minor, or dominant chord
	0:42	12-6	Afro-Cuban groove with syncopation for a half-diminished chord
63	0:00	12-7	Reggae groove for a minor chord
	0:31	12-8	Reggae groove for a major or dominant chord
	1:02	12-9	Reggae groove for a major, minor, or dominant chord

Track	Time	Figure	Description
	1:20	12-10	Drop-one reggae groove for a major or dominant chord
	1:38	12-11	Drop-one reggae groove for a minor chord
64	0:00	12-12	Soca groove for a major or dominant chord
	0:19	12-13	Soca groove for a minor chord
	0:30	12-14	Soca groove for a major, minor, or dominant chord
65	0:00	12-15	Ska groove for a major, minor, or dominant chord
	0:16	12-16	Ska groove for a major or dominant chord
	0:37	12-17	Ska groove for a minor chord
66	0:00	12-18	South African groove for a major or dominant chord
	0:21	12-19	South African groove for a minor chord
	0:33	12-20	South African groove for a major, dominant, or minor chord
67	0:00	13-1	Waltz accompaniment for major, minor, and dominant chords
	0:16	13-2	Waltz accompaniment for major, minor, and dominant chords
68	0:00	13-3 a	Grouping in 5/4 meter
	0:11	13-3 b	Three-two grouping in 5/4 meter
	0:22	13-3 c	Two-three grouping in 5/4 meter
	0:32	13-4	Groove in 5/4 meter for major, minor, and dominant chords

(continued)

Track	Time	Figure	Description
	0:44	13-5	Groove in 5/4 meter using a three-two grouping
	1:06	13-6	Groove in 5/4 using a two-three grouping
	1:29	13-7	Groove in 5/4 using sixteenth notes
69	0:00	13-8 a	Grouping in 7/4 meter
	0:16	13-8 b	Three-two-two grouping in 7/4 meter
	0:27	13-8 c	Two-three-two grouping in 7/4 meter
	0:36	13-8 d	Two-two-three grouping in 7/4 meter
	0:46	13-9	Groove in a 7/4 meter for major, minor, and dominant chords
	1:01	13-10	Groove in 7/4 meter using a three-two-two grouping
	1:18	13-11	Groove in a 7/4 meter using a two-three-two grouping
	1:34	13-12	Groove in 7/4 meter using a two-two-three grouping
	1:50	13-13	Groove in 7/4 using sixteenth notes
70	0:00	19-1	Bass line in the style of Bootsy Collins
	0:15	19-2	Bass line in the style of Donald Duck Dunn
	0:28	19-3	Bass line in the style of James Jamerson
	0:54	19-4	Bass line in the style of John Paul Jones
	1:11	19-5	Bass line in the style of Joe Osborn
	1:23	19-6	Bass line in the style of Jaco Pastorius

Track	Time	Figure	Description
	1:43	19-7	Bass line in the style of George Porter, Jr.
	2:01	19-8	Bass line in the style of Francis Rocco Prestia
	2:20	19-9	Bass line in the style of Chuck Rainey
	2:45	19-10	Bass line in the style of Robbie Shakespeare

Troubleshooting

If you have trouble installing the items from the CD, please call the Customer Service phone number at 800-762-2974 (outside the U.S.: 317-572-3993) or send e-mail to techsupdum@wiley.com. Wiley Publishing, Inc. will provide technical support only for installation and other general quality-control items.

Appendix B

Really Useful Pages

*T*hroughout this book, I show you how to create your own grooves, accompaniments, patterns, and solos. This appendix contains blank notational pages that you can use to record the notes (pun intended) of the grooves and licks you create based on the information you receive from this book. Don't just copy the bass lines — change them and even improve on them. Let your creativity flow. You can start out by changing some of the bass grooves in Part IV, and then eventually come up with grooves that are entirely your own.

I include pages of different notational systems in this appendix so that you can choose your favorite. Figure B-1 provides an overview of where the notes are located on the staff. In case you have a five- or six-string bass, I include the low notes B, C, and D (even though they're outside the regular four-string bass range) because you occasionally encounter them when reading musical charts.

Figure B-2 is a page that shows a staff with accompanying grids — the form of musical notation I use throughout this book. This page is great for writing down notation and grid fingerings for your own grooves.

Figure B-3 is a page of grids for the regular four-string bass. If you don't want to be bothered with writing down notation, just use these grids to keep track of your grooves, scales, and licks.

Figure B-4 has grids for the five-string bass, and Figure B-5 has grids for the six-string bass, just in case you get yourself a bass guitar with an *extended range* (which is what the five-string and six-string basses are called) and you feel left out. The grids for the five-string bass have five vertical lines (representing the five strings, low to high: B, E, A, D, G), and the grids for the six-string bass have six vertical lines (representing the six strings, low to high: B, E, A, D, G, C).

Figure B-1:
The notes
on the
bass staff.

B C D   E F G A B C D E F G A B C D E F G A B C

5- & 6-String
Basses only

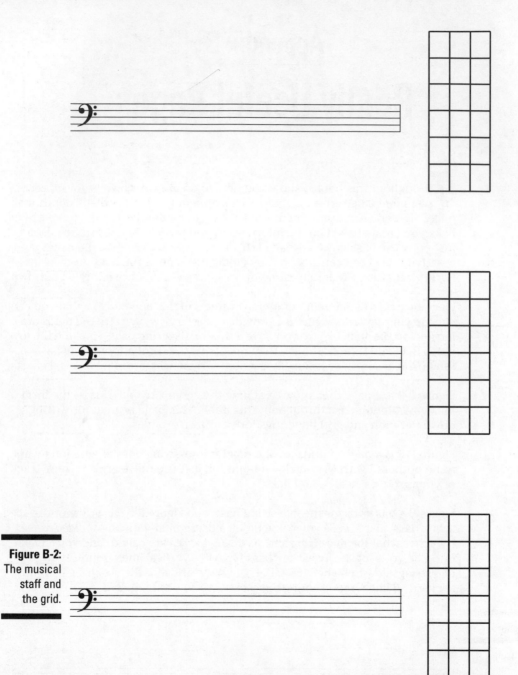

Figure B-3:
The four-string grids.

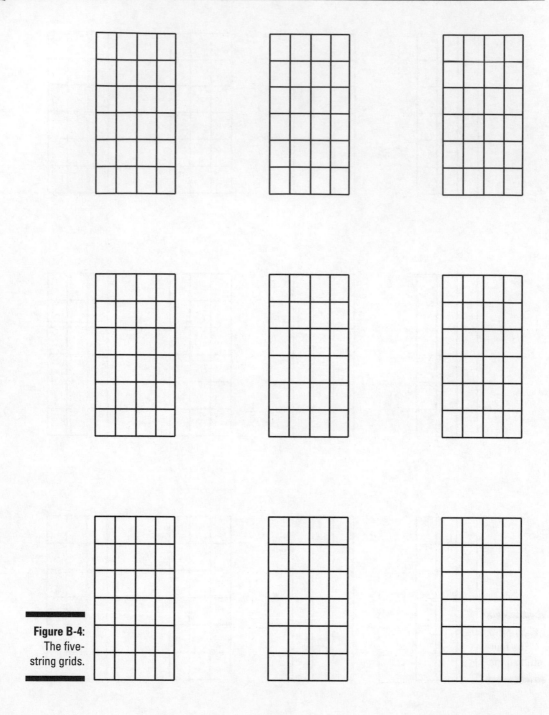

Figure B-4:
The five-string grids.

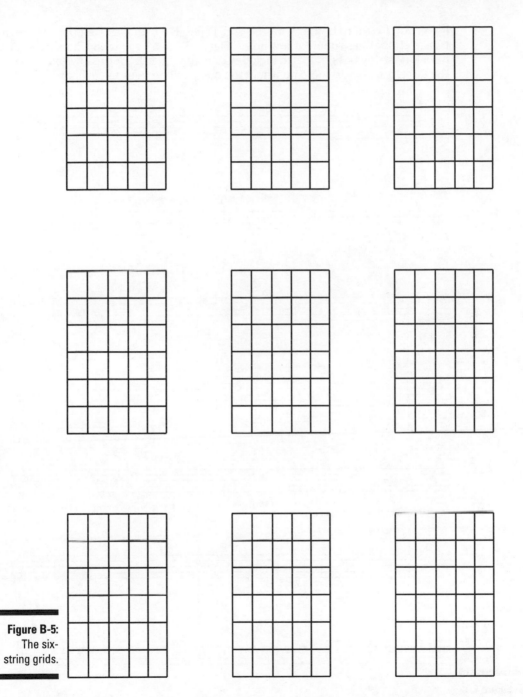

Figure B-5:
The six-string grids.

If you don't want to bother with the grid, Figure B-6 provides staff paper (with a bass clef) that has room for low notes. Figure B-7 is a page with a musical staff for a four-string bass that also includes tablature lines underneath. You can use the tablature lines to indicate where the notes fall on your fingerboard.

Figure B-6:
The musical staff with bass clef.

Figure B-7:
The musical
staff with
bass clef
and four-
string tab.

Figures B-8 and B-9 are staff pages with tablature lines for five- and six-string basses. You can use these pages if you have an extended-range bass and prefer tab notation. See Chapter 3 to find out more about tab notation and regular notation.

Figure B-8:
The musical
staff with
bass clef
and five-
string tab.

Figure B-9:
The musical
staff with
bass clef
and six-
string tab.

I highly recommend making copies of these pages before you write anything on them. Keep the copied pages in a file so that you can find them anytime you want to jot down a bass line. After you master the bass and are ready to pass the torch to the next fledgling bassist, these pages will make a great teaching tool.

With that, I wish you well, and may your bass lines be heard by millions of fans.

Index

hip-hop
  description, 204
  groove, 204
  groove for a major or dominant tonality, 205
  groove for a minor or dominant tonality, 205
holding a bass, 24–27
humidity, protecting against changes in, 247, 254

• I •

icons, used in the book, 6
I-IV-V progression, 175
international styles. *See* world beat style
interval
  definition, 40
  half-step, 16, 82
  identifying, 40
  names and configurations of, 41
  whole-step, 82
intonation, adjusting, 250–251
inversion, 17, 118–121
Ionian mode
  description, 89, 90, 92, 93, 126–127
  D-major scale, 134
  in fusion, 198
  in R & B, 194

• J •

Jackson, Anthony (session player), 199, 259
Jackson, Jr., Al (R & B drummer), 284
Jamerson, James (Funk Brothers)
  with Benny Benjamin (drummer), 284–285
  finger-style playing technique, 29
  history, 280
  Motown sound and, 196–197
jazz
  blues walking pattern, 185
  two feel, 184–186
  walking bass line, 183–184
Jones, John Paul (Led Zeppelin), 169, 285

• K •

Kaye, Carol (studio musician), 32
keeping time, 11
key, finding particular, 38
Khumalo, Bakithi (South African style bassist), 217

• L •

lacquer, 247
Latin style, 211
leading tone, 183
Led Zeppelin, 169, 285
Lee, Geddy (Rush), 171
Lee, Will (session player), 282
left hand
  coordinating with opposite hand, 16, 77–80
  finger permutations, 77–78
  position, 27–28
  shifting to play two octaves, 103–104, 111
locking in, with the drummer, 11
Locrian mode, 89, 91, 92, 93
looks, importance of, 258
luthier, 246, 264–265
Lydian mode, 90, 92, 93

• M •

magnets, 14
maintenance
  adjustments, 248–252
  cleaning, 243–246
  of finish, 247
  repairs, minor, 246–247
  screws, tightening, 246–247
  service agreement, 264
  storage, 253–254
  string, 241
  tool bag, 252–253
major 2nd interval, 41
major 3rd interval, 41
major 6th interval, 41
major 7th chord, 88–89, 90, 164–165

• T •

Wiley Publishing, Inc.
End-User License Agreement

READ THIS. You should carefully read these terms and conditions before opening the software packet(s) included with this book "Book". This is a license agreement "Agreement" between you and Wiley Publishing, Inc. "WPI". By opening the accompanying software packet(s), you acknowledge that you have read and accept the following terms and conditions. If you do not agree and do not want to be bound by such terms and conditions, promptly return the Book and the unopened software packet(s) to the place you obtained them for a full refund.

1. **License Grant.** WPI grants to you (either an individual or entity) a nonexclusive license to use one copy of the enclosed software program(s) (collectively, the "Software," solely for your own personal or business purposes on a single computer (whether a standard computer or a workstation component of a multi-user network). The Software is in use on a computer when it is loaded into temporary memory (RAM) or installed into permanent memory (hard disk, CD-ROM, or other storage device). WPI reserves all rights not expressly granted herein.

2. **Ownership.** WPI is the owner of all right, title, and interest, including copyright, in and to the compilation of the Software recorded on the disk(s) or CD-ROM "Software Media". Copyright to the individual programs recorded on the Software Media is owned by the author or other authorized copyright owner of each program. Ownership of the Software and all proprietary rights relating thereto remain with WPI and its licensers.

3. **Restrictions on Use and Transfer.**

   (a) You may only (i) make one copy of the Software for backup or archival purposes, or (ii) transfer the Software to a single hard disk, provided that you keep the original for backup or archival purposes. You may not (i) rent or lease the Software, (ii) copy or reproduce the Software through a LAN or other network system or through any computer subscriber system or bulletin-board system, or (iii) modify, adapt, or create derivative works based on the Software.

   (b) You may not reverse engineer, decompile, or disassemble the Software. You may transfer the Software and user documentation on a permanent basis, provided that the transferee agrees to accept the terms and conditions of this Agreement and you retain no copies. If the Software is an update or has been updated, any transfer must include the most recent update and all prior versions.

4. **Restrictions on Use of Individual Programs.** You must follow the individual requirements and restrictions detailed for each individual program in the About the CD-ROM appendix of this Book. These limitations are also contained in the individual license agreements recorded on the Software Media. These limitations may include a requirement that after using the program for a specified period of time, the user must pay a registration fee or discontinue use. By opening the Software packet(s), you will be agreeing to abide by the licenses and restrictions for these individual programs that are detailed in the About the CD-ROM appendix and on the Software Media. None of the material on this Software Media or listed in this Book may ever be redistributed, in original or modified form, for commercial purposes.

FOR DUMMIES®

The easy way to get more done and have more fun

PERSONAL FINANCE & BUSINESS

0-7645-2431-3

0-7645-5331-3

0-7645-5307-0

Also available:

Accounting For Dummies
(0-7645-5314-3)

Business Plans Kit For Dummies
(0-7645-5365-8)

Managing For Dummies
(1-5688-4858-7)

Mutual Funds For Dummies
(0-7645-5329-1)

QuickBooks All-in-One Desk Reference For Dummies
(0-7645-1963-8)

Resumes For Dummies
(0-7645-5471-9)

Small Business Kit For Dummies
(0-7645-5093-4)

Starting an eBay Business For Dummies
(0-7645-1547-0)

Taxes For Dummies 2003
(0-7645-5475-1)

HOME, GARDEN, FOOD & WINE

0-7645-5295-3

0-7645-5130-2

0-7645-5250-3

Also available:

Bartending For Dummies
(0-7645-5051-9)

Christmas Cooking For Dummies
(0-7645-5407-7)

Cookies For Dummies
(0-7645-5390-9)

Diabetes Cookbook For Dummies
(0-7645-5230-9)

Grilling For Dummies
(0-7645-5076-4)

Home Maintenance For Dummies
(0-7645-5215-5)

Slow Cookers For Dummies
(0-7645-5240-6)

Wine For Dummies
(0-7645-5114-0)

FITNESS, SPORTS, HOBBIES & PETS

0-7645-5167-1

0-7645-5146-9

0-7645-5106-X

Also available:

Cats For Dummies
(0-7645-5275-9)

Chess For Dummies
(0-7645-5003-9)

Dog Training For Dummies
(0-7645-5286-4)

Labrador Retrievers For Dummies
(0-7645-5281-3)

Martial Arts For Dummies
(0-7645-5358-5)

Piano For Dummies
(0-7645-5105-1)

Pilates For Dummies
(0-7645-5397-6)

Power Yoga For Dummies
(0-7645-5342-9)

Puppies For Dummies
(0-7645-5255-4)

Quilting For Dummies
(0-7645-5118-3)

Rock Guitar For Dummies
(0-7645-5356-9)

Weight Training For Dummies
(0-7645-5168-X)

Available wherever books are sold.
Go to www.dummies.com or call 1-877-762-2974 to order direct

FOR DUMMIES®

A world of resources to help you grow

TRAVEL

0-7645-5453-0

Hawaii
0-7645-5438-7

Walt Disney World & Orlando
0-7645-5444-1

Also available:

America's National Parks For Dummies
(0-7645-6204-5)

Caribbean For Dummies
(0-7645-5445-X)

Cruise Vacations For Dummies 2003
(0-7645-5459-X)

Europe For Dummies
(0-7645-5456-5)

Ireland For Dummies
(0-7645-6199-5)

France For Dummies
(0-7645-6292-4)

Las Vegas For Dummies
(0-7645-5448-4)

London For Dummies
(0-7645-5416-6)

Mexico's Beach Resorts For Dummies
(0-7645-6262-2)

Paris For Dummies
(0-7645-5494-8)

RV Vacations For Dummies
(0-7645-5443-3)

EDUCATION & TEST PREPARATION

Spanish
0-7645-5194-9

Algebra
0-7645-5325-9

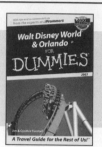
U.S. History
0-7645-5249-X

Also available:

The ACT For Dummies
(0-7645-5210-4)

Chemistry For Dummies
(0-7645-5430-1)

English Grammar For Dummies
(0-7645-5322-4)

French For Dummies
(0-7645-5193-0)

GMAT For Dummies
(0-7645-5251-1)

Inglés Para Dummies
(0-7645-5427-1)

Italian For Dummies
(0-7645-5196-5)

Research Papers For Dummies
(0-7645-5426-3)

SAT I For Dummies
(0-7645-5472-7)

U.S. History For Dummies
(0-7645-5249-X)

World History For Dummies
(0-7645-5242-2)

HEALTH, SELF-HELP & SPIRITUALITY

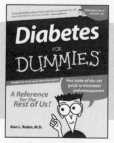
Diabetes
0-7645-5154-X

Sex
0-7645-5302-X

Parenting
0-7645-5418-2

Also available:

The Bible For Dummies
(0-7645-5296-1)

Controlling Cholesterol For Dummies
(0-7645-5440-9)

Dating For Dummies
(0-7645-5072-1)

Dieting For Dummies
(0-7645-5126-4)

High Blood Pressure For Dummies
(0-7645-5424-7)

Judaism For Dummies
(0-7645-5299-6)

Menopause For Dummies
(0-7645-5458-1)

Nutrition For Dummies
(0-7645-5180-9)

Potty Training For Dummies
(0-7645-5417-4)

Pregnancy For Dummies
(0-7645-5074-8)

Rekindling Romance For Dummies
(0-7645-5303-8)

Religion For Dummies
(0-7645-5264-3)

Available wherever books are sold. Go to www.dummies.com or call 1-877-762-2974 to order direct

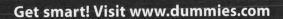